FRO
BERGEN-
TO
BAGHDAD

THE LETTERS OF ALEX ARONSON

FROM BERGEN-BELSEN TO BAGHDAD

THE LETTERS OF ALEX ARONSON

edited by
Alan Mendelson
and
Joan Michelson

MOSAIC PRESS
OAKVILLE — NEW YORK — LONDON

CANADIAN CATALOGUING IN PUBLICATION DATA

Aronson, Alex, 1934-1978
From Bergen-Belsen to Baghdad

ISBN 0-88962-490-9 (bound) ISBN 0-88962-491-7 (pbk.)

1. Aronson, Alex, 1934-1978 - Correspondence.
2. Europe, Eastern - Description and travel.
3. Middle East - Description and travel.
I. Mendelson, Alan. II. Title.

G490.A76 1992 910.4 C92-093154-5

Published by MOSAIC PRESS, P.O. Box 1032, Oakville, Ontario, L6J 5E9, Canada. Offices and warehouse at 1252 Speers Road, Units #1 & 2, Oakville, Ontario, L6L 5N9, Canada.

Mosaic Press acknowledges the assistance of the Canada Council and the Ontario Arts Council in support of its publishing programme.

Design by Ruth Scheffler
Typeset by Aztext
Printed and bound in Canada.

ISBN 0-88962-490-9 BOUND ISBN 0-88962-491-7 PAPER

MOSAIC PRESS:
in Canada:
MOSAIC PRESS, 1252 Speers Road, Units #1 & 2, Oakville, Ontario, L6L 5N9, P.O. Box 1032, Oakville, Ontario, L6J 5E9, Canada.

In the United States:
Distributed to the trade in the United States by: National Book Network, Inc., 4720-A Boston Way, Lanham, MD 20706, USA.

In the U.K. and Europe by:
John Calder (Publishers) Ltd., 9-15 Neal St., London, WCZH 9TU, England

Table of Contents

Alex Aronson
1934-1975

Preface

This volume contains all the letters which Alex Aronson wrote to me from 1962 until 1974. It also contains other documents which have a bearing on his life and tragic death. These letters were not written with an eye to eventual publication, and so they contain spontaneous expressions and unguarded opinions. Over the years, both Alex's views and my own which are reflected in the letters changed. I have made no attempt to alter or modify opinions which either of us espoused, even when those views now appear regrettable. Alex's own honesty was remarkable, sometimes painfully so. He would not have tolerated any whitewashing of his views, or mine.

This is not a critical edition of Alex's letters. The English in which Alex communicated with me was outstanding by any standard. The editors of this volume have decided to preserve the Dutch flavor of Alex's English. That is, we have resisted the temptation to smooth out all awkwardnesses or to replace unidiomatic with conventional English. Occasionally spelling, punctuation, prepositions, or the verb 'to be' got the better of Alex. Whenever Alex inadvertantly became obscure, we have attempted to recover his meaning with the fewest possible words. Alex tended to write very long sentences and paragraphs. At times, we divided up prolix passages; they have not been changed in any other way.

Edited passages (where more than a word or two are involved) are indicated by the use of square brackets. Parentheses in these documents contain the author's own words. The editors have used italics to elucidate private remarks or contemporaneous events, especially when those events have receded from public awareness. We have not thought it necessary to provide background on such well-known events as the Six-Day War or the assassination of Martin Luther King, Jr.

In most cases, we do not include the surnames of personal friends. The given names which appear in this book, however, are real. This book would have been impossible without the cooperation of Alex's family and friends in Holland. The editors would like to express heartfelt thanks to Alex's mother, Mrs. Sara van Straten-Cohen; his father, Mr. Leo Aronson; his widow, Mrs. Elisabeth Aronson; and his first-cousin, Mr. Gershon Eisenmann. The production of this book has not been without pain for Alex's family; I can only hope that they find some solace in these pages. We should also thank Rev. Ype Schaaf for his meticulous attention to many details. In addition, Amnesty International was most helpful in allowing us to use its files.

Joan Michelson wishes to express her appreciation to the Memorial Foundation for Jewish Culture for a grant to aid her research and to Wolverhampton Polytechnic (U.K.) for research leave to work on this project.

I would like to thank McMaster University, Arts Research Board, for their financial support. I would also like to record my deep appreciation to my wife, Sara; my uncle, Joseph L. Mendelson; and the rest of my family for their keen interest. I am grateful to Howard Aster of Mosaic Press, Hanan Bar-On, Patricia Crawford, Sheryl Dick, Grace Gordon, Louis Greenspan, Hans van Nie, Erin Phillips, David Runia, Gérard Vallée, and Barry Walfish. I thank them all, particularly those who did not know Alex personally, for they seemed to share my belief that his life should not remain unchronicled.

For years I dreamt of bringing the correspondence of Alex Aronson to life again. I did not do this simply because Alex was my friend. Etty Hillesum's *Letters from Westerbork* puts in words what I have found difficult to express:

> One always has the feeling here of being the ears and eyes of a piece of Jewish history, but there is also the need sometimes to be a still, small voice. We must keep one another in touch with everything that happens in the various outposts of this world, each one contributing his own little piece of stone to the great mosaic that will take shape once the war is over.

These sentiments were written in Westerbork in 1943, the very year Alex himself passed through that place.

Alan Mendelson

Hamilton, Ontario
15 October 1991

Two Views of Alex

I

by Alan Mendelson

"Cut is the branch that might have grown full straight,
And burned is Apollo's laurel bough,
That sometime grew within this learned man."

Leendert ("Alex" or "Lex") Aronson was born in Amsterdam on 20 December 1934, the son of Sara (*nee* Cohen) and Leo Aronson. Before he was three years old, his parents were divorced. (His father re-married in 1937; his mother, nine years later.) In 1943, Alex was deported with his mother and his maternal grandparents via Westerbork Transit Camp to Bergen-Belsen. Alex and his mother survived for two years. This, in itself, was an accomplishment, for of the four thousand Dutch Jews who were deported to Bergen-Belsen, less than a third remained alive at the end of the war.

To my knowledge, Alex did not discuss his experiences of the war with the friends of his adult years. Alex did, however, share some of his experiences with his first-cousin, Gershon Eisenmann, when they were both boys. Mr. Eisenmann has recently written me a moving account of those years in Alex's life:

Lex was strongly attached to our grandfather. He was more than a grandfather to him; I would say he was at that time his father figure. As I remember my grandfather, he was a very nice and pleasant man, always optimistic and happy, and he had not many reasons to be that way, as he had a hard life. Our grandfather died of exhaustion in Bergen-Belsen in the early summer of 1944.

In early April, 1945, when the Allies were nearing the neighborhood of Bergen-Belsen, the Germans transported everybody who could still walk a little bit out of Bergen-Belsen in two trains. Their intention was to drive the trains into the River Elbe. This never happened, and the trains drove aimlessly through Germany. The first train was freed by the Allies. The second train — and this was the train in which Lex and his mother and many other Dutch Jews were — left Bergen-Belsen on 10 April. It drove on for 13 days until it was freed by the Russians near the village of Tröbitz in eastern Germany, about 60 kilometers from Leipzig. They stayed there about two months. During that period, Lex's mother fell seriously ill with typhus, and it was there that Lex, ten years old, nursed his mother. After she recovered, Lex himself fell ill with typhus, and she took her turn nursing him.

As for my grandmother, when the train left Bergen-Belsen, all the old sick people who were dying were left behind. We never heard about her anymore. However, when my aunt was forced to leave, a Dutch Jewish doctor, who knew the family, told my aunt that her mother would not live for another three days.

Between 1945 and 1947, Alex was in Switzerland recuperating from tuberculosis. Returning to Amsterdam, he attended the Hogere Burger (Jewish Secondary) School (1948-51). In 1952, he received a certificate in chiropody. For the next three years, he studied nursing at the Jewish Hospital in London. Then, in 1955, he suddenly left London to join his father and step-mother who had emigrated to Israel four years earlier. For a few months, he worked at the Rambam Hospital near Haifa.

Years of wandering ensued. To reconstruct Alex's movements between 1956 and 1960 in any detail would be impossible. Once Alex showed me one of his two valid passports. There was not a single blank page; not even a blank corner of a page. I know that during this period Alex travelled to India where he worked with followers of Gandhi in the re-distribution of land. I also know that he travelled extensively in Arab countries. In 1962, he proudly told me that he had seen the Golan Heights "from the other side," by which he meant Syria. His favorite theme at that time was the nobility of ordinary Arabs whose hospitality he had enjoyed in several countries. But Alex did not give himself over exclusively to travel. He also published a booklet of poems, written in English, entitled *Surrendering My Love*.

At the beginning of 1961, Alex decided to hitch-hike to Albert Schweitzer's village in Lambaréné, Gabon. It took him months to get there, but he arrived, after a delay in a Cameroon prison for a customs infraction, on 26 April 1961. For four months, he worked in the village and studied the New Testament with Schweitzer, who had written a pioneering work on Jesus.

Greece had a special appeal for Alex; he had even bought some land in Fannari, a small village in Thessaly. On this land, he built a cabin. It was a place of sanctuary for Alex and his friends. At any rate, one night in the Spring of 1962, on one of his trips to or from Fannari, Alex found himself in the Athens Youth Hostel. There he met a friend of mine by the name of Sharon. At the time, both Sharon and I were studying in a program for American students at the Hebrew University of Jerusalem. She had decided to visit Greece during her spring vacation. That vacation was to change all our lives.

Not long after Sharon returned to the University, Alex appeared in Jerusalem. He was, as Sharon had claimed to me earlier, larger than life. Even at that time, I was struck with his irrepressibility. He did the things which most of us only dreamt about. He had hitch-hiked through India and Africa. He had talked to Schweitzer and Martin Buber as if he were their equal.... How often sober second thought, or the light of reason, would stop the rest of us in our tracks. Not so with Alex.

To Alex, everything was possible. He never alluded to his early years when nothing was possible. And yet, as his life spreads out before us now, it seems that with Alex, more than with most, his end was in his beginning. Bergen-Belsen was his first "real" school. It "taught" him to revere life, to disrespect laws, to question authority, and to challenge customs which seemed to stand in the way of the higher good as he understood it.

When our academic year was over, Sharon and I dutifully left Israel. One of our first destinations was Fannari, "Alex's village" in the mountains of Thessaly. To get there we had to pass Mount Parnassos. It was easy to see why the ancient Greeks had seen their gods in those places; it was also clear why Alex sought solitude there.

We spent unforgetable days in Fannari. Then Alex, Sharon, another friend by the name of Joe, and I continued our journey westward. In Italy, Alex left us, reaching Amsterdam a month before we did. Back in Amsterdam, in his mother's house, Alex again showed us his hospitality. By this time, it was obvious that Alex was in love with Sharon.

The relationship between Alex and Sharon was difficult from the start. He was always challenging her for what he perceived to be her Americanisms, her need for security, and her desire for some (modest) creature comforts. Sharon had a genuine affection for Alex, but his repeated challenges threatened to engulf her. Against this background, Alex's letters to me begin.

Alex must have been ready for marriage. About a year after the events recorded above, Alex met Elisabeth van Dieijen at an Albert Schweitzer village in the French district of Dordogne. They were married two months later. On 14 December 1964, in Piraeus, Greece, their son Alwin was born.

For some time, Alex appears to have immersed himself in family life. Then in December, 1968, he left Holland to work for eight months in Gabon, Biafra, and Nigeria as an aid-worker for the International Committee of the Red Cross and Terre des Hommes. On 8 February 1970, he made his often-postponed debut in the United States. At that time, I was a graduate student at the University of Chicago. So Alex spent two weeks with me in Chicago. Then he spent another few months fund-raising, travelling, and working elsewhere in the country. In May, 1970, Alex returned to Holland. Not long thereafter, he set off again, this time to India (November, 1970 - January, 1971).

My next, and indeed my last, personal encounter with Alex took place in the Spring of 1974. I was living in Oxford, England;

on a trip to Holland, I went to visit Alex in Friesland. I spent a pleasant day with Alex and his family. He was as hospitable as ever. Unfortunately, I left with an indescribable sense of sadness, for I realized that Alex had reached an impasse in his life.

About three months after my visit, Alex wrote to me to announce that he was going to Kurdistan. Late in August, 1974, he left Holland, this time in his own car. In this volume, we reproduce letters (in English translations) which Alex wrote to his family as he moved to the east.

It was his last journey. On 24 March 1975, Alex was arrested by the Iraqis, somewhere in Kurdistan. The next nine months of his life are shrouded in secrecy. There was a trial and a conviction. During his six months in prison, Alex managed to have several messages smuggled from jail. These messages provide us with our final glimpses of Alex.

For months, those close to Alex tried energetically, but vainly, to discover his whereabouts. Only on 15 March 1976 did the Iraqi Embassy admit that he had been executed. The exact date of his execution in Baghdad is not known either to family or to friends. In April, 1976, Alex's mother flew to Baghdad to obtain the release of her son's remains. During her stay in Iraq, Mrs. van Straten-Cohen kept a journal. We are proud to be able to publish an English translation of it in this volume. On 26 May 1976, Alex Aronson was laid to rest in the Jewish Cemetery in Muiderberg.

For more than thirteen years, I looked forward to letters from Alex. Long after his romance with Sharon waned, we continued to correspond. I could never tell in advance what idol he would try to shatter, what outrageous idea he would explore, what dream he would act upon. I always thought that his letters were a testimony to something triumphant in the human spirit. The more I re-read them now, the more I feel his spirit, still restless, still challenging those he left behind.

Even today, when disaster strikes, Alex seems to be there. Each time an innocent man is kidnapped, jailed, or executed, Alex is there. Right now, fifteen years after his death, Alex is back in the arid mountains of Kurdistan.

I began to think about the problem of evil at the beginning of my correspondence with Alex. For many years now, I have taught a course on that theological problem to undergraduate students. Yet only recently did I realize that I did not have to turn to classic texts for examples. For I had known a good person whose life was a series of encounters with evil in its many guises. Alex came of age in a cauldron of evil. He exposed himself deliberately to the evils of war, disease, despair, famine, and inhumanity — especially as experienced by children. On one level, he was more conscious of evil than most people; he must have been more pained by its existence, for it never let him rest. At the same time, he underestimated the capacity of ordinary people to do evil. His need was to help suffering humanity. His fate was to see the face of evil, suffering betrayal, imprisonment, and death.

Nearly thirty years ago, Alex wrote to me: "Life is bound to be stopped some day and what will remain of us? A book, a painting, a thought, a picture...." This is Alex's book.

II

by Joan Michelson

I met Alexander Aronson in Holland in August, 1964. He was then a tall, big-boned, dark-haired, heavily-bearded thirty-year-old, recently married and soon to become a father. Since his marriage, he and his wife, Elisabeth, had been living in a tramcar which Alex had fashioned into a four-room home. He had put up internal walls to make two bedrooms, one for Elisabeth and himself, and the other for the French orphan they were fostering. He had also built an extension to serve as his study and guest- room. Later I was to learn that this was characteristic of Alex: however little he had, he always made provision for others. And he expected others to visit — especially disparate members of his international community. I was counted among these. "Come," he telegrammed me in Jerusalem. "Bring nothing but smiles."

At the time, I was an undergraduate student en route home to the United States after a year of study at the Hebrew University of Jerusalem. Sheltered by my American childhood, protected by poetry, hitch-hiking with a portable typewriter, I arrived for a week's visit with this friend of a friend. I don't know what I expected, but certainly I didn't expect to be disturbed for decades afterward.

I remember Alex towering over me. Through his dark-rimmed spectacles, he seemed to be reading my character. Some of his observations tallied with my own way of seeing. Others, however, I contradicted, stubbornly holding out against his inspired and assertive convictions. He was wrestling with how to live and questioned how I was living. He despised the blinkered, the parochial, and especially the unconscious acceptance of established modes. He sought human values wherever they could be found, and he looked for them across an international landscape. He directed me to study Indian mysticism, as well as the Jewish philosophers, Christian missionaries along with Arab farmers. In order to undertake this study, he thought I should to drop my suspect university degree course, abandon or at least marginalize my personal training program in the craft of writing, and travel to outposts to learn through living.

He didn't mean that I should join the Peace Corps and so set off for the Third World supported by American defense funding. His model was more individualistic. He saw himself as a disciple of chosen masters: Albert Schweitzer and Mahatma Gandhi, to name two. I was to follow his own example here, possibly as his disciple or, at least, assisted by his guidance. Then I would no longer be a "butterfly" as he accused me on the eve of my departure, or, as he wrote to our mutual friend Alan after I had gone, "an immature... unpredictable... American girl... happy in her unhappiness" and unaware of how "VERY young" she is.

Alex spent his formative years in Occupied Amsterdam, in Westerbork Police Transit Camp and in Bergen-Belsen Concentration Camp. Of that period in his life, I know very little. His father, who survived in hiding, told me that Alex was with his mother in "that hell." "That hell," he said. Shaking his head, he looked down as if to read something from the low glass table between us. Rev. Schaaf, a friend of his adult years, used the phrase a "closed chapter," pointing out that even Elisabeth, Alex's wife, remained an outsider because she hadn't been "there." According to Rev. Schaaf, Alex's only reference to the Camps was a joke about money. The Dutch government pays a pension to all victims of the Second World War. In spite of the fact that Alex was only 10 when the war was over, he convinced the physicians that he should receive this pension. It was sufficient for a recipient to live a modest life. Alex told Schaaf that he was able to join the Frisian S.O.S. (an organization similar to the Good Samaritans in England) as a volunteer, because he had this pension. And, Alex added with a smile, why shouldn't society pay him for the rest of his life? Especially when it supported humanitarian ventures all over the world.

During the week I spent talking with Alex, he didn't discuss the Camps; and in the letters which follow, Alex hardly ever refers to the Camps, the War, or indeed, his past. Those references that do appear are brief and, more often than not, connected to the public or communal. For example, discussing the Hindu practice of fasting for purification, Alex notes that he knows what it is to be hungry. Similarly, but with no personal reference whatsoever, he comments on National Mourning Day for the dead of the Second World War. "Two minutes of silence have just passed in which everything went dead. No vehicles moved; no man walked; no child said a word. Why, oh why can't such a moment be prolonged?..."

At the end of my holiday, I left Alex and his Europe, only to take them home with me, alive in my mind and imagination. Alex didn't show me any scars or old snapshots. He was not like another survivor I met who showed me a snapshot of himself as a skeleton released from Auschwitz. No, Alex bore his experience in a different way.

As things turned out, I never saw Alex again. By the time I returned to Holland, expecting to knock on his door the way I had fourteen years earlier, as if he would still be there sucking on the same pipe stem and smoking the same tobacco, he was dead. The man who told me, a man who stepped out of his car into pouring rain, put a stiffened hand to his own throat and sawed across it. "Espionage," he said, with a nod like a punctuation mark. Then, as if that were the whole story, he said "Good day," got back into his car and drove off.

It is impossible to determine to what degree the Camps shaped Alex's character. For a long time, I was baffled by the apparent contradiction: that a Holocaust survivor could chose a humanitarian path. Eventually, however, I came to see that it was refugees Alex sought to save and heal, especially children, and that, as he himself had been, they were victims of wartime or other atrocities. As mentioned above, Rev. Schaaf sees the Camps as a "closed subject." Yet he refers to the Camps in order to explain why Alex couldn't work in an authoritarian set-up. Alex's father also links Alex's background to his subsequent life-style. In a letter to me, his father explained that as Alex hadn't had a "real normal youth, he was not always standing with his both legs on the floor.... (This) resulted in... (his) not always us(ing) the normal and legal ways to gain his purpose."

The story or history of Alex's ways of gaining his purpose is contained in the letters and documents which follow. Rev. Schaaf described him as shrewd. I wonder if any child could have survived the Camps without both wile and luck, on top of learning the lessons described by Primo Levi in his memoir of Auschwitz: to care about nothing, but the most immediate; to recognize when theft is the only way of provisioning; to recognize when the laws of the ordinary moral world are invalid; to know that one is either an "Organisator," gaining the esteem of the powerful, or one is a "mussulman," spiritually dead and physically dying, blank-eyed dragging a body into the dirt.[1] To survive, Primo Levi explains, "one has to fight against the current; to battle... against exhaustion, hunger, cold, and the resulting inertia; to resist enemies and have no pity for rivals; to sharpen one's wits, build up one's patience, and strengthen one's will-power."[2] This was part of Alex's heritage. Hard enough for an adult; terrible for a child.

"Look, Old Jew," Rev. Schaaf once told him, "you should have become a rabbi." By this, he meant that Alex had a *yiddische Kopf*, that he was clever, imaginative, and possessed Talmudic reasoning. To gain his purpose, which his father identified with the single word "humanity," and Schaaf described as "caring for people," Alex had to depend on both his shrewdness and his quick wit. These stood by him, helping him out of the tight spots he inadvertently worked himself into.

Three times he landed in jail. The first time was in Cameroon in 1961 which he was crossing on his way to the Schweitzer Hospital in Gabon. The second was in Pakistan in 1975 when he was returning to Kurdistan from India. His strategies proved successful until, only months after his release from the jail in

---

[1] In *Survival in Auschwitz: The Nazi Assault on Humanity* (trans. S. Woolf; Collier Books, 1961, pp. 80-81), Levi discusses the word "mussulman." He writes, "This word, I do not know why, was used by the old ones of the camp to describe the weak, the inept, those doomed to selection." The terms used to describe the powerful were "Organisator,", Kombinator," and "Prominent." This book was also published under the title: *If This is a Man.*

[2] Idem, p. 84.

Pakistan — an experience which he described as "torture" — he was arrested by the Iraqi authorities.

At the start of his final trip, Alex was explicitly warned of the risk he was taking. Schaaf tried to convince Alex that, since the 1967 war, Arabs considered all Jews to be Zionists. As Zionists, they were to be destroyed. Although Schaaf understood and admired Alex's character and wouldn't have discouraged Alex from previous risky adventures (such as his flight to Biafra in 1969 to lead transports of children to safety in Gabon and Cote d'Ivoire, or his journey to Nigeria later in the same year to work with the Ibo children), regarding the proposed trip to Kurdistan, Schaaf had strong misgivings.

At that time, Schaaf had known Alex for over a decade. In 1961, Schaaf was in Africa working for the Bible Society in the Cameroons. Alex was on his way to Albert Schweitzer in Gabon when he was caught in the town of Edéa without an entry permit. As Rev. Schaaf recalls, permits were products of bureaucracy and "Alex was not much interested in bureaucracy." At any rate, Alex was pushed into a corral with one hundred and fifty other prisoners. Since there was no Dutch Embassy in Cameroon then, Alex telephoned the Bible Society. Schaaf went to see Alex in prison and offered to contact the vice-consul on his behalf. "Don't bother," Alex said, "I can talk myself out of this."

It seemed to Schaaf that Alex experienced that period in prison as a "curious" one, by which I believe he meant that it was unusual, in some sense, novel. It interested Alex because it fed his curiosity. There was no privacy. You could purchase many things... a bottle of wine or even a woman. According to Schaaf's recollection, after three months, Alex was freed. He then continued on his way to the Schweitzer village in Lambaréné, Gabon.

Alex went to Kurdistan as he had gone to other danger zones because he was an international aid worker who had to substantiate goals he had set for himself. After watching a television feature on the plight of the Kurds, he made a quick decision. Within a month, he was packed and ready to go. His plan was to set up his own hospital for refugees. This proved more difficult than he had anticipated. The approaching winter weather made the territory he planned to explore impenetrable. Under the circumstances, he was advised to wait until the spring. He followed this advice by making a winter trip to India. When he returned, a week or so later than he intended due to his imprisonment in Pakistan, it was the beginning of March, 1975. As he made his way towards the front, foreigners were being advised to leave the country.

An item published in the "Guardian" newspaper quotes an Agence France-Presse report that he was arrested on 24 March in possession of political and military reports to his "Zionist superiors." None of us who knew Alex believes that he could have been involved in espionage. His life was too clearly focussed. He had trained as a nurse; he had worked with Schweitzer and in Schweitzer homes; he had worked with Gandhi's followers in India; and in Holland, with his wife Elisabeth, he had opened his home and set up homes for injured, disturbed, and lost and runaway children.

Rev. Schaaf summed up Alex's character as follows: "Alex proved to be a man with idealism and excellent common sense. On the one hand, he did not want to be a tough businessman like some members of his family; on the other hand, he was a clever businessman himself. So the semi-official way the Kurds operated suited him perfectly."

When Alex told Schaaf that he had met a man from the Kurdish resistance and that he was going to Iraq, he warned Alex that because he was a Jew, he was in danger. Schaaf continued, "Alex's answer was typical: 'Precisely as a Jew, I want to prove that help can cross borders. And don't forget, I always find a way out.' That last sentence came with a big smile. Well, he was wrong and paid for that miscalculation with his life."

Alex was buried in the Jewish Cemetery in Muiderberg, on the outskirts of Amsterdam on 26 May 1976. On his rough-hewn gravestone, it is written that he died for the sanctification of God's name, a martyr for his people. His mother felt that this epitaph summed up her son's life and fate.

Although Alex's wife disagreed with his mother, she accepted the gravestone marking and attended his religious funeral service and burial. Further than that, however, his wife felt she could not go. The following October she wrote to Alex's parents explaining that she could not attend the unveiling of the gravestone because the "Muktidas" in Alex could not be there. MUKT, as Alex explained in a letter to Alan, means FREEDOM; DAS means SERVANT or SLAVE. Muktidas was the name Alex's best friends called him, and it was the one he felt he really earned. Gandhi's successor, Vinoba Bhave, had given it to Alex as a sign of appreciation. So Alex identified himself as a Servant of Freedom. In his wife's understanding, as a Servant of Freedom, Alex belonged to the universe.

There is a pleasing irony in the thought that a child who survived the Nazi Camps, could become a Servant of Freedom. But this turns bitter, knowing, as we do, that this Servant of Freedom was arrested, imprisoned, tried behind closed doors and hanged.

Alex, playing a trumpet at the age of six, pictured with his grandfather, who perished in Bergen-Belsen, and his first-cousin, Gershon Eisenmann.

Alex with Albert Schweitzer, Lambaréné, Gabon, 1961.

Letter of Introduction by Dr. Albert Schweitzer

(Eds. The following letter was written by Dr. Albert Schweitzer on 8 July 1961. It is rubber-stamped in the upper right-hand corner with the author's name and address. The latter is given as Lambaréné, République Gabonaise {site of Schweitzer's famous village; geographical coordinates are .45°S, 10°E}. This document is a letter of introduction which Schweitzer wrote for Alex to a medical colleague in nearby Port Gentil, Gabon.)

Doctor René Kopp
Port Gentil

Dear Friend,

Permit me to recommend an unusual person who will be spending some time in Port Gentil. He is a twenty-eight-year-old Dutchman of Jewish origin. Mr. Alexander Aronson is travelling the world to gain first-hand experience. He already spent one year in India studying contemporary philosophical systems. Since then he has come to me to learn my philosophy of humanism. He has been here since 26 April. Now he wants to return to Holland. Since he lacks money for a ticket, he is looking for an opportunity to do any kind of work as an extra on a freighter, a kind of work he has already experienced. Here too he worked. I am recommending him to the stevedores and to the representative of the shipping company Hugo Lines. Permit me to recommend him also to you for one or two meals. He is a very interesting person. I have profited from what I have learned from him about modern India and its thinkers. With my best thoughts for you and your wife, your devoted,

Albert Schweitzer

[P.S.] He speaks German, Dutch, French, English, and Hebrew. Also he is conversant with Jewish theology. If you could find a corner in the hospital to place him, that would be a blessing. He doesn't have a penny. I've given him some money, but I wonder what he will do after he has spent several days in Port Gentil.

It took Mr. Aronson four months to get here, walking and hitch-hiking from Algiers to Lambaréné.

[translated from French by Dr. G. Vallée]

Section One

Single in Amsterdam

October 1962 - November 1963

stand upright, speak thy thought, declare
the truth thou hast, that all may share,
be bold, proclaim it everywhere;
they only live who dare.

ALEXANDER L. ARONSON
(MUKTIDAS)
Andreas Bonnstraat 25
Amsterdam, Holland
18 October 1962

Dear Alan,

I don't know whether you have any regular contact with Sharon, but I thought I would tell you anyway that it is finished between the two of us. Though she thought she had made up her mind three weeks ago, it appears that she can't stand the influence of her surroundings and is completely overcome by the perfection of American life and society. When you two were here in Europe, it was you who, as I called it, "played the American" (don't mind the sarcasm) and she was the "idealist." Yet I have the strange notion that you especially are going to be harder on your own people and your own society and system than she ever was. Am I right? Though of couse I am sorry that now I will not have the opportunity of visiting the States and seeing with my own eyes what I am, apparently unjustly, thinking about it, I am in a way happy that a final decision has been made. Even if it be in the negative. It is not very pleasant not to know what you are up against. And I am sure it is a good thing we (or rather she) broke off at this early stage. Also because, when the distance is greater, it doesn't hit so hard.

How are you getting on with your love life? Is musical Holland or Israel favorite?

(Eds. Alex is joking about the fact that at this time Alan had expressed a fondness for two female musicians, a Dutch cellist and an Israeli student of the piano.)

And how are studies? I did write to [Albert] Schweitzer and [Martin] Buber about the problem of evil; but so far no response.

For a few weeks, I have worked in different places, thereby making more money than I did in the Amstel Hotel. It leaves me, moreover, much more time to do whatever I want to do for myself. Chiropody-practice is constantly increasing, and I am even doing some private Hebrew tuition. Next week I intend to take a few days off to go to the south of France to meet Dr. Magreet van der Kreek, a Dutch medical doctor who married a Frenchman, worked five years in Lambaréné with Schweitzer and is now trying to put up a home for orphans.

Now plans for going to the U.S. have been dropped, I am trying to figure out what to do in the coming year. I might go back to Greece to complete the job (toilet, etc.) on my cabin there. And I am trying to get two friends to join me, one a carpenter, the other an art-painter. So if ever you think of returning to Europe, I shall be very glad to see you there, and I hope you will not have to wait till night when you wish to use the W.C. again.

(Eds. A few months earlier, Alex had purchased a white ceramic toilet bowl in Athens and had brought it by bus and foot to his cabin in remote Thessaly. It was the only toilet of its kind in the village. Alex was planning to build walls around it. But in the meantime, the toilet stood over a hole in the open; it could only be used after dark.)

I tried to get a copy of *Zorba the Greek*, but it is not available here. Would it be possible for you to send a copy of it to me? In return, I would be only too happy if I could send you something from Holland, though I doubt whether they will tolerate wooden shoes at your university.

I am sending this letter to your parents' address [in Washington, D.C.], for I think this is the surest way for you to receive it. If not, then write me which address would be better.

I shall not be continuing correspondence with Sharon. It would be too difficult on the two of us, and I don't believe in "friendly relations" with a person one has once loved. So you shall be the only contact I have in the U.S. and hope we will correspond regularly. Believe me, I would have been most happy if you were the one that was going to replace me with Sharon because I have observed how much you are suited together. A pity that neither of you has this notion.

Do you have the address of Joe? And what is news about him?

(Eds. Joe was another American who had been studying at the Hebrew University during the academic year 1961-1962. He visited Alex in Greece with Sharon and Alan. As a pacifist, he later objected to the war in Vietnam and spent two years in a Federal prison.)

Write me something about your studies, too. I am very interested in starting some violent discussion with you.

Greetings and respects to your parents, all friendship to you,

Fraternally,

Alex

P.S. <u>With</u> beard.

(Eds. Alex had cut off his beard and mailed it to Sharon because she preferred him beardless. He now thought he could grow it back.

Alex's stationery was professionally printed. Pride of place went to his maxims for the conduct of life. {Those who knew Alex agree that he remained remarkably faithful to these dicta.} Only then did he get down to the business of giving his names and address. Until his marriage, Alex lived in the attic of his mother's house at Andreas Bonnstraat 25 in Amsterdam. Here he entertained Sharon, Alan, and others mentioned in these pages. Alex used this stationery for over a year. The editors indicate his use of this stationery by reproducing the first line, as in the next letter.)

stand upright, speak thy thought....

Amsterdam
27 November 1962

Dear Alan,

Receiving your letter was a great thing, and I waited especially until I got *Zorba* so that, in this letter of mine, I could thank you both for the letter and the book. Even more I appreciated the dedication you wrote inside it. Both from it and from your letter I saw that you at least understand me and my ideas. Not many people do.

But let me first answer your letter. About Sharon not much should, or could, be said. I miss her more than I had ever thought possible. Yet I could hardly expect her to change her ways so completely that it would suit me, and I know myself only too well to realize that if I ever would change mine, it would mean a certain death to me. I could best refer you to the characters of Larry and Isabel in Somerset Maugham's *Sharp of the Knife* which, I think, could have been a biography of myself while Sharon plays the part of Isabel. Don't think I blame her. I love her too much for that even now. Yet I wouldn't want you to tell her this.

(Eds. Alex clearly is referring here to Maugham's novel The Razor's Edge, *1943.)*

The matter of my beard you have realized very correctly. It is not so much the thing itself (though Sharon may tell you it is) as the idea it stands (hangs) for. Would Sharon have the "belief" you have, we might have made an excellent pair. Without it, it is better (for the two of us) to leave things as they are. I have never doubted that she loved me and tried to "do right" as you put it. I realize now that I have done a great wrong to her to shave off my beard in the first place. I hope she'll forgive me.

Reading your "revelation" of yourself (for the confidence of which I am more grateful than you may think), I can't help thinking that we are less different than you supposed. True, our ideas may differ, but we must have many things in common, otherwise we would never understand what goes on inside the other. Your writing about America enlightens me a lot, and I hope you'll continue the same. Perhaps I may still someday come across the big water, and I am sure with your continued instruction I may see it in a different light (and a clearer one). Usually I do not make up my mind about something of which I know nothing by personal experience. America is the only land which violates this principle. I am sorry to see myself so subjective on this country. Please make it change.

Please rest assured about anything I may want to send to you. It will never be in return for something. I do hate this terrible bourgeois custom too much myself. If I do present something to somebody, it is to satisfy my urge to do him or her a good turn.

Today something very beautiful and true which I want you to know about. One of the radio corporations opened an action for a village which is going to belong to and be inhabited by invalids only. This action consists of a 23-hour program (now well near its end) in which more than 400 artists will appear in Amsterdam's largest hall, and all these hours led by a very popular reporter (a woman). People come and go bringing presents and money. To start with, they had counted on a total donation of 4 million guilders, but, with still 5 hours to go, they are well over the 8. And all this collected by "small people." Children bring their weekly savings, sometimes that makes not more than 60 cents; workers, laborers work one hour extra for the benefit of this village and their employers double the amount; an impoverished former Olympic champion swimmer brought her golden medal as the only thing of value she could offer; a bride (invalid herself) came in a wheelchair to bring the money she had first intended for a bridal-gown (then somebody donated another bridal gown to her). It is all very confusing and touching. The "big people" too didn't stay at home (for everyone comes to this hall to bring his or her gift). The owner of the land on which the village is to be built (and the sale was already agreed upon for 800,000 guilders) suddenly thought better of it and decided to donate the land rather than to sell it. And so on. The queen sent a telegram promising a gift and the show finished ten minutes ago with a speech by our female minister of social work. Do tell me whether there was anything in the American press about it. (P.S. It is finished now with a final sum of 12 million.)

Well, Alan, write to me again soon. I am wishing you already a Merry Christmas (which I celebrate every year as one of the greatest events) and a Happy New Year. Regards to your family and greetings to you,

Fraternally,

Alex

Amsterdam
6 January 1963

Dear Alan,

First of all, wishing you a very happy New Year. I suppose you are back at the University so therefore this letter is addressed to you there [Brandeis University, Waltham, Massachusetts]. Thanks for your card and what you wrote on it. Though I had the impulse to write to Sharon more than once, I knew to check it. And what you supposed (that she might surprise us both) came indeed to pass. Partially at least. I received a letter from her yesterday. She is not very sure of herself. Strangely enough, you may think, I have tried to discourage her as much as possible in the answer I sent to her today. To discourage her from giving up America with its "security" and to discourage her from getting herself involved with the bandit I really am. ("Vagabond" is maybe a better word.) Of course, I left her the chance of choosing my way of life, but in a manner that makes it very clear that all material comfort and security might be unobtainable. For you see, though I really did want Sharon very badly, I have realized during the past few months that it would be my spiritual ruin if I were to give in to the "American way" even in the least bit. I think I love my freedom (myself?) too much to be able to abandon it for a longer period. Though I do feel that my time of wandering is now finished, and I am ready to settle, I intend to do it my way. And I am archaic enough to want my wife to follow me, if not to agree with me, in everything I do. And if the result will be that I won't get a wife, I am ever so sorry but shall have to accept that as the consequence. Do I lack in love? I don't think so. I might be afraid to give it all at once.

At present I have a guest from India, a good friend whose guest I had often been in Baroda and who is now working in England. He doesn't find life too pleasant there. There seems to be a great color-bar. But if you ask me this is not only inevitable, but (like us Jews) they bring it on themselves. "Do in Rome as the Romans do" is a proverb they may have heard of, but consciously ignore. They can't place themselves mentally in the places of the rightful inhabitants of the country. In England, they believe themselves to be rightful inhabitants instead of just guests. I know there is a lot to say about consequences of colonialism, but if you ask me that is all rot. I have seen myself that, though colonialism has indeed profited a lot from the dark continents, it has brought plenty of "good" too. (I put "good" in quotation marks because I am talking about it from the worldly point of view.)

I know (and you do, too) how I feel about some tourists who invade a country (it doesn't even have to be my own) with their noise, their cameras, their touristic attractions, etc. And they are not even staying a long time. Then how must it be when your place is invaded by similar people who intend to spend the rest of their miserable lives there? O, I wholeheartedly agree with Article 13 of the Declaration of Human Rights, but I believe there should be an addition, or at least a warning to the effect that persons emigrating to a new country should either completely conform to the local customs (even more completely than the inhabitiants themselves) or take the risks.... I don't think, for example, that I would like my toilet to be sat on by a person who doesn't know how to pull the chain or who is not interested in learning how to use the flush. Please let me have your ideas on the subject.

About pre-conceived notions, the following: I agree with you that however objective the observer may be, the color of one's skin remains. But you shouldn't think that any true emotion will be stopped by skin-color. Color is a good protection against "love at first sight".... No, Alan, I am not reading the liberal press. I just listen to the news from all sides, and leave it up to my experience which fails very rarely to sift the ridiculous from the possible truth.

Loving one's country is not vanity or escapism. It usually is plain stupidity or ignorance of the existence of other countries. Generally it is derived from the natural nostalgia for "the old times" — times of one's youth which will always remain, however wise the person.... I believe you fully when you write the good points of your country. But it was not necessary for you to write them. I would have known that there are good things in USA as well. Unfortunately, I have the habit of seeking out the weak points everywhere. Which makes me very unhappy at times. It is not pleasant to play the gadfly to everyone like old Socrates. But some people like me just have to.

Your letter makes me want to come to the States just to see you. But I shall wait till you have finished all your studies. Then I promise you to come on condition that you will spare a full month at least to show me all you want me to see. For if you would tell me only where to go and leave it up to me to see it, the same thing would happen again: I would come back with mainly the bad things I noticed.

Alan, do write me soon again. I love hearing from you. Best wishes to everyone you love.

yours ever,

Alex

stand upright, speak thy thought....

Amsterdam
13 February 1963

Dear Alan,

If not for fear of being misunderstood, I might have started this letter with "beloved Alan." It is not customary here in the West and, I suppose, even less in the States, for men to address each other like this, so I leave it at this hint of my warmest brotherly feelings for you. For I regard it as a very great honor for a man to entrust a girlfriend of his to a friend. Maybe it is the greatest mark of trust and friendship between men. I believe there is quite a bit of literature on the subject. I recall one book I recently finished by Lin Yutang, *A Leaf in the Storm: a Novel of War-swept China* [1941], which deals with it.

I do not recall the moment of which you say that I made indirect acquaintance with HER [Sandy W.]. At least I do not suppose you mean Sharon. Strange, but I still see you and Sharon as the perfect pair. Reading from her letters I believe she is going through quite an ordeal of inner turmoil now (with which love has nothing to do). She has started to "grow up," meaning, of course, her search for what perhaps most properly can be called the "self." I did NOT write to her anything hurtful "point-blank," yet I do think I made her realize that we do not suit very well together. Two more letters have been written since, and I think we have, at last, reached that state in which we can remain intimate and yet never be more than friends.

It is funny but, with the exception of one cousin from whom I sexually feel great nauseation, I have never yet been able to become intimately friendly with any girl without the sexual question becoming a deciding factor. I have always felt greater true (selfless) affection for my male friends because there is no question of sex becoming involved. If it were not for my sincere regard for nature and its creations, I might have had myself castrated, so much do I feel that it is in my way. (And with "it" I mean the natural urge to "cleave".) It is one of the things I trust old age will give me. And YET and yet and yet..... What would life be without the constant struggle to receive sexual love? For the only ones who are able to see humanity with loving eyes are the ones who either are in love, were in love, or want to be in love.

To speak personally, I myself feel I have had my fill of it. Talking the subject of "love" over with a fellow laborer in the factory I presently work in (about my work more later) the man, who is a real working class guy, remarked, "One cannot say one doesn't want to marry. Marriage is like shitting. You may not want it, but the urge to do it comes up suddenly." (Unlettered men usually do have more common sense than we philosophers.)

"Life," the same kind you were writing about, has been very kind to me of late. There is a girl who gives me an occasional kiss when she feels my loneliness too great. I teach her Hebrew (and very fast too). There are my records I listen to with dreamy eyes. There are some very fine discussions which I attend. There are some fine performances; this week, the first performance in Holland of *The Persians* by Aeschylus. And finally there are the classes I now frequently, though not regularly, attend. For I had myself officially registered as a student at the Amsterdam University (Faculty of Philosophy and Letters) with the understanding that I will not participate in exams.

The education system here in Holland, I think, is exceptional. One can attend any classes one likes, when one likes and take exams too the same way. The classes I follow are 1) Democracy, Aristocracy and Monarchy in Greece, 2) Interpretation of Herodotus, 3) History of Slavery in Greece and Rome, 4) Interpretation of the *Qur'an*, 5) Cicero, *De Republica*, and 6)History of Ancient Greece. They are really very edifying. At the same time, of course, I work doing (besides my private Hebrew tuition and Chiropody) manual labor, changing my job about every month. (Part-time labor is less wanted by laborers and, therefore, better paid.) Of course I earn and save for the sole reason of continuing my little cabin in Greece.

Be it therefore to your knowledge that I shall remain in Holland at least till June/July. After that about 2 months in Greece (Fannari) and about 1 week in Israel, to return to Amsterdam in September. So when your friends come here, let them write in advance when they can be expected. So as not to have to inconvenience my guests by sleeping on the floor, I bought last month a foldable camp-bed, quite comfortable. And I am having quite an influx of guests which greatly gratifies me. As for your particular *haverah* [Hebrew, girlfriend; here, a reference to Sandy W.], she will naturally be as welcome as you are yourself. Your writing has made me quite anxious to see what she is like. If she is the same girl you mentioned to Sharon while you were in Israel, I might know her (a bit) from Sharon's criticism of her at the time (don't remind her). There is no way of getting to know a girl from a man in love with her, but, here I agree, neither from another girl.... That's it for today. Tomorrow I shall reply on some philosophical details you touched upon. One more thing: I am sending you a small present, a sort of show-of-esteem. It is something you will certainly like and value. It is, in short, aesthetic (Damn it, how do you spell that word?). There is only one condition: that it shall never be used (copied, multiplied) for commercial intentions. The condition isn't mine, yet I agree wholeheartedly with the original owner.

(Eds. The small present was a copied tape of a private recording of Gandhi's voice which, Alex explains in a letter written on 16 March 1963, "used to be in possession of Mirabehn" [Miss Madeleine Slade].)

Yom Shabbat [Hebrew, Sabbath]
16 February 1963

At the same stand where you got Beethoven's "Les Adieux" for me, I just bought Dvorák's "From the New World" Symphony for 5 guilders, and it shall be the company of my pen while writing this....

Did I write to you that I was unhappy? Or did I just say that the increase of knowledge (or, rather, awareness of the True) leads to loss of happiness in general. I meant the latter. For I am happy as far as an intellectual can be happy. If I do miss something, it is from my own choice...the security of a home, for instance. Now it is the modern trend to deny that "great art grows out of physical hunger" and to call this a "romantic idea," but I shall refuse to agree with this. For facts and experience have proved to me that it is not a romantic idea at all, but a hard fact. There is a very terrifying fact as a parallel: i.e., that love for something has never unified or pushed people to action, but hatred has. Even so physical poverty has proved to be of greater incitement to greatness than just the want to create. Take the Olympic games. The greatest fastest runner cannot make the time a man makes who is pursued by a dangerous animal; the highest Olympic jumper cannot scale the walls of a prison over which a condemned prisoner escapes. Three grey mice, three grey mice.... I saw the fact proved at primary school where I had quite a teacher who used to experiment with our powers under different circumstances. Also this, why is it that the greatest inventions are made in wartime (margarine, penicillin)? Nothing, I repeat, is a greater urge to create than the hard struggle for preservation of the only tangible thing that we may call ours, the body.

However to return to the question of security of a home, don't you think that this same security can damage a thinker insofar as it cuddles his awareness of bare facts to sleep? True, this doesn't have to result from security alone, but you agree that the danger is there. It must be a very strong personality who can survive.... As for going from pillar to post, if one but chooses one's goal in advance and strives towards it, it doesn't have to be a "going from pillar to post." Going from one country to another is just a means, never a goal. One day one gets so far (as I believe I myself now got) as not to *need* to wander anymore, unless it be now and then just to revive and refresh one's perceptional powers. I indeed do insist that wandering is an *absolute essential* for everyone who intends to emerge as an individiual from the sea of society-anonymous. If the resulting loneliness (never "emptiness" though) causes one to stand alone for a long time, it is too bad. Yet you must realize that, if you fulfill your intention to "wander" (the early Russians had many such "stranniki") even for one year (which may or may not be sufficient), you will *never* emerge the same as you went into the wanderer's (searcher's) life. And as it is easier for a man to follow and lead this kind of life, than for a girl, the result is that there are few, if any, girls of this disposition. So that one may find it very hard to satisfactorily marry. Sometimes, when loneliness will get to be too much, one may compromise and settle with an ordinary girl. It will be the ruin of one's achievements of wandering. It may give happiness, if one is too small a personality to regret the loss.... To find the other part to make a spiritual unity will be the great ideal. I lost faith in ever finding one. They usually become nurses, social workers, spinsters, all of whom I detest. If I would find her, she would find in me the most devoted husband, ready to sacrifice himself, his freedom foremost, yet (and that would prove her suitability) she would never need nor want any such sacrifices.

That is as far as I wish to go in this letter. It is easy to say what one wants, needs, loves, does. Yet when ultimately two personalities of the opposite sex meet, there can be no telling what the resulting formations of mind, body and thoughts will be. They may be the union of two split atoms, bringing about an enormous explosion. They may just run round each other, finding no point of contact at all. They may absorb one another. They may, like two magnetic poles, cleave to each other. And that last, idealistic result...who knows, it may happen to me, to you. But never forget, life is bound to be stopped some day and what will remain of us? A book, a painting, a thought, a picture...

Write soon again,

Alex

stand upright, speak thy thought....

Amsterdam
11 March 1963

Dear Alan,

If I didn't know you so well, I would have thought that you were trying to sell me something. I am, of course, very happy to read all those good things about a girl who is going to be my guest [Laura], yet you should know that I always prefer to know the bad sides (weak sides) of a person I have got to live with for some time. *It makes accepting those weak points easier than when you come to their discovery suddenly.* At the same time I hope you are not weaving too many fables around us. When sending someone to me please, and I repeat, please, tell him, her, them, my soft spots in the first place.

I am too self-sufficient, self-centered, a confessed egoist, and sometimes very hard-headed. Yet, though I may indeed have a rather high opinion of myself, I certainly will not go as far as calling myself or letting myself be called the First Man of Europe. There are, as a matter of fact, a few individuals whom I look up to with the greatest respect and who earn that title honestly. These are few I regard as being better than myself. Greater is the number of individuals I know on whose level I put myself. And I know but too well that there are numbers of individuals of my potentialities whom I do not yet know though usually, sooner or later, same-levelled people do find each other. But enough on this subject. If it were not that I regard you very highly as a friend, I would not have written this to you. Very little is necessary to give a wrong interpretation to words written about oneself.

One very important change has taken place in my program, for I have accepted a job as travellers' guide during the summer months. I am going to conduct tours, believe me or not. ME, the one who is so much against conducted tours. However, my reason for accepting was mainly that the conducting of my tours is being left entirely to me. Though there is some sort of schedule, the choice of program, places, and things to be visited by the herd is left to me. It will be a great experience to see how herd-minded tourists will react to the shepherding of an individualist. Probably it will end in the surrender of the individual, though the chances are there (though very minute) that the crowd will discover new potentialities. And it is on those chances that I am building my plan.

The countries I shall be passing through are Germany, Austria, and Italy and the period I am engaged for is from 14 May till 9 October. I do not know what will happen in October. I might go to Greece by train. I might have again to change my program. If you were to ask me what to advise your friend [Laura], I should say, *send her here by plane right away!* I suppose that she could afford a one-way air passage to Europe. She shall be my guest from here onwards. The pleasure would be mine.

One more thing. If your friend [Laura] doesn't like beards, don't send her. Enclosed — a snap of myself at my worst. Maybe it frightens her off! Even for friendly intercourse (I mean psychical) alone, physical disgust can be decisive. I, on my part, wouldn't even be able to talk in a nice way to a girl with untidy appearance and unkempt hair. Writing this makes me understand Sharon's disgust with beards. It might not have been psychological after all, but purely physical. Talking about Sharon, I hope you have not quarelled with her. Your letter did give that impression. Please remember that I still like her too much to tolerate criticism of her by third parties without frowning.

As you see on the envelope, I wrote U.S.A. in brackets instead of Massachussetts. For you see either there exists a Union of States and then the Union is of prime importance, or each state is a separate entity and then Union is of so little importance that it need not be mentioned and is only a political fact. (This is the case in India. No one there will call himself an Indian, but a Bengali, or a Assamese, or a Punjabi.) In America I believe the feeling of Union is less important. Please your views on this as well as on my reply to you in my last letter. Discussing with you is great. Regards and friendship.

Alex

stand upright, speak thy thought....

Amsterdam
16 March 1963

Dear Alan,

It was good to get your nice letter, and I shall start at once answering it, though it may take a few days. There is a lot to reply to you on.

To quote you: "to do something worthy of the memory of a great man." You may not know it, but this is a typical oriental thought. It can be found in the *Veda*: "Man must find himself a *Guru* (teacher) whom he attaches himself to and who will guide him throughout." Even in our own *Pirke Avoth* [*Ethics of the Fathers* 1.6], we find "make yourself a teacher and get yourself a friend" (and not "buy" yourself a friend as some author I could mention construes it). I want to remark, however, on one essential difference between your remarks and my quotations. You want to do something worthy *of the memory* of a great man while my quotations clearly indicate the necessity of finding a live teacher. This, I believe, is of great importance especially in view of your desire "to find inspiration from human sources." Remember that anything done *in the memory* of someone leads to organized religion (Moses, Jesus, Mohammad). [The same applies to the future; in that case people act in the expectation of a great man (Messiah). There is also a danger in taking one's inspiration from "human sources."]

[That danger lies in] the "deadness" of the Master. In order to see the Master as perfect, people begin to spin legends. Gandhiji is, at the moment, being deified in India. Fortunately there are still people alive who knew him intimately, him *and* his faults. When they are dead, his scriptures will be analysed so as to suit man's need for finding "a perfect Man." Remember what has been done to poor Jesus. If he would know it, I am sure he *would* come back to earth. All this does not mean that one may not take a dead man (or several dead men) as an example to form one's own personality. Gandhi is indeed my great light. But when it comes to deeds, I would *not* do them in his memory.

Just one more question that may seem contradictory to what I wrote before. You say that you don't hold to theology, but what is theology if it is not = the history of human sources?

Don't read biographies of Gandhi (or of anyone)!!! Read what he wrote about himself. I am enclosing a shared list of the things that would be of help to you. The tape I sent you has a story. It is a copy of a private recording which is in the possession of Holland Radio. The latter is a copy of an original which used to be in the possession of Mirabehn, a 70-year-old friend of mine who worked with Gandhi for 25 years. She once gave it to the Gandhi Center in Vienna, but the lady in charge of that place (an Indian) went to California, and it is supposed that she took the record with her. Very probably two more copies exist with the B.B.C. and All-India Radio.

Ask Sharon about my opinion of *Catcher in the Rye.* I think it is *the most worthless rubbish ever written.* I didn't get further than the first four chapters, after which I threw it away. So don't send it to me. I would like you, however, to get me this Dostoevsky story you wrote about, "Notes from Underground." I looked up all shops and libraries today. It cannot be had.

I've had *two* letters this week from Sharon. I know now that she must be still very much in love with me. It frightens one to know that one's impression can be so great. I suppose that the only cure will be my going to the States, if only to wipe away the good memories with my beard. And I presume that my many bad sides are being forgotten.

Your remark about married girls: I too know some. But even there where sex between the girl and myself is out of the question, I must ever realize the danger of the intellectual intimacy becoming too great. The husband, when he cannot share it, may feel greatly injured.... (I experienced one such case.) The slight of intellectual intimacy may even be heavier to a husband than when his wife sleeps with another. For in the former he may feel personal inadequacy in addition to injured propriety. Anyway, one should always be careful when dealing with women. They usually do more harm than good to the efficiency of one's intellect. Yet they can sometimes be great arousers of flames which light the fires of creation. An artist, when he really wants to put a soul in his composition, must feel some sort of fever that annihilates reason. No great work can come out of deliberate composition. Technique and skill alone are not enough to create masterpieces. Indeed, the greatest creations do not stand up in the "light of day" just because their human short-comings and incompletenesses are then seen more clearly. That's why we go to a dimly lit concert hall, or listen to records in the dark of our rooms: to grasp the imaginative motives of the composer. (That's why we make love in the dark.) That's why we can understand Heine only when we are, have been or want to be in love, and Oscar Wilde's "Reading Gaol" only when we have been imprisoned.

So if you do have a "fever" make the best of it and let your "wild ideas" run amok as much as they like. Be NOT afraid to live on the brink. Remember too that the brink, in a way, is a zenith as well. Sitting in a valley is, theorectically speaking, only right for those who indeed wish no more than to contemplate and speculate on that which is beyond. Aren't we all in a valley when our discussions lead us on to the subject of "God"? We must realize, however, that there are matters we can and must contemplate from up high, standing upon a mountain. And we should NOT hesitate to put ourselves on that spot. If we do hesitate, we commit a crime towards ourselves, toward reason.

One more thing I disagree with. Hunger, you say, doesn't promise anyone the reward of insight into reality. But why do you think do we Jews fast on Yom Kippur? Why do the Indian saints practice fast? I once wrote an essay on abstinence. The essence was that not only is it the poor and hungry who know life best (and who incidentally are most human themselves), but one can force insight into life's reality by fasting and abstinence. (There are rules that must countermand the dangers involved in the experiment, as Gandhi also clearly pointed out.) I can see from your reasoning that you have never been hungry. ("Man doesn't live to eat. If I were really hungry, I'd find it very easy to think that." Only an always-fed person could say that.) The only thing that I could wish you is that some day you will experience the beauty of hunger. When you come to Europe, I shall gladly oblige you by sharing the experiment, though God knows I know what real hunger is.

(Eds. To this letter Alex appended a reading list. The editors have added certain bibliographical information in brackets.)

By Gandhi himself

Autobiography [or, *The Story of my Experiments with Truth,* 1948]

In Search of the Supreme [3 vols.,1961]

The Gospel of Renunciation [compiled by R.K.Prabhu, 1961]
What Jesus Means to Me
All Men are Brothers [*The Life and Thought of Mahatma Gandhi as told in his own words,* edited by K.Kripalani, 1960]

By D.B.(Kaka) Kalelkar
Stray Glimpses of Bapu [1960]
Even Behind Bars [by Kakasaheb Kalelkar, 1961]

By Mirabehn [Madeleine Slade]
Bapu's Letters to Mira [1949]

Navajivan publications are available in America at American Friends Service Committee, Cambridge, Mass., and Philadelphia.

Amsterdam
20 March 1963

Dear Alan,

Just this short note as a preliminary answer to your last letter. I shall write a more explicit one when I receive your reply to my last letter which I suppose crossed yours on the way.

Please read my last letter carefully. I believe I wrote in it: "*If I didn't know you better* I'd think you wanted to sell me something." So need I be more generous if I already admit in advance that I am cognizant of your real meaning?

My apologies to your *yedidah* [Hebrew, female friend, a reference here to Laura] because of my mistaken remark about "affording the air-trip." I *am* very sorry if I will not meet her. But why not? She'll come to Holland anyway, won't she? And I may have a spare weekend. By the way, I could even take her in "my" bus to Italy. I do not approve of contact lenses. Wearing glasses may indeed not be so beautiful, though I know a girl to whom it is very becoming. But at least wearing glasses is honest.

I shall leave it at this till I get your next letter. There is still a lot

I want to say concerning your *haverah* [girlfriend, a reference to Sandy W.] and love in general. If you need consolation very badly, start reading [Heinrich] *Heine*. It helped me!!!

Yours,

Alex

stand upright, speak thy thought....

Amsterdam
24 April 1963

My dear Alan,

Received this afternoon your gift [a copy of Dostoevsky's "Notes from Underground" in the translation of C. Garnett]. Thanks greatly. After working my body like a slave this day I am now settling down to read it. I won't take time to eat, but will suffice with my great friend, the schnaps bottle... a good companion to the lonely. While reading I shall tell you my comments. They may, of course, change as I approach the end.

First chapter. The man seems to be utterly unhappy, needs someone perhaps. **Second.** He is highly intelligent, yet I don't think I'd ever agree with him. **Third.** Confirms my previous idea. "Merciful Heavens! but what do I care for the laws of nature and arithmetic, when, for some reason, I dislike those laws and the fact that twice two makes four?" He is saying the same here as Will Brangwen (D. H. Lawrence, *Rainbow*). But how different in manner, and why do I agree with the latter and disagree with the narrator.

(Eds. Alex is scrupulous about distinguishing Dostoevsky himself from the fictional narrator of "Notes from Underground.")

Fourth. I think he realizes himself what I said about him under "first." **Fifth.** Reading this chapter, I suddenly feel a strange sensation. All this I have discussed before. I know even where: in Ne'veh She'anan in the hills near Hebrew University. It must have been in a dream, yet I recognize the same sensation and reflections. Is it the influence of my bottle? I doubt it. Yet I have had this feeling, of returning ages in time, before, without having tasted a drop. I like the little bit about his trying to make himself fall in love. The fact that he tried shows his need for projecting love. Woe to the man who realizes this, he truly can be pitied. **Sixth.** "I love all that is *good and beautiful*." This must appeal especially to you, the aestheticist. It does to me. But don't let this phrase fool you into believing you must identify yourself with this man. **Seventh**. I would have recognized this reference to Plato anywhere.

(Eds. This is the passage Alex is referring to: "Oh, tell me, who was it first announced, who was it first proclaimed, that man only does nasty things because he does not know his own interests; and that if he were enlightened, if his eyes were opened to his real normal interests, man would at once cease to do nasty things, would at once become good and noble because, being enlightened and understanding his real advantage, he would see his own advantage in the good and nothing else, and we all know that not one man can, consciously, act against his own interests, consequently, so to say, through necessity, he would begin doing good? Oh, the babe! Oh, the pure, innocent child!")

Did you underline this passage for me? And if you did it for your own purpose, is it your intention that I should return the book to you? Or may I keep it?

(Eds. Alan intended that Alex should keep the book.)

I do believe I act out of self-interest. Sometimes I even pride myself on it. At least I never wind any bandages around that fact. I think I need a bit of fresh air. Continue tonight or tomorrow.

26 April 1963

While Robert Casadesus hammers away at "Les Adieux," I continue. Meanwhile I heard that Ben-Zvi died. Who shall be his successor? I hesitate to put my bet. Probably Abba Eban or Nahum Goldmann....

(Eds. Alex is referring to the death of Mr. Izhak Ben-Zvi, elected President of the State of Israel in 1952, and re-elected in 1957 and 1962. Alex now returns to his discussion of the seventh chapter of "Notes from Underground.")

"Will you take it upon yourself to define with perfect accuracy in what the advantage of man consists?" I think one can [define the interest of a human being], basing one's theory on the Indian idea of *dharma* (want me to explain what it is?). Naturally man's interest changes depending not only on the person, but even on the particular minute in the person's life when the definition is wanted. Generally speaking, I think that the interest of a person may be seen in terms of two rules. A) It has to lie in the line the person follows (at that moment) to the goal he aims at. B) It must satisfy a (consciously or subconsciously felt) desire. It may happen that these two (conscious and subconscious) collide. In that case I believe the person is automatically made aware of the subconscious and will follow its desire.

I don't think the *interest* of a person can be identified with the *good* for the person. The former, to me, is left entirely to the discretion of the person himself while the latter can be discussed by others. Take suicide. Some may say it's not a *good*, yet a man may at a certain time say that it's in his *interest*. Therefore I disagree with the narrator when he puts the question this way: "And what if it so happens that a man's advantage, *sometimes*, not only may, but even must, consist in his desiring in certain cases what is harmful to himself and not advantageous?" About the "golden pins" I keep silent. This is our friend Freud's department.

(Eds. Alex is referring to the undergound man's comment that Cleopatra "was fond of sticking gold pins into her slave-girls' breasts and derived gratification from their screams and writhings." The narrator's point here is that, if anything, civilization has made human beings more bloodthirsty.)

27 April 1963

Eighth. I fully agree here with his idea of reason and free will. He will do it in order to *establish his right* to wish for the most idiotic things.... He puts it very nicely and leads up to my own idea, that of the supremacy of man's individuality. **Ninth.** I like this formulation of the "twice-two-is-four" problem.

(Eds. Alex is expressing his approval of sentiments such as the following: "Man is a frivolous and incongruous creature, and perhaps, like a chess player, loves the process of the game, not the end of it. And who knows...perhaps the only goal on earth to which mankind is striving lies in this incessant process of attaining, in other words in life itself, and not in the thing to be attained, which must always be expressed as a formula, as positive as twice two makes four, and such positiveness is not life,

gentlemen, but the beginning of death." Years passed, and Alan got to know Alex better, but this passage still seems to epitomize something at the core of Alex's being.)

But who, except the few of us who battle to preserve our own ego, will agree? Yet I don't think that gives us a need to creep into each others' mouseholes (to identify, if you like.) Rather the opposite, I should say.

Did I say I'd ever agree with him? Oh, but I do now!!!

So much for the first book. You noticed how I cycled around to complete agreement with the narrator? Was that your intention? The rest of the book, though I will presently continue reading it, probably won't need such exact comment on my part. Suffice it for me to say that I understand now why you identify here. If you do, we have a lot in common. Your environment, however, must make it a lot harder on you than on me, I suppose. Tell me, for I may learn from it, what the greatest conflicts are with which you have to cope. I know mine, and how hard it is to break with custom, with the "what-shall- the-neighbors-say" mentality, and last but not least (I have not yet got so far myself) with one's own family. I think I shall only be able to make the break complete when I find a wife strong and equal-minded, who could catch that part of me that would become unattached and swinging in the winds.... Sharon obviously would not be able to fulfill that part, I agree. Yet she would probably be such an addition to the opposite side (that of the custom-neighbors-family) that the whole of one's weight would topple over. And as the man said, how do I know that that isn't really what I want? What's your opinion?

28 April 1963

Tonight rehearsing for the singing which I'll do in tomorrow's commemoration service for the dead president [Izhak Ben-Zvi]. It's been a long time since I've sung. I hope my voice still carries. Anyway, cotton wool is cheap. The day before yesterday I found a piece of triplex-wood lying in the gutter. Turning it over it proved to be a painting. I loved it and had it entirely restored. Costs are 15 guilders which is not too much. No signature on it, but it must have been quite a painter who made it. It presents a landscape with dark woods, a small pool and an old farmer's cottage. Quite common in Holland, yet beautifully caught.

My room undergoes small changes now and then. Additions

like these are not uncommon. This month shall be the last I live in it; at least for 1963. I arranged with my mother to keep it alive and liveable so that any chance-visitors will always find here a pleasant repose. I hope many will come. My intention is to come to the States next Christmas. Do you know a certain retired professor named George Boas (Johns Hopkins)? I am going to be introduced to him as well as to "other persons of fame." I just wonder.... Tell your friend I just found out from UNESCO that there are regular student-flights from Athens to Tel-Aviv (every week) and between Greece and Italy (every other week).... I myself shall go from Holland to Italy every month. It may be interesting for her to get UNESCO's "Vacations Abroad" in which a lot more information.

Shalom rav,
[Peace be with you]

Alex

stand upright, speak thy thought....

Amsterdam
4 May 1963

Dear Alan,

Today National Mourning for the dead of the Second World War. Two minutes of silence have just passed in which everything went dead. No vehicles moved, no man walked; no child said a word. A moment of great beauty in which everyone felt at peace with the world. Why, oh why, can't such a moment be prolonged?

Your letter gave great joy and quite a lot to do. I hope my mind will retain all details that come into it while reading, so that you can partake in my reactions.

Starting with your remarks about quick judgment. First of all, I did write down my responses to "Notes from Underground" from the very first chapter. I did it for you to be able to follow my reasoning and for myself — to discover where I failed. Yes, it does make life harder to be this way, but it makes it easier on my personality to maintain itself. Who said that it is not the weak who can afford to change opinions, but the strong? Gandhi, in one of his letters, says that if he is heard to say something which contradicts one of his previous utterances, it should only be regarded as a sign of progress in his education. It is interesting to note this progress in the writings of all great men. In the New Testament we see how Jesus' mind was shaped even by short encounters. For instance, the brief meeting with the gentile woman who begs him for his miracle. ("Even the dogs eat of the crumbs that fall from the children's table.")

(Eds. Alex is referring to Matthew 15:21-28 or Mark 7:24 - 30.)

You have a tendency, Alan, to regard a book as something holy. Don't. It isn't organic. It is the record of a person's mind, which itself is very fragile. No, I do *not* judge books by whether they lead up to ideas that are mine. I judge them by whether they lead up to any idea at all *and* by whether they succeed in making this idea understandable to the reader.

Naturally, when the book leads up to my idea, it will be a great help (morally sustaining, too), but I may even learn more from a book which expounds an opinion different from my own. Take *Lady Chatterly's Lover* for instance. I *completely* disagree with Lawrence on the question of the importance of sex. Yet the book made me aware of those who think differently. It even gave me occasion to put up my fences against their ideas.

Jesus was a great man.

Twelve o'clock midnight. In order to be able to answer your letter and the question of Eichmann and capital punishment in general, I went to see the "Judgment at Nuremberg" with Spencer Tracy as Judge Haywood. I am too tired to start writing now; the film gave too much for my mind to digest at once, but I'll start first thing tomorrow.

5 May 1963
National Liberation Day

Something on the radio which I can't identify, but it is nice. Capital punishment... or? "Of the ninety nine war criminals sentenced at Nuremberg to life imprisonment, not one is jailed anymore." This was the conclusion of the film I attended yesterday night. Is that justice?

At school I learned that the spirit of a law should be considered before the letter of the law. Life later taught me to replace the word "law" with "justice" for law may be wrong when given by a bad governor. (I herein disagree with Socrates' regard for law.)

The music on the radio was Haydn's Symphony in A Major. A Schubert symphony follows.

One should follow the spirit of justice. What happened at Nuremberg — the sentencing of the criminals and their later release — is what I would call the "letter of the spirit of justice." When talking to Martin Buber on the subject of Eichmann, before the end of the trial, he said, "Death is not punishment, first of all. Secondly, a crime so big really cannot be punished. If the judges want to keep their moral integrity, they should not answer hatred with hatred. It's important for them to keep their hands clean. Capital punishment will lose them the right to judge...."

There are plenty of other great men to support this. I want to mention only one more quotation from the very great author Alan Paton (*Too Late the Phalarope*): "If man takes unto himself God's right to punish, then he must also take upon himself God's promise to restore." Which doesn't say that I'm religious. But this is pure sense because it is based on a promise the existence of which cannot be disproved. (Nor proved, but that's beside the point here.)

So I am against capital punishment, and I tell you I always was. But imprisonment is no punishment either. Here in Holland only 4 criminals of war still serve their life sentence. Their rooms are provided with shower, toilet, radio, t.v. etc. "If that is what my war crimes are going to give me, I am going to be a war-criminal." I have heard it said.

The best way of punishment in such capital crimes I have always thought to be the Japanese Hara-kiri (suicide). But a western character, if he's really bad, will never kill himself when he is asked to. The westerners, moreover, lack the eastern sense of "saving face." What then should be done to remove a war criminal from society? (You see I am not talking of punishment any more.) Let them walk around freely, I say. With an iron mark or some Cain's mark. Of all the punishments we nowadays have, I don't think any one is adequate. It's the whole system that should be changed.

Don't be sad about me and "my bottle." I'm well aware of what it might lead to, yet it never will to me. I consciously use it as a temporary release of some mental disturbance which may or may not pass some day. If that disturbance would be only a sexual one (I mean, if it would be only sex that isn't getting its fulfillment), I would be at rest in the assurance that old age would mend it. But unfortunately that function doesn't count with me. When loving a girl I have always counted intellectual intercourse as the deciding factor. You may not believe it — but, in my 28th year, I am still a virgin. This is strictly between us. Anyway, no one would believe it, counting the number of girls I have courted.

During my travels I have adhered to the strictest discipline. I could because I felt myself standing on a much higher level than the people whom I came in contact with. Nowadays, leading the life of a wage-earning civilian... feeling myself, from time to time, uplifted in my correspondence out of the miserable bourgeoisie that surrounds one here, I can again believe in myself. Some day when my present aim, to earn in a short time enough to make me financially independent for the rest of my life — I have counted on ten years of slavery — I shall again be able to become my entire self.

I have realized the danger: to become addicted to slavery, to feel safe amongst a crowd. When I get near that point, and it is a long way off yet, I shall break with my intention and not hesitate to become myself even if my present aim has not been reached....

(Eds. In what follows, Alex is obviously referring back to "Notes from Underground." In Chapter 8 of that work, a piano-key is taken to symbolize life without desire, freewill, or choice. As the narrator says, "The whole work of man really seems to consist in nothing but proving to himself every minute that he is a man and not a piano-key.")

Talking of a piano-key, what would you think of a piano-key club? As many members as there are keys on the piano. I would know 3 or 4 who could be considered. The thing might grow into a nice group of fellows. Something like the Thirty-Six Just. Answer s.v.p.

(Eds. Reference here is to the Jewish legend that at any time there are 36 just people living on earth. A contemporary treatment of the subject was The Last of the Just *by Andre Schwarz-Bart [1960].)*

Alan, I wish you were here now. We would have a marvelous time, and I would be the beneficiary. Started recently a new sort of communication — incoherent, maybe, to those who don't know the writer. Just noting down the thoughts that come into my head, following no specific pattern. Of course the prime condition is to leave out no single thought so that the recipient may be able to follow it; even bad things coming into one's mind should be recorded. (Influence of Dostoevsky's *Idiot*?)

Tomorrow's another day; going to bed now. But before I forget: all correspondence should be sent to this address [in Amsterdam], even when I am away. My mother collects everything and forwards it to me wherever I might be. I shall get my mail about twice a month. A letter might remain unanswered for a month, but no more.

8 May 1963

I'm not getting any further with this letter. Quite a few other letters have to be written in between. Hardly any time to get to my reading. Gave up the newspapers quite a while ago after your example. Indeed, it leaves more room for fresh air. We use newspaper for the toilet here so now and then I get a bit of "outside information," the latest being that America has introduced new brassieres for girls of 9 (nine) years old. Sounds exciting.

I didn't know of Norman Thomas. Glad you wrote me something about him; another Person I shall have to meet in America.

(Eds. Norman Thomas, the Socialist candidate for President of the U.S. in all elections from 1928 until 1948, had spoken at Brandeis University. Alan had reported his speech to Alex.)

The day after tommorow, I shall go to see Gré Hofmans, the woman who was friendly with our queen, treated our youngest (not 100% normal) princess with faith, and was thereby the cause of quite a scandal here, as you might remember.

9 May 1963

The idea of a piano-key club doesn't leave me. There are Grand pianos and Upright pianos. It is understood that club members should be well aware of distinctions between keys. They should in fact possess keys. Well, I'm raving again, as usual when I am tired.... Till Tomorrow.

(Eds. At this time, Alan owned a piano-key which he had salvaged from an old upright. He tied a string to this remant and hung it from the ceiling where it turned and swayed.)

11 May 1963

This is going to be the last part of this long letter. Have just written a short note to your *haverah* [girlfriend, a reference to Sandy W.] to ask if and how we might meet before I leave Holland. For I now know that once my job has begun (11 June), there will not be a spare minute till I finish on 14 September.

Have I answered your letter on every point? Yesterday, I met with Miss Hofmans. She's great and truly inspiring. I can see why she offended "society" and how open she is to abuse and slander. It needs some very honest mind to appreciate what she stands for. I might tell you more about her later. When I was with her, I became aware of the certainty of my impending trip to U.S.A. Seems to have become unavoidable now. I shall come on a tourist visa. Yet there must be an opportunity for me to earn my stay during the (3?) months I'm "over there." Do you have any suggestions?

Well, Alan great friend, this must be it for the time being. Do write to me again when you find time, which I hope is soon.

Yours ever,

Alex

P.S. Saw a three-year-old child in synagogue today. Could have been you when you were that age. Truly two drops of water.

(Eds. This letter is undated and is not headed with the printed dicta {"stand upright... "}. His new heading is rubber- stamped: ALEXANDER L. ARONSON, INTERNATIONAL UNDERSTANDING, AMSTERDAM - HOLLAND, ANDREAS BONNSTRAAT 25.)

July [?] 1963

Dear Alan,

This shall be a very concise letter, half in telegram style. No time. Full stop. My herd is completely occupying me from morning till evening. More so than other guides who can take a day off when they feel like it. I try to live up to my own standards and show them more than they really bargain for. I seem to be in the hands of a favorite guardian angel. Last week I had to take a group to a place near Stuttgart, but refused to go with that particular driver with whom I had an unpleasant experience before. I got a tour to Garda instead and a colleague took my trip. They crashed off the autobahn, 10 people killed and the courier mortally wounded in hospital. Hope to be able to see him today when I return to Holland via Stuttgart where the accident happened.

My program has changed.... I have an extra trip added to it which will occupy me till 28 September. This last trip starts on the 17th. So if your, so beautifully described, Laura is willing to come on an eleven-day trip to Iesolo [Adriatic coast, to the northeast of Venice] she is welcome. After this trip, I could show her Amsterdam. All this, of course, at no cost to her (or to me). I just have to know it well in advance so I can give you directions for where she'll have to meet me and at what time. The schedule is pretty close. When I return one group to the airport, the plane that takes this group back to England brings me a new group. So I have an hour between groups which makes the last and first day of trips quite hectic.

You may pass my picture on to her. Tell me if your supply is exhausted and I'll send you some more snaps. Tell her that if I don't see her in Holland, I shall certainly come to Paris. Meanwhile your *haverah* [girlfriend, a reference to Sandy W.] was in Amsterdam with another friend and visited my mother, who liked her. Unfortunately I missed them by one day, for I had an unexpected break of three days. I wish I knew some nice girl going to America; then I could repay the compliment. In fact I do know one who is a very good *yedidah* [female friend] of mine, is in Israel now, and will thence go to Canada. Enough girl- talk. Let's be sensible and not spoil our precious time. After all, I do believe that everything is predestined, even meetings with girls.

I don't agree with your idea of evil of others being in you as well. This sounds too much like the dogma of original sin. I do certainly not agree with the idea of one being responsible for the actions of all men. Yes, it is up to everyone to pursue justice for himself as well as for others, but this is a *personal* challenge which everyone has to decide on and which should not be imposed.

When it is imposed, like in dogmatic religion, it is prostituted by priests and the like.

Yes, we could say there are saints and devils. But remember that it is not only the fate, but the *dharma* [Hinduism, ultimate law or purpose of life] of a saint to be persecuted. And remember, when you try to find justice for a saint, the only thing you do is help his adversaries. Silent adoration does a lot more for the saint as well as for yourself. More later.

Greetings

Alex

(Eds. Alex kept preparing to make a trip to the States. He wanted to see Sharon and Alan, but also America itself. Again and again he worked out the details in his letters. This type of forward planning is as characteristic of him as his seemingly impulsive and hasty departures.)

Amsterdam
? [sic] August 1963

Dear Alan,

A short entr'acte letter. This is just to say that I have been to the U.S. Consulate. Things which I need:

A) Ticket to the U.S. (provided for)

B) Return ticket or guarantee for the same (provided for by my bank here)

C) An official invitation by an American saying that I am invited by him and that during my stay in the U.S., boarding and lodging are provided for by him

D) *If possible* a request from any employer to the local immigration authority to grant me a working permit for a year so that I can work for that employer.

This last will enable me to do something by way of earning my expenses in the U.S. It takes six weeks for the authorities to grant this. Any employer's request will do; I am not obliged to keep to one job once I am in the U.S. If you don't know anybody willing or able to do this, I can only enter the U.S. on a visitor's visa, not permitting any labor whatsoever. "C" is essential in any case.

You can rest assured that any invitation or guarantee you can provide me shall not be imposed upon. Once I am in the U.S., I shall know how to work my way through the places you will want me to see.

I intend to come over before Christmas which I wish to celebrate there. It is a Holy Day which means a lot to me and my philosophy.

In a letter to Sharon, I suddenly hit upon a new idea concerning Man. That is, it is not a duality of flesh and soul, but a trinity of Man, Existence, and a Meaning added to it — not by the Existence-part, but by the Man-part of it. I am still working on this. Has anybody ever thought of anything similar? Literature?

Dancing Eyes [Laura] already haunts my imagination, which shows you in what state I must be in.

The History of the Labor Movement in the United States [a book written by Laura's father, Philip S. Foner] is a work of perfect research. But to me it is the work not of a communist, but of a reactionary republican. The spirit of the book has a lot in common with Gandhi's conclusions.

Yours,

Alex

stand upright, speak thy thought....

Amsterdam
21 August 1963

Alan, Alan,

What have you done to me?!! Do you want me to commit suicide that early? Should I become a complete drunkard? For with your red letter [a letter written in red ink], I got a reply from Laura AND a picture of her. Good God, but what shall I do after those few days she will visit me? Those few hours when poems shall again flow out of my pen like so many drops of rain? Alan, dearest and most beloved friend, can you stop her coming here? For if she is not like that picture, I shall get mad, and if she is anything like it, I shall be forever enslaved, whether she encourages me or not. I have not drunk a drop of liquor now but I am crying in unison with the Dutch rain. And my mother, for once, understands and agrees with me, and she tries to comfort me with the idea that in reality she looks less like Mona Lisa than in this picture. I pray my mother is right for such beauty should really not be allowed to walk around unveiled. Says my mother who doesn't read anything but *Wuthering Heights* stuff: "A beauty like that invites crime."

From Dostoevsky this phrase would come as a commonplace, from her it is a true vision. Go slow, *langzaam* [Dutch, slow], says you, have a sense of the dramatic. You FOOL, don't you know that everything governed by sense drowns when the winds of feeling blow? Yes, I've said, "I'm willing to give up a lot of what I hold precious." And I repeat it again and again, for well do I realize how feeble reason is when it has to combat that indefinable Ulysses that some say comes from the heart. If it were only a matter of sex, one could cut off one's penis, but has anyone ever succeeded in letting the heartbeat stop, even one second, and live? No, boy. Books teach a lot, and you can even use them for a shield around your body against that what comes from the outside. But you are helpless when the attack is made from that powerful fifth column within....

A night of blissful sleep has passed, and the sharp edge of the shock has worn off. Of course, I do not mean it when I ask you not to let her come. The damage has been done anyway. Your letter, I'm afraid, shall not be of much help. I am so unfortunate as always to give myself away. Also I realized that American girls may flirt and pet without meaning anything more serious than temporary pleasure. Here, as soon as a girl lets herself be kissed and touched, it means that she cares a hell of a lot for you. Which explains to you my (I realize now unexpected) immediate genuine friendship for Sharon. By the way, her friend Sandy C. came here, and I am afraid neither one of us was very faithful to Sharon's memory. She is very nice, and after her two-day stay it seemed like we knew each other a lifetime. She told me she met you while you were in New York.

She and Sharon are going to share an apartment in which I am invited to stay. Complications?

In her letter Laura writes, "Although I don't know you, I have so much respect and affection for Alan that I have complete faith in his judgment about people."

This fact only shall probably help me in restraining myself than anything you wrote in red. Remembering that it was you who recommended me, I cannot but try to live up to the picture you must have given her about me. And I wouldn't want anyone to blame you because of me. So rest assured, all shall be well. And if I get to be destroyed, nobody shall be any the wiser for it.

No, I'm not angry at your words. Only people who love and respect each other can afford to pronounce them or listen to them in the right spirit. And don't blame yourself *ever* if you need to scold an older person. It is an old Jewish custom prescribed by the Sanhedrin.

Don't ever let yourself get "Alexandrized" (or whatever the past principle). Be an individual; be Alan; it is good enough....

*(Eds. Here Alex uses a classical Greek verb, **Alexandrizo**, which means to be a partisan of Alexander. Clearly Alex means that Alan should not be unduly swayed or influenced by him.)*

Pray for me on the 16th. I shall feel like on judgment day: *hatimah tovah.*

(Eds. In thinking about his impending meeting with Laura, Alex pictures it in apocalyptic terms, and he employs the traditional Hebrew greeting reserved for use at the High Holiday Season: may you [in this case himself] be inscribed for good. This greeting evokes a most solemn Hebrew prayer.)

Alexander
[signed in Hebrew]

Amsterdam
1 September 1963

Dear Alan,

Just a reply on the official things. More intimate letter will follow later. I went with the information your letter contained to the U.S. Consulate General. Their reply is as follows: you must have been misinformed. Everyday they issue so- called H-visas. These are temporary worker visas with no immigration implied. They can be issued for 3,6,9, or 12 months depending on the request of the employer. These H-visas, moreover, do not come under any quota scheme. (By the way I would otherwise fall under the Israeli quota and not the Dutch for I have an Israeli passport.) DO NOT INFORM OR AQUAINT THE DUTCH CONSULATE OF MY POSSIBLE COMING. As far as the Dutch officialdom is concerned, travelling is taboo for me.

In order to get me an H-visa, the only thing required from your immigration authorities is a PETITION NO.12g-B. Sandy C.'s father is in a position to do some hiring so I believe it better to let her do this part of the formalities. I am sending all information to her. I do need this OFFICIAL invitation to stay in the U.S. as your guest. For the unofficial one in your letter, I am very grateful, yet hope never to abuse your father's hospitality. But do send me the thing for counsulate's eyes. I'll tell Sandy to write to you if she fails. Then you can take up the thread later if that be necessary. Here follows the information you will want in filling out forms etc.

Name: Alexander Ben-Aharon [Hebrew form of Aronson]
Address: Andreas Bonnstraat 25, Amsterdam
Born: 20 December 1934 in Amsterdam
Nationality: Israeli
Passport: Israeli No. 85673 issued in Beersheva on 3 August 1957 valid till 14 August 1965

A little bird told me that many H-visas are issued to mother's helps (unobtainable in the U.S.). Why not introduce me as a Butler or House-servant? Remind officials of Our Man Higgins if they object.

Your man,

Alex

P.S. Laura will make acquaintance with a beardless me. On the way to a bar mitzvah, I had an accident and broke my jaw. (This was yesterday.) Painful and unable to eat more than porridge, but shall be able to look normal by the time she arrives.

(Eds. It is obvious from this letter that Alex held dual Dutch-Israeli citizenship. At a later time in his life, some mis-information on this point was spread, for the claim was made that Alex was not an Israeli. The denial of Alex's Israeli citizenship was clearly intended to save his life.)

Amsterdam
[Early September 1963]

Dear Alan-my-lad,

Back home in Amsterdam and for the umpteenth time out of a job. I was made to quit, wanted too many things my own way. That was not appreciated. Of course, I had expected it so it did not come out of a blue sky. There is still a chance that they will give in to some of my wishes: more expense money for porterage, more liberty during excursions, etc. There is a lot to the job which goes straight against my ideas, and I naturally take the consequences. Pity, the going was good while it lasted. As it is, I have earned the journey to the U.S. For the rest — my living expenses there and my return here — I still have to find some way, and I will....

Wrote a letter to your lassy with the dancing eyes [Laura], telling her the trip to the Adriatic had to be cancelled, but not to worry for I'd make her time an unforgettable one anyway, or something to that effect. I am really looking forward to her coming. I am ready to fall heavily in love at any given moment now. Not that I stopped loving Sharon, but I am very suspicious of my feeling for her and think that it may be just the shadow of my desire to love. The state of mind I am in is really very dangerous, for I am ready to give up a lot of what I hold precious in exchange for a bit of real love. It is so hard to find!!! I can imagine how you feel when you are having a crisis in connection with *your* emotional center. She [Sandy W.] did come here with a male friend, though my Mother said there seemed to be nothing between them. But, Alan, girls are so strange and unreliable. Were it not that we need them so much, I would spend the rest of my life hating them. If I do not find a girl for myself soon, I might get myself a pet monkey. One needs an outlet for one's surplus emotion.

During my last trip to Austria, I made a discovery in a record shop, and you will have it in your mail-box soon. Really great!

(Eds. Alex had found a record of Martin Buber reading hasidic tales in German. The record was entitled "Wo ich gehe — du!")

Talking about names, I prefer Alan to Al. Alan Paton is my favorite writer. Once a person tried to call me Al, too, and I slapped him (an American soldier in Massawa, Ethiopia). Alexander is not my real name, you know. The L. stands for Leendert, an old Dutch name which I despise for its suggestion of bourgeoisie, but that is what I am really named. Since my childhood, however, I hated it, and my mother always called me Lex [*lex* in Latin means law] to which I put an "A" because I am so opposed to written law. So the name Alexander was born about ten years ago.

Yet now my best friends call me Muktidas which you know is a name I have really earned. It was Ghandhi's successor, Vinoba Bhave, who gave it to me as a sign of appreciation. The meaning is Servant of Freedom. MUKT = FREEDOM in mainly the spiritual sense. DAS = SERVANT or SLAVE.

Said old Shakespeare: What is in a name? But isn't it like the clothes one wears? It not only makes you for the outer world, but it can even form one's whole personality. The soldier is a brute because he wears a uniform and is called sergeant. That's the difference with the Israeli soldier: he does wear a uniform, but they call him Moishe anyway.

I am at present racing through (don't you write "thru"?) a few books by Laura's father. Not properly reading, for I have better books that call my attention. So far I can't form an opinion.

Enclosed another picture of me to replace the one you sent to Dancing Eyes. Taken at a last-night party for one of my herds. At the time, I had swallowed about 8 bottles of beer, but you see I still behaved. So even while being scratched, I still did not become a barbarian. I believe Freud was wrong when he said, Scratch a European and uncover a barbarian. *Any* person when properly scratched will produce the barbarian, or rather, primal qualities.

(Eds. Alex obviously has in mind an adage like "Scratch a European and find a barbarian." What is not so obvious is whether Freud actually said this. The key words of the adage do not appear in this context in the six-volume Concordance to the Psychological Works of Sigmund Freud.)

Look at a mother, when harm is done to her child; look at a man, when his chosen mate is endangered. They do not lose their "civilization"...at least I don't think so. But their natural senses become sharpened to the quick. And that is probably what Freud meant by "scratch." Not scratch at the civil varnish, but scratch at the person's *life*.

I don't understand the feeling of murder, because I never felt it yet. I do know the feeling of killing which, I want to make clear, is not quite the same. Murder is aimless; killing is protective (whatsoever it may protect, from property to love). Or perhaps, in calling killing protective, I might be right in calling murder acquisitive?

Alan, I stop. My head isn't fixed to it any more, and it wanders off to Greece. Please realize that I am waiting for your parcel of long dark hair ONLY [Laura]. But I know that anything or anyone sent by you would be worth the effort.

Xairete [Greek, be glad or rejoice]

Alexandros
[signed in Greek]

INTERNATIONAL UNDERSTANDING...

Amsterdam
16 September 1963

Dearest Alan,

Laura and I both writing to you, sitting opposite each other in the same little attic that you honored with a visit, so you know how. She in the easy chair in the corner near the window, I sitting near the little table at the door.

She didn't come by ship, but managed to get a free passage by air to Paris and decided to arrive here *dafka* [Hebrew, precisely then, with the suggestion that there was something slightly perverse about the timing] on shabbat by train. Before that she had notified me by a telegram of 15 words (of which 7 were unnecessary) which train she was coming on, and I managed to pick her out of the crowd though she doesn't look a bit like her picture. Fortunately, for I wouldn't have had a peace of mind if she'd turned out to look anything like it. But she is very sweet, and we understand each other very well. She has contact-lenses which I have persuaded her not to make use of, and she now uses her old specs again. Last night we went to "The Good Hour" [a café in Haarlem]. We both enjoyed it. She agreed with your calling it aesthetic. I believe she loves you a lot.

I do have a copy of the Buber record on tape, for I now possess such a machine. It is quite handy, and I'll take it along with me to Greece, together with a portable record player that works on batteries, my favorite records, and nearly all my books. A Dutch friend will go with me to help with the building. I hope to get a lot of work done in two months, though God knows for what purpose I am doing it all.

Don't send me Hannah Arendt's book on Eichmann. As it is, I haven't even read half of all the books I possess, though I keep on buying those which I so much want to read. Got lately all Gandhi's major works sent over from India (20 of them) and bought a lot here besides.

Your writing about sex, love, etc. gives me a great wish to have discussions on these subjects with a group of Americans who are willing to give themselves entirely in these discussions. Could you gather around you a group of people as follows?

A) Equal number of men and women and boys and girls

B) None of them should be the "traveling kind" as you call them, but all of them ready to open up and, if necessary, to become personal

C) Not exceeding 10 persons in total.

The subjects I would wish to discuss with them are:
1) Segregation, 2) Love and marriage, and 3) Sex.

Here in Amsterdam such groups already are in existence, and they work out very well. Maybe you can start such a group at your university, and then I can come over for the hours that above subjects can be discussed. This is just a thought of mine; what do you think? The idea is for me to get an insight into the average American's way of thought.

I don't want to answer you on paper on your charge that I am less honest (perhaps with myself?) on the question of men/women relationships. It too easily leads to misunderstanding, but I shall continue our discussion on that subject orally. *Inshallah* [Arabic, God willing].

The Consulate here gave me the necessary papers for an H-visa, and said they don't agree at all with the view held in the place you were advised. I filled out the things concerning myself and then sent them to Sandy C. Meanwhile I hope you send me your invitation in some more readable form (for the consulate). It is ABSOLUTELY ESSENTIAL for you to remember that, whatever they may say in the U.S., here counts what is said here.

So far in reply to your last letter. You may understand how little I am really inclined, with Laura sitting here, to write at all. I feel a great urge, but I am afraid to lose myself again. Right now I can't afford to fall in love, or rather to love at all and then to become disappointed. There isn't much that keeps me alive, and I don't want to lose the little values I still possess. This may sound indeed self-conscious, but, spiritually speaking, I am desperate... and the spirit is what counts, or rather, what I want to count.

Tell me to be less self-conscious, and you are saying the same as "be your age" or "behave as any ordinary man would." Though I know I could do it (with more ease even than to maintain my present being), I also know that it would be the death of Alex A. and some nincompoop called A. Aronson, Esq., would wander aimlessly around. And you wouldn't want to know him.

Don't reply me on this. You may understand it better when we meet again. Enough about myself.

Today, after letters have been written, Laura and I will go to the flea-market, Rembrandt house, and Anne Frank house. Tomorrow the Van Gogh museum. I think she has faith in my program for she never has any opposed suggestions. She is good. I like her.

Thanks,

Alex

Amsterdam
22 September 1963

Dear Alan,

I suppose you must be very much in love with Laura yourself. Else how could you have written such beautiful things of her? By this you may have guessed that she has become a disappointment.... I LOVED having her with me AS I LOVE EVERY GUEST, but to get such a regard for her as you seem to have is impossible.

Right now I am having a terrible time because a wisdom tooth in the lower jaw had to be pulled. An aftermath of my little accident. The pulling wasn't done too well, and I am writing this during my third sleepless night. I hope it won't last too long for this Monday I shall leave for Greece. A Dutch friend who is a good mason will go along for three weeks to help with the building. I myself will stay there till the end of November.

Have applied for a tourist visa for the U.S., but will have to wait for an invitation WHICH IS ESSENTIAL. Also for a clearance from the U.S. consul in Israel. All that may take a month, if I ever do succeed. I am getting impatient with your country. But then, I suppose, it would be the same over here. Do send all your letters from now on to Yatros Alexandros, Fannari (Karditsis), Greece (Thessalia). He is a person I met last year... beardless yet still quite a character. I decided to renew his acquaintance. But seriously I don't feel half so naked as I did without beard last year, which is good.

26 September 1963

Bought at last my ticket for the ship to the U.S. Unfortunately I had to accept a later ship than I planned in order to get a cheap fare. Believe it or not, the fare is only $130. The ship leaves here around 15 December so that I may have to pass my birthday, and probably that of Our Lord too, aboard ship. They don't get as far as New York. The waiting now is for the visa. *le-shanah tovah* [Hebrew, Happy New Year].

Alexander
[signed in Hebrew]

Fannari
[= Fanárion 39°N, 21°E]
12 October 1963

Dear Alan,

Your letter just arrived as I was sitting in the café where we so often used to sit, the one up high that used to be opposite the church. "Used to be," for the great snow fall last winter made the church collapse. The tower still stands and rings every hour. My own cabin is 100 per cent all right, thanks to the care of my neighbors who kept it clean of snow all winter. My Dutch friend is now helping me with the building of kitchen-shower-WC as I had planned. We just spoke to the local priest, and he agreed to sell the old church doors (anno 1871) to be used by me. Continuously raining, foggy, windy and nothing to be seen of the sun. This hampers the work a lot, and my first load of sand (to be used in the cement) was completely washed away. A big loss, but one that I have meanwhile overcome.

Your letter gave me a lot to think about. About the part in which your Sandy [W.] figures, I will not reply but this: I pity you and am happy for your sake. This is not a contradiction....

About my trip to you. My ship leaves around December 15th and arrives 10 days later in Hampstead Roads, Norfolk. I have asked Sharon to meet me there ALONE. She might not want to, but

I'd hoped she cared enough for me to save me embarrassment of having others present at our first meeting on her territory.

You must know that I am against the purchase of Rembrandt reproductions. The stuff they sell "ready-to-hang" at the Rijksmuseum is tourist-trash. Please, Alan, allow me to pick reproductions for you. And don't you dare try to re-pay me in cash. There will be enough for you to give me once you lead me into a book- or record-shop. I've already discovered the Folkway series, and I want to dig in it deeply when I get the chance.

Your characterization of me is perhaps correct. [I do have a sacred mission] to shatter idols. But you have forgotten one important thing: I am doing this as an adult, on an irresistible impulse and *against* my own inclinations. God knows how I would like to be "normal"...an all-accepting nobody.

My writing, I suppose, is very bad right now, for it is night, and I am straining my eyes by the light of an oil lamp. Shall continue tomorrow. My companion just had a clever idea and took the oil lamp from the wall and set it on the table so I can continue now.

Concerning the National Geographic Map of the Classical Lands of the Mediterranean, let me say that I'd be interested in it. It sounds good, at least. But is it historically correct?

Your statement of invitation [for the U.S. consul] is, in one word, darling (with all the sentiments included). I believe it will do, but I won't know until I return to Amsterdam. Meanwhile I hope you'll continue writing to this here address. Your letters are a welcome diversion from everyday Greek life.

My day is as follows: Waking up (with a pain in the back) at 5:30, fetching water, washing, and boiling the milk (one bottle brought daily by a dear little girl) till 6 a.m. Reading till 6:30. Writing till 7 a.m., drinking the cooled milk, mixing cement. My friend takes the work over at 7:30, and I go about doing the daily chores: laundry, food, cleaning, shopping. When my friend Peter, a Mennonite who converted to Judaism, goes on October 22nd, I shall do less work at home. (Incidentally Peter is a sailor now serving the Dutch Rabbinical Kasruth Control, autodidact and a jewel.) I will probably spend my time then travelling around Greece visiting good friends.

My cooking here is very satisfactory; people wonder about a man being able to make tasty things. But then cooking is one of my hobbies. And I made an oath never to eat from tins any more. No canned goods whatsoever, which my American hosts will probably regret, but I am this way.

Fannari
November 1963

Today I left the world. Having worked last night till llpm putting the finishing touch to the completed kitchen/toilet by whitewashing the walls, I suddenly felt I had to flee from Fannari. (Interruption for a bread, olives and something saltish that I faintly recognized as *smoked herring*!!!) I absolutely had to be alone for a few hours, and I have become so much involved in Fannarian life that the only hours I really had to myself were the siesta hours (12:30 to 3:30pm). So this morning I got up with the idea of spending my Sabbath elsewhere. Not in Trikkala or Larissa, where there are Jewish communities, as was my habit.

Shabbat has become very dear to me as also Jewish company on that day. Old age? My idea, then, was to spend the day in the tiny village somewhere on top of the Pindos mountains where I am now. To get here one has to walk one hour from Fannari along the road to Kappa and then to drink a strong retsina in a roadside coffeehouse to gather strength for the two-hours stiff climb (2,000 ft). Just before reaching this village (1,000 inhabitants), you turn around and say goodbye to the world. Then you follow a bend in the road to a mountain crag where you are curiously received by a nosy, but friendly race of poor farmers weakened by rheumatism and continued intermarriage. When you are here for the first time, you are led to one of the four village "Americans," local sages of 65-85 years old who spent their youth in the U.S.A. and still know a few words of "English." As it was, I had been here before and had some friend to go to.

Panajotis Passialis is one of the three village barbers, a young man of 26, married, with a not too healthy looking child and an 85-year old "American" father. Passialis seems to have been the adventurous family of the region, for, besides the old man here who will show you a row of ancient medals, there was that brother of his who went to South Africa and married a black Congolese woman. This "African" Passialis had a son (now dead) called

Lamberos, a half-blood who shared my cabin in the Albert Schweitzer Hospital in Lambaréné where we had a fine friendship. It was he who gave me the address of his Greek relatives and thereby became the indirect cause of my Fannarian venture. For on my way to this mountain village one and a half years ago, I had to pass through Fannari and became so enamored with the beauty of the view that I decided to make myself a retreat there and then.

My friend Panajotis here helped me to get the piece of land and now, after building on it again, I have come to see him before leaving Greece this year. Call it my yearly pilgrimage to eternity, for here you really are outside yourself — as you may notice from my style. It is, moreover, the ideal place to visit before undertaking a journey to America, for the atmosphere here, because of the old "Americans," is U.S.-minded....

Interruption. This time for a walk through and around the village. First, of course, to the central coffeehouse where I am heartily greeted by people who remembered welcoming me last year. (Advice to hitch-hikers in Greece: always go to a central coffeehouse, wherever you are. It will save the expenses of food and lodging.)

Meeting with a young fellow who speaks English rather well. He was in the army in Athens and Turkey (NATO-plan) and "studied," which probably means that he visited the Athens University Library one day. (Like the typical Indian surgeon who advertizes "Ram Singh MBBS, FRCS {failed}".) Now he will go back to Athens to open a restaurant there. Of a rich family, naturally, but he knew a lot of the local history and showed me around in the way I like, bringing me first to the primary schools, housed separately in two small buildings, and then showing me a large 40-room palace, abandoned (but still retained) by a rich local family who moved to Athens. I was offered a small house and, though it was something I could afford (because of its low price, not my bank account), I decided not to take a "summer-house" here or anywhere. The beauty here is so great that it would become boring after a while. So I prefer to keep this village in reserve for rare yearly visits.

My own paper is finished. I am getting some scraps from my host. Slept peacefully last night and had a very satisfactory bowel-movement just now. Lots of olive oil and Turkish coffee. Our tour last night ended in a coffee-house where we sat for two hours, sipping ouzo embroidered with "little nothings," platters of pickled eggplant, etc. One of these platters contained, to my surprise, salted chick peas. Result, me turning the wheel of a coffee-mill for half-an-hour to make *hummous.* It turned out quite well.

Over the blue window pane [in the coffee-house where I am writing] hangs a colored print of 1920... "With the compliments of Joe Pizzurro, manufacturers of Maccaroni and Bread, 232 East 29th Street and 236 Elizabeth Street (near Prince Str.), New York." Moreover, last night I dreamt that we were visiting New York together. I am getting in the mood for your country (which is just as well). Got a not-too-nice letter from Sharon telling me she cannot come to meet me in Norfolk [Virginia] since she has not been so far in the U.S. before. Rather stupid to admit such a thing. Anyway, I noticed on the map that Washington is much nearer to my port of landing and so you are the one person after Sharon who has the right to introduce me into "la terre sainte" of the U.S. It will probably prove even better after all to have your friendly and typical American face awaiting me than one which could provoke antagonism. For you too, however, the same goes, do meet me alone and don't let my attention be diverted by other or new faces.

Interruption. This time for a long walk amongst and over surrounding mountains. My host and the English speaking youngster accompanying me, thinking to themselves, "How far does that foolish foreigner want to go now?" They, getting tired after a four-hour climb... and I, getting drunk on the continuous beauty that surrounds us. Four hours of savage life; scraping the rocks and being scratched by thorns; sliding down muddy paths and stumbling over uneven tracks. Four hours of calling hello to laboring farmers and jumping over small rivers. Four hours of life, viewing my own Fannari like God from up high and wishing for wings to fly like a bird.

Returning to Gralista to rest in a coffee-house (you see how important a part these inns play here in Greece) and getting again filled with that feeling of love for mankind, this time caused by a great number of ouzos. I tasted the satisfaction of being allowed to pay for a round of drinks, the sure sign that one is accepted and is not an outsider any longer. In the only store of the village, I bought you a notebook with the map of Greece on its cover and an old-fashioned cigarette lighter, though I don't think you smoke. Finishing now this letter before taking my siesta. Shall write again to say when exactly my ship arrives and what is its name. Love from your

Alex

(Eds. Enclosed in this letter were three dried pressed leaves.)

Section Two

Early Married Life

December 1963 - September 1964

stand upright, speak thy thought....

Amsterdam
10 December 1963

My beloved friend Alan,

This letter will bring you a great disappointment, for it will tell you that I shall not come to your country; but I hope it will also give you a bit of joy, on my account, when you learn the reason for it.

Everything was settled for my departure to the States. I had got my visa, bought my boat ticket, received my vaccinations, saved my pocket money in dollars, packed my suitcase. In short, I was ready.

Then, two weeks ago, coming back from Greece, I passed by the Albert Schweitzer village, a house for refugees and orphaned or abandoned children. The idea was to visit a Danish friend of mine who worked there as a carpenter, but he was gone when I arrived. So I did not meet him. But on the third day of my stay there (I had been asked to remain for a week to help with a few odd jobs), I met Bess. After we knew each other a full week, we realized that we just have to marry. And we will. Our ideas and ideals are the same, our characters for nearly 100% identical, and we were born in the same month, she on the 10th (today birthday celebration here), I on the 20th. There is one drawback... She is not Jewish, and I shall therefore have to break with my Mother and her orthodox family completely. Which I do without any hesistation because I feel that when I shall be completely free from them, I'll be able to develop myself better. Those whom I cherish most, my more intimate friends like you and a few others will, I trust, remain by me. We, that is Bess and I, have been offered the post of Father and Mother of the orphanage in France. The way matters stand right now, we may move in there in about three months. The wedding shall be very soon yet *nothing* may be whispered to the wind. I do not want my Mother to know anything about it till the very last moment.

In Holland one may not marry without parents' consent till the age of 30 which is still a way off for me. (Bess is 34.) So I shall have to tell my Mother about it the day before it happens. No need for me to ask you to keep it under your hat for the time being. You are the first and only one to whom I tell this, for I feel I owe it to you. I am writing to Sharon about my not coming; no more. I shall write to her all the rest when everything is settled to my satisfaction which may take up to one month.

Now to reply to your two letters as far as it still is appropriate. First of all, the reproductions which you requested will be sent by sea. Try to get me a complete catalogue of Folkway records, and I shall tell you what you may send me in return. This is only to set your conscience at ease. I don't agree with your statement that all reproductions are incorrect and incomplete. To show you what I mean, I shall enclose one which I would have chosen.

(Eds. Alex sent reproductions of two paintings by Rembrandt, "Titus, son of Rembrandt, dressed as a Monk" and "Portrait of an Oriental.")

Since I cannot get a map of classical lands, you may send me one which you choose yourself. Another thing which I am sorely in need of is the *Dictionary of Classical Antiquities* by O. Seyffert.

I can still answer you in a general way about the idea of disappointment. It is true that when one has not seen a good friend for a long time, one is liable to idealize him or her. (With girlfriends, another factor, that of sexual images, comes into the picture.) At any rate, when the acquaintance is renewed, there is a tendency to become disappointed — at the lack of obvious qualities which one had thought that friend possessed; at the change of physical features; at the coldness of the unknown that hovers between you and him (or her).

I have experienced this kind of disappointment several times and am continually afraid of it. Yet I have found it usually very helpful to be very reserved at the first reunion and to forget the former friendship altogether, although of course one can never cipher away entirely the pleasant feeling of expectancy.

To put your conscience at ease concerning your not having been able to come to Norfolk (if I would have come), let me tell you that I would not have forgiven you if you were to come there with so much work ahead. Not to speak of the fact that it would have burdened me unbearably to have deprived your mother of you for those two days. So please never write to me any excuses for doing, or not doing, something. Our friendship suffices to warrant the rightness of what we decide.

To return you a compliment, I am sending you a *yedidah* [female friend] of mine with whom I am on a very sound brother- sister footing. She is 22 years old, just back from Israel and is overwhelmed by it. She may sound a bit too firm and materialistic for a girl, but *is not*. Please write to her and discover a fine person who will NEED your friendship. Israel has given her a perception of people that made her give up many of her former friendships....

Please do forgive me for not coming. In a way, it is a disappointment for me, too. The joy which causes it, however, is so great that I feel completely happy. Regards to your parents.

Yours ever,

Alex

Poortugaal, [Holland]
22 March 1964

My dear Alan,

Hurrah! Got your two letters and shall answer immediately, for I delayed writing on purpose to hear whether you had received the reproductions. I am glad that these were to your liking, for I had lost the letter in which you wrote which ones you desired, and just chose them to my own preference. Boy, I wish you could see my room here in which I am writing to you now.

I am so very happy. The wedding went very well. I received your telegram the moment we stepped out of the townhall where the ceremony had taken place. It was not too stuffy in there thanks to our adopted French son (2 1/2 years old) Jean-Paul who mimicked the official and did everything to draw everyone's attention to himself. An hour earlier, I had a nice adventure with my black hat which was blown off by a strong breeze across a barbed wire fence into a muddy ditch at the foot of the dike (where we now live). So I stepped into the townhall with my (only) shoes unrecognizable by *botz* [Hebrew, mud].

On the whole, we were both very glad that everything went a bit topsy-turvy for neither of us likes convention. Elisabeth and I are so very much alike in our thoughts and ideals that we are still continually surprised. Of course, now that we have been married for nearly two months, we get to discover our differences as well, but these, too, are all very much to the completion of each other's self.

This week I am starting work as a male nurse in the local home for the aged. Staying in Amsterdam doing my job there and coming here for the weekends only, as I had planned, did not turn out well. I got homesick the minute I left the house. This house, by the way, is a converted streetcar (sleeping room, in daytime playroom for the boy, living room, kitchen) with an added shed. The shed contains our hall and toilet (which I built myself two weeks ago) and my room that breathes the same atmosphere as my attic in Amsterdam (now dismantled). Unfortunately, a large new road will be built very soon. It will pass this lovely free spot (orchard of my parents-in-law outside the village), and we shall have to move all our things in a year or two.

Anyway, we had not intended to finish our lives here but we are going to start a children's home somewhere. Of course, everything depends on our finances. We are thinking of a real home in the sense of a family with lots of kids in France or Greece, but in order to start properly we need at least $2,000 for the first year. After that, I hope to be able to earn a regular wage to pay for daily needs. We have a good start in Greece where I had a kitchen and toilet added to my cabin last year. I just got the offer of a prefab wooden house to be put there (in addition to the cabin) so that at least we need not worry about space to live. I also bought the neighboring plot last year so there is plenty of room to expand. In August Bessy and I are going to Greece and Israel for a visit of orientation. In the meantime, she continues as leader of a kindergarten, and life here is very sweet.

I got the National Geographic Map of Classical Lands. It has a prominent place in my study on the wall next to the map of Israel. I use it frequently. I hope that the dictionary will be found, for it is supposed to be a good one. As a gift I received from Bess a marvellous first edition of Whiston's *Josephus* bought at our Amsterdam flea market. A pity that this part of Amsterdam will also be removed shortly.

(Eds. The full title of William Whiston's translation is The Genuine Works of Flavius Josephus, the Jewish Historian: containing twenty books of the Jewish Antiquities, seven books of the Jewish War, and the Life of Josephus, written by himself.)

Alan, friend, this is it for today. I hope you will find the opportunity to write to me soon, for your letters are a constant shot of energy into my spiritual muscles.

Love from Elisabeth and Jean-Paul.

yours,

Alex

Poortugaal
17 May 1964

My most dear friend,

This week I received your second letter and so urgent it was that I feel the need of sitting down to answer it now on this beautiful day in May while the sun is shining brightly on my back. The child [Jean-Paul] at the moment stands beside me, looking on the play of this typewriting business. How long we shall be able to keep him is not known. Officially he should have been out of the country a long time ago, but the mayor, as yet, doesn't dare to lift his finger against him. The child has become very popular with the people here, and I do not think they would let him be "deported" back to France without interference. I have also engaged a lawyer to take official steps in the departments, but I doubt whether he will have any success. Anyway, if necessary, we shall let our little one "dive" into one of the many homes that have been opened to him in hospitable defiance of the law. Until, of course, we shall leave ourselves and take him along wherever we may go.

My tribe, if you so wish to call it (it is rather a circus, you know), consists at the moment of Bess, the child, myself, Beaucould (the mother dog), her two six-month-old black children and her two two-week-old children, and The Cat, whom we call Pussychat (a mixture of Jean-Paul's Dutch-French language).

My environment is not so very difficult to picture. The room, outside of which I am now writing to you, is a replica of my attic in Amsterdam, in my Mother's home. That is to say, most of what is in it and its atmosphere are the same. A little more "aesthetic" because it is all wood. The orchard that surrounds our tramcar home is in full bloom; this week the cows entered the meadows behind our rear window.

I am so completely happy that I continually wish for a speedy death. Very egotistically, of course, but if it were not for Bess, I would have put an end to myself knowing that life, as it is now given to me, cannot be improved upon. There are daily anxieties, of course, material matters which people like myself and Bess shall always have to put up with as long as we live.

Last week we had another possession thrown upon us by sheer coincidence. A wagon with gypsies spent a few nights here in the village. Every village in Holland has a small piece of land set apart for passing gypsies. Some of these "camps" are merely flat sites for easy wagon-parking; others have electricity, running water, and toilets. When we saw these gypsies, both Bess and I had conceived the idea of asking them whether they knew of a nice wagon for sale. And they did. So I went with them to another gypsy camp to bargain with the owner of a large wagon. And the sale came off.

So now we have a real gypsy car standing behind our tram wagon. There is a lot still to be repaired since we want it to be fixed properly before we begin our wanderings in it.

Our plans have changed several times since I wrote to you last. Undoubtedly, they will change again before we leave here. As it is now, the program, though not fixed, will keep us here in Holland at least till August/September. We may be gone for a week or so in between to take a breath of foreign air—a deep breath which will give us energy to stay here so long.

Please tell your friends that they are always welcome here. We have room for about twenty guests now, though not beds for all. Anyone sent here by you must be prepared (if needs be) to sleep on a carpet and to eat dry bread. I don't think it will ever come to that since guests usually come singly or in twos. Neither do I want to frighten your friends away. ON THE CONTRARY. Everybody passing Holland shall be MOST welcome; and when they are sent by you I shall be the more happy to entertain them. Laura will come here after the exams (in June), and I have an idea that she will not come alone, but will bring a friend along with her. We have had a very fine, though rare, correspondence since she left for France, and I feel somehow that Europe has done her a lot of good.

As for you, I gather that you are still not fixed up with a more constant nymph. I shall be glad to see the one you call your muse now. Be sure that I shall give you my verdict. I hope that it shall be someone worthy of you, for you know that I think a lot of you. American girls, I find, are a bit "too easy" on the whole. Of course, there may be exceptions. I doubt whether an American girl would be suitable for you. If it were up to me, I would fix you up with a French girl.

There is one thing that disturbs me in you and that is your lack of interest in "originals." It is, I find, not so much the value in money that should be the attraction of an original painting or letter, but the thrill of directness: i.e., the spiritual contact that comes to one through an original book, painting, or any object that has passed itself through the hands of a Master. I have here a letter written by Gandhi himself. It is not the value that I cherish. It is the fact that The Master himself has rested his hands on this paper, that it has absorbed a few drops of his sweat. This gives me the feeling of having contact with Him as if he were still alive. "For what man knoweth the things of a man, save the spirit of man which is in him?" Thus Paul in his letter to the Corinthians [I Cor.2.11].

Concerning those records, do not hurry to obtain them. I have got lots of things to occupy me and, though I shall be glad to receive them, I am not waiting for them. There is one thing I would be very eager to have here with me and that is your own person. Isn't there a chance of your coming here again? Although I know that you must be very occupied, I hope you will some time write to me a short dissertation on your view of the "History of Ideas." Tell me also your view on whether you see a practical application of it in life. Personally I regard philosophy as a great help when great decisions are to be made.

Listening to the music of Vivaldi. Life is brimming over with happiness. I wish I could have many people here to share it. If I were rich, I would invite many chosen friends to a secluded spot here or in Greece where I would set up a "centre for happiness." But I am starting to dream. I feel floating on thick air. I am not drunk, unless drunk with milk and honey. So I wish you may feel some day when you have found the woman of your choice. A great quietness....

Bess is now sitting by my side, peeling potatoes, a lovely blonde creature, home-like and my equal in thought and action. Well, dearest Alan, I must stop for energy in writing is fast fleeing from my head, and I must turn to other pleasures.

Write again soon and tell me something about your new president [Johnson]. How is he behaving on domestic questions? And what are the prospects for the coming elections? Here it is said that Nixon again will have a try at it and may have a good chance.

Love from the whole family Muktidas,

yours affectionately,

Alexander

P.S. My beard was shaved off when I fell on a station-platform last summer and broke my jaw. I kept it off in view of a meeting with Sharon whom I didn't want to disgust at first sight. I stopped shaving on my wedding-day. Bess had no antipathy toward it. She now grows her hair long to please me.

(Eds. A feature article about Alex and his wife, Elisabeth van Dieijen, was published in the "Trouw" newspaper on 22 July 1964. At the time, they had been married for six months and were living in Poortugaal, Elisabeth's home village to the south of Rotterdam. The two-year-old Jean-Paul was living with them. He was the French child they had brought back with them from the Schweitzer village in France where they had met the previous December. This article was translated from Dutch.)

The Couple Aronson-van Dieijen of Poortugaal Start a Home for Displaced Children

In the French district of the Dordogne, in the Albert Schwietzer village, a Dutch cow is at pasture. Her name is Kivapo...she is a present from the children of Poortugaal. She is a living symbol of friendship, faith, and sympathy. Kivapo came to Dordogne, far from Poortugaal, because a brave Miss van Dieijen told the children about the great Albert Schweitzer and his charitable work for humankind.

Together with her husband, Alex Aronson, she has unfolded ideas about helping suffering. Their first idea has already materialized. Jean-Paul, until lately a weak, ill, and neglected French boy, is now a striking example of Dutch health. One of our reporters has written up the adventures of the couple.

Letter to the Queen for Jean-Paul

She was Bets, the ringmaster of the children's circus in Poortugaal, and he had received the name Muktidas from his Indian teacher. The name means "a servant of liberty." Since February, they have been man and wife, the thirty-year-old Alexander Aronson and the thirty-four-year-old Elisabeth van Dieijen. They live in a house at the bottom of Welhoeksedijk, just outside the village of Poortugaal, midst fruit trees and rich grass. Two weeks ago, Elisabeth was still a teacher at the nursery school. Alex remains a nurse at the Old People's Home in Siloam. At the town clerk's office (where I asked how to get to their house), there was sneering. " 128 Welhoeksedijk! It's practically a slum. And she, the Miss of the nursery school." (I thought, "Little child in the cold, we will help you.")

They gave us just enough information to keep us from getting lost. At number 128 Welhoeksedijk, a red and white house hidden at the bottom of the dyke, we found an old man. He told us to go down the path until we came to a tramcar. "It's my daughter," he explained.

We heard the high voice of the child, then saw the little hideaway. Mrs. Aronson-van Dieijen is not the kind of person who waits for visitors at the door. "Come in," she said, nodding us towards two chairs. "I hope you don't mind if I carry on." There was a jumble of things which she was busy moving, not bothered by the clutter or untidiness.

Bets explained that she read an article about the Albert Schweitzer village in Dordogne in *Margriet* [a Dutch ladies' weekly]. That was three years ago. She thought, "That's for us." So they went to work at the local nursery school. The children painted plates and had a sale to raise money which was spent for the cow. Once she had a first cow grazing on the grass in Dordogne and giving milk, she pressed on for a second. "Children in need," she advertised, "Please help." A second cow came from Dutch soldiers in Fontainebleau.

This kind of activity is familiar to Elisabeth van Dieijen. "It's difficult in Holland because of all the rules and regulations," she said. But she has always been involved in welfare on an international level.

Last November she met Alex Aronson in Dordogne. It appeared that he had the same ideas about helping the suffering. Three months later, they were married and went to live in the tramcar in Poortugaal. They had the idea of starting something together.

The first of these "somethings" is standing in the grass screaming. This is three-year-old Jean-Paul whose mother could not look after him.

Jean-Paul

"If only you knew how difficult they make it for us to keep him here," Alex Aronson says. "The government has declared him to be an unwanted foreigner. No one in authority seems to appreciate that we have taken in a neglected French child. Now we've written to the Queen. Whatever happens, we will never let Jean-Paul go back to the gutter." He is a determined man in possession of a big black beard. There is too little room in Holland for him to achieve his ideals. He finds himself hemmed in by laws and regulations of all kinds, especially for the kinds of initiatives he and Bets would like to develop. "We have to go abroad," he says, nodding at the window through which the new buildings of Meenwenplaat [Rotterdam] and the Pernia oil refineries are appoaching. It's oppressing him because they are coming closer all the time.

Albert Schweitzer

Alex does know. He has seen much of the world: Africa, where he worked with Albert Schweitzer; Asia, where he was taught by a follower of Gandhi; Amsterdam where he was born; and London, England, where he earned a degree. Elisabeth and Alex are not the settling type. But they have a definite goal: to start a home for homeless children, not a shelter or institution, not in the way of Josephine Baker, but for a large number of children who miss something in their lives.

They want to leave early in September. Indeed, they would have preferred to have left right after their wedding in the spring, but Elisabeth had to complete her school year at the nursery. This trip will be a belated honeymoon as well as an orientation voyage to discover where the best place for them is. First, they will go to Greece, then to Israel where Alex's father lives. Alex knows Greece very well. "I have a little cabin in Fannari in Thessaly on a 70-meter-high mountain. I am completely at home there. The people in the village have seen me coming and going for years. It's a very primitive district, but I do everything myself."

Greece

"Why would we choose Greece? There is a great need there. There are many displaced children, as well as orphans. Also there are many poor children who need nursing care. How we are going to start, we don't yet know. It will take money, but we will battle our way through that. We have had vague pledges from friends. More than that, I don't want to say because of course we don't know if it will work. Nobody can know. The thing to do is to start small."

Their own children's home. That is their dream. No government will prevent them from bringing their ideals into practice. "Governments are always against everything which has not proved to be successful," Alex says. The government should see how Jean Paul has developed. He jabbers a French mixed with Dutch. He moves like a young cat. He is their best advertisement. "We hope that we can give Greek children the same good fortune."

Poortugaal
23 July 1964

Dearest Alan,

Seeing you yesterday on television made me think of this long overdue letter. "How's that?" you ask. Yes, my dear friend, your image came to me via a lovely movie called "Virgin Islands" and the man playing the main part was your double—John Cassavetes. If you have seen the film you may understand what I mean. It really was you.

I have got the idea that this letter is going to be written with lots of interruptions. There is, of course, the small matter of my job that keeps me busy from seven in the morning till about four p.m. I enjoy the work: playing nurse to people old of age. They range from 65 to 97 years old. Boy, if you get them to talk about old times!!! After my daily work, there are naturally some household chores to be done for the wife who is getting heavier day by day. For, and this will probably be a pleasant surprise to you, a little Muktidas has announced itself, and we await him or her (I hope for the latter) around the middle of December.

Can you imagine how happy we are? We just can't stop quarreling from morning till night for sheer love. I am very much satisfied with married life and can full-heartedly advise you to do the same. My Elisabeth is a very good cook and a very ardent housewife though I am constantly trying to teach her my ideas about order in the house (which she doesn't seem to be able to adopt). This is sometimes very tiring, but it is a failure of hers that I accept, considering her many good sides. Another thing about my love that I have to put up with is my own inability to take inspiration from her. However we talk and agree with each other, she just doesn't activate me. The fault, very likely, is with me. Or rather, with my proximity to her. If we would be separated for a long time, I am sure that my spirit would surge to great heights, as it did when I was so very much in love with that Swiss creature who made me write many poems, when I was far away from her.

I suppose it is because I am being too well fed, with food as well as with love. I am getting so that I sit on my chair with a smoke, a cup of coffee, good music on the radio or the pick-up, and my wife in front of me, washing or darning or peeling potatoes. At such a moment, I feel myself spiritually dead, though there must be a good side to my realizing it. I get thrown back to my old self when a visitor arrives with whom I have no daily contact, and who makes me take up conversation on different subjects in which I am well versed....

After writing this I talked it over with Elisabeth. She told me she experiences the same thing. She used to do a lot of painting, but hasn't been able to draw a simple design since we have lived together. Strange, isn't it? Or perhaps not. The formula for an increase of spiritual power was phrased by Jesus in the New Testament. It was known even before his time in old Indian philosophy. That is, the decrease of worldly pleasures will automatically force the spirit to counterbalance man's need for any comfort. This is proved by the fact that the poorest among men are the most faithful believers. This, by the way, is to me also the reason why a new religion, in order to be successful, has to be started among the poor. Do write to me what your History of Ideas says about this.

On the first of September, we shall start our tour through France, Italy, Yugoslavia to (of course) Greece and Israel. It is final at last. I am still not sure whether finances will carry us all through, but we just do not wish to put it off any longer. I realized that, once the new world-citizen is born, we shall not have much freedom any more. Besides, there is still the matter of our Jean-Paul, the French baby whom we have succeeded in keeping with us till now. Against government's wishes. Pressure has become very strong, however, and if we do not bring him out of Holland very fast, he shall be deported like any unwanted foreign criminal, notwithstanding his 3 years. Officials here are very much afraid that some day he will become a charge to the country, though we have given all possible assurances and guarantees. The fact is, however, that here in Holland there is quite a child-problem already (the reason of which, I do not wish now to discuss). This is not to be talked over with anybody else, since it is kept absolutely secret, but about 4,000 children per year are being "sold" to America. The few who know this do not wish to make a scandal out of it, because they (or rather, we) know that these "exported" children are getting good homes. They are also getting futures that couldn't ever be given them if they were kept here in Dutch "institutes," "homes," or whatever you may wish to call places where a few hundred orphans or children from incapable parents are "kept."

Both Elisabeth and I still cherish the idea of establishing a real HOME for some of the unfortunate. Yet every new bit of information we get points to an increase in essential capital required to begin the project. So I don't see the realization of our dream yet. I know I am getting lazy and lose a lot of my fighting spirit living IN society, instead of above it, as I used to do when single. But how the heck shall I change it??? This coming trip, I realize, is important to both of us to refresh our spirits by letting fresh impressions of misery on the way awaken our better impulses. For I am sure that the worst that can happen to a man like me is the replacement of impulses by "reason."

Yesterday I received a postcard from Laura informing me that there won't be a chance for her to come to Holland again. Great pity, for I would have loved to see what Europe and Israel had done to her, if anything. But she has already left Europe, and since I think she might have flown, it is quite possible that you have seen her already. Do report to me about her "being."

Alan dear, I think you write wonderful letters and could even write poetry about your "muses." Why is it that man must always be in love with someone or something in order to evoke the utmost of his abilities?

Please do not worry too much about finding those records. There is absolutely no hurry and certainly no "must" in getting them. Just think of them as items of luxury which one can do without. Another thing is the following. I just got a list of "Mentor Books" which is a series of paperbacks. I would love it if you got me the following items: *The Papal Encyclicals* (edited by Anne Fremantle), *The Bhagavad Gita, The Tao Te King, The Sayings of Confucius, The Teachings of Buddha, The Upanishads*. Also, urgently, *The Authentic New Testament*. Lost my copy yesterday.

If you can get them soon, I would be happy. If you could, send them NOT to Holland, but to Post Restante, KARDITSA, Greece (Thessaly). Not to Fannari because I doubt if they understand the idea Poste Restante.

The idea is that I will have some more good reading to do in my little place which we undoubtedly shall visit for some weeks. Since you took the New Testament as one of your subjects (you know it is one of my pets), I am perhaps a bit late in advising you to get yourself the Schonfield translation in this series. Hugh Schonfield is a good friend of mine, or rather, he was. (We lost contact about three years ago.) He is a real yid and a very unusual one, for he is a yid with ideals, who translated the New Testament in a quite Jewish fashion, showing more of the background of the Book than any translation has achieved so far. I do not like all of his ideas and translations, but still regard his version as one that really HAS to be read and studied. Another one of his beautiful translations is the Song of Songs which you also MUST read. Hugh Schonfield, by the way, is the founder and president of the Commonwealth of World Citizens. Once I was a very active member. I lost touch with them some time ago since my interests in idealistically motivated organizations waned.

(Eds. Alan bought these books in Washington.)

Back to our conversation about "originals." Of course, I realize that wanting an original is based on man's desire to possess. One may possess a thing for the sake of the thing itself... but one may also wish to possess a thing for the idea or the force that stands behind it. It is not the artistry of a person that decides whether he is capable of assessing the value of an object. And your argument that a thing in your possession deprives others of seeing it does not have to work at all. What is your opinion of all the Stradivariuses laid up in museums, useless? For everyone to see, yes. But I would rather have one given to a person like Menuhin to play upon and to draw inspiration from.

If you wish, there are opportunities enough to put an owned article into museums for some days or weeks. The best exhibitions here are not the ones owned by museums (usually I find a museum so crowded with beauty that I get sick of it), but the exhibitions of private collections that are on view now and then in a specially reserved room.

Somerset Maugham wrote somewhere that beauty, pure beauty when seen a long time together, is very wearying. Do you know why? Because it is up to the person who looks at it to decide for himself whether a thing is beautiful or not. Beauty is not absolute. It depends upon the watcher. A quite useless, to me ugly, object may have a very real beauty in your eyes. A letter of Gandhi, interesting for others to look at, curious for historians to see, is a thing which (to me) links my spirit with the writer of it. Then, if you do not wish a hand by Rodin, to HAVE it, it doesn't mean that you deny yourself a possession, but simply that your wish to feel contact with the Master is not very strong.

I believe very much in originals. I got myself one of those Goya prints, and it is opposite my desk at this moment. It depicts the Horror of War; a man taken up a ladder to be crucified while a body that was hanging on it before is being slung down. A priest tries at the last moment to convert the poor creature. Not that it would have helped him. He would have got only the privilege of being hung by the side of the neck, to die immediately, instead of getting the rope around his throat, to be slowly strangled. A soldier takes one of his boots off to try it on himself. Yes sir, this picture would have been great, even as a reproduction. But this is an original by the Master himself. To me this means that the air of the scene is in my room when I look at it. The man who saw it, that man touched this paper and printed it himself. It is alive.

Perhaps I am over-sensitive...but the most treasured item in my room is a stone, taken from the ruins of an old synagogue of which my grandfather (whom I loved very much and who is still my guiding spirit) was the *Gabbai*.

(Eds. Alex is referring to his maternal grandfather, Hartog {=Herman or, in Hebrew, Tsvi} Cohen, who died of exhaustion in Bergen-Belsen early in the summer of 1944. Tsvi Cohen had been the Gabbai in the Linnaeusstraat Synagogue in Amsterdam. Alex mentions his grandfather again in one of the last notes he wrote from prison. A gabbai was a synagogue warden, originally probably a dues collector.)

Two broken tiles on a bit of cement on which I painted the verb from the Psalms that He gave me when I was born. "Some trust in chariots, and some in horses, but we, in the name of the Lord our God, SHALL REMEMBER [*nazkir*, Psalm 20.8]." If it were not for the fact that I am married to a *shiksa* [Yiddish, non-Jewish woman], I would get VERY religious continuing this letter. I cannot afford that now.

Let me end this discussion by remarking that to my belief every single person, you included, has his sacred spot or spots. And any object closely connected to this spot would become a holy relic to him. If only to chase away his own fears of becoming disconnected from his own sacred spot [a man turns to] art, a person, a religion, or whatnot. Perhaps I may even go so far as saying that this "relic" or "originals" business is, in some way, equivalent to the crucifixes of the southern Catholics, the paper images of the Chinese ances-

Linnaeus Straat Synagogue, Amsterdam, built in 1927-28 by architect J.S. Baars and destroyed during the War. Alex's grandfather served as gabbai (warden) of this synagogue. Source: R. Wischnitzer, The Architecture of the European Synagogue, #210.

Interior of the Linnaeus Straat Synagogue. Alex kept a piece of rubble from this synagogue among his most prized possessions. Source: Wischnitzer, The Architecture of the European Synagogue, #209.

Alex's greetings to Alan on the Jewish New Year, September, 1962. Pictured is the street where Alex lived until his marriage.

Alex during the summer of 1962.

tors, or the puppets of Terah. But that, of course, is going too far for this, innocent, discussion of ours.

4 August 1964

Hurrah, your muse has contacted me. Got a letter today from a certain Joan Michelson, and I gather that she is it. She intends to come at the end of this week. So I wired her that she is welcome any time. Joan met Laura and the latter has not discourged her to see me. This week is full of guests anyway. My father and his wife have come over from Israel. My brother with his wife has come too. And finally my youngest brother, who has been here a year to study, will join the family reunion tomorrow. The idea is to get a picture made of Papa with his three sons and their wives. We are all very happy to be together again, if only for a few days. Shortly Elisabeth and I shall be in Israel again ourselves, and this is a good first acquaintance for her with Israeli life and thought, while it is on her own grounds that she meets it.

Reading your friend's letter, I fear greatly for her intelligence unless it is the first time that she uses the typewriter. Don't be afraid that I am going to prejudge her, though. You shall have my thoughts about your muse when she is gone back. Somehow I am happy to see an American face at this stage of my life. Any face would have done, but the fact that there is some spirit of yours in her (this would have already been for she writes, "I am Alan's friend") makes me look forward eagerly to her visit. I hope to give her something that you may recognize when you see her again. Spiritually I mean. Anyway I still have some hopes of seeing you again in not too distant future. I have sort of a feeling that you are going to be here shortly.

Alan, dear, do write to me again soon, please. Your letters are a constant uplift of warming fire in a world that is so very pleasantly lit already. My love and respects to your parents,

Yours ever,

Alex

P.S. Just this. When asking for the Brecht House Un-American Activities Committee record, I was under the impression that it was a real recording of Brecht's interrogation before the committee. If I am mistaken, then don't bother about it.

(Eds. Bertolt Brecht appeared before the House Committee on Un-American Activities on 30 October 1947. Brecht cleverly dispelled the Committee's suspicions about him. What interested Alex was Brecht's facility in dealing with those in authority, not Brecht's ideological commitments.)

About Burl Ives: aren't there any 45 r.p.m.'s of his with guitar only? If not, just choose the one that you think is the most "aesthetical." I have got good faith in your taste. Do play the records once or twice on your own pick-up so that you can honestly write on the outside of the package that they are *second-hand records*.

If your finances don't hold, please write to me, and I shall mail you the amount required. For the books requested in this letter I am giving something to cover expenses along with your muse.

Love once again

Fannari
? [sic] September 1964

Dear Alan,

Here we are again at a point which we have in common, my cabin in Greece which is slowly emerging into a new denomination called "bungalow" — like the little ugly duckling into the swan. Stirring me into activity is Dvorák's "From the New World" Symphony. And here are my three white mice again.

Yesterday I went with Elisabeth to the village Gralista from which I wrote to you last year. She preferred it to Fannari and, in a way, so do I; but to me it is too much out of the way, too difficult to reach to have my homestead there. The road to Fannari has been greatly improved and from Karditsa it now takes me twenty minutes in the Morris. The climb around the mountain to the cabin remains the same 15 sweatful minutes. Besides the wooden hut which you know, there is the additional toilet-kitchen in brick, built last year.

The past week has been occupied working out some of Elisabeth's ideas: a large cupboard against the wall inside the cabin that she herself supplied with a beautifying curtain and a balcony around the hut which has given the whole a great aura. Underneath it, in the coming week, we shall build a shed; later on it will be changed into a guest room. Pictures will be taken when the work is completed, and you will naturally receive some. Yesterday was a "tourist" day, and we gave ourselves some much needed diversion. Today will be dedicated to music and script.

I got your parcel of books the day I arrived in Karditsa. Lovely. I doubt whether I shall be able to read them all through, but they have found their place. My parents-in-law sent me a letter telling that the records had arrived too. Thanks a lot. I am forever on the lookout to find something worthy of you. A little parcel is on its way with Greek "little nothings."

Beethoven's "Pastoral Symphony." A minute to sort out some stamps. A few weeks ago I started to to collect stamps again so that my son/daughter... will have a nice collection to start with. When you write again, do put some nice ones on the cover of your letters instead of using the printed air letters.

Elisabeth and I have decided on the naming of our child to come. If a girl (which I hope for) she will be named after one of my greater lights, Mirabehn (Lady Madeleine Slade who was so named by Gandhi whom she served for twenty-three years in India). If a boy, he will be named after my Grandfather (Tsvi) who is still guiding me from above and, as a second name, I wish him to have your name, Alan, in a slightly altered fashion: i.e., Alwin which means Noble Friend. I hope you agree to this small change; I hope too that you will agree to be his godfather, if and when he shall be born in December.

Already two people have prophesied that it shall be a boy. If the popular idea is right that an infant is a boy which makes much ado inside his mother, then it will certainly be so. For one can see the unborn baby jumping up and down Mama's belly from the outside. Judging from his movement, he will be either an actor or a dictator. In either case, the happy father shall find suitable purpose. The funny thing is that both Bess and myself feel like parents of a live baby already. It is a very rare experience to have created something in one's image. Something that breathes and lives. Did anyone say that there are no more miracles happening today? He is a fool who doesn't see the daily miracle of nature's everlasting progress.

Looking out over the fields at my feet, hearing Beethoven's "Pastoral," I share God's disgust at those who do not enjoy every second of life given to them. In moods like these, I have often the desire to enter into the eternal. If I ever die (and sometimes I doubt whether I ever will), I hope it shall be in the great happiness which now surrounds me, having my loving wife at my side and in the midst of my own creations, in the communication with my best friend and his world.

I read Joan's letter to you about me. In a way she observes very well and is extremely exact. I love the way in which she knows to put down her observations and, as long as she remains single, she will continue to write marvelously. Yet I believe you to be wrong to call her your muse. She is happy in her unhappiness, looking from the exterior much like you and thinking much like you, but lacking your aloofness from possessiveness.... I try not to be insulting, for I do not know how intimate you are with her at this moment and, moreover, I DO like her. But I believe it to be destructive for a man to get involved with her, and I have the idea that she has the same idea about herself. Yet there is one thing, or rather, two things that may change her. First of all, she is VERY young (I don't think she realizes herself how young she really is and how immature) and, secondly, she is an American girl, which means unpredictable. I don't believe in the education the American girls and boys get. They think and act too much sex. It is too prominent in their minds. It may be a sign of the times, for American youth did not have a war and its aftermaths to fight like us here in Europe.

I am too far removed from present-day youth here to judge how they act and react. It may be that they, too, will have a time like yours is having now. Fortunately (my opinion solely), we have "The Beatles" and their like which can craze the minds so far as to exclude the need for other outlets. I suppose that American youth have outgrown these "outlets" and have realized how they are being fooled. With the result that they are now fooling themselves, a fooling that is far more serious and can have far more serious consequences because it is not a momentary illusion, but an intrusion in body and mind.

Beethoven's Ninth. *Ja — wer auch nur eine Seele / Sein nennt auf dem Erdenrund! / Und wer's nie gekonnt, der stehle / Weinend sich aus diesem Bund.* ["Ay, and who a single other / Soul on earth can call his own; / But let him who ne'er achieved it / Steal away in tears alone."] One of the great.

A week later. I want to get this letter on its way. So I am stopping and just closing the envelope. Next time more of the same, probably from Israel.

Love

Alex and Elisabeth

(Eds. In this letter, Alex enclosed a list of the "little nothings" he was sending. A month or so later, the objects arrived. As Alex himself describes them, the objects included "2 boxes of matches, 1 old-fashioned cigarette lighter in use by the villagers in the interior, 1 chip of the mountain Olympus, and a little piece of camel's meat prepared in old Turkish fashion." The latter was probably meant to remind Alan of a dish Alex himself had prepared in Fannari. The main ingredients of that dish were eggs and canned camel meat. By serving such a meal, Alex could "shatter" several idols at the same time.)

Section Three

Fatherhood

December 1964 - April 1966

(Eds. Alex wrote the following letter shortly after the birth of his son. Written from the point of view of his newborn, this letter was addressed not to Alan, but to Alex's parents. Perama is a refugee camp in Greece. The letter has been translated from Dutch.)

Perama
24 December 1964

Dear Opa and Ama,

This is my first letter, and Papa said I have to write it in my parents' name. Let me apologize that they aren't writing because they are so busy. Papa is occupied cooking and washing, while Mama is at the breast pump trying to cope with her surplus milk. But let me introduce myself since you know only the details Papa sent in the telegram. My name is Alwin Tsvi. You wrote that you thought it beautiful, but what about the meaning? The first is a modern version for the Old Dutch Adelwyn and that means Noble Friend. It's after great-grandfather Cohen [Alex's maternal grandfather who died in Bergen-Belsen], who lived like a noble man in his mind; and after Papa's best friend, an American named Alan, who is more or less my godfather. Papa and Mama agreed that a child should have a meaningful name, and they hope that by carrying this name, I will be a noble friend to many.

I am typing this on Papa's machine because it's quicker and clearer for you to read. My handwriting is bad due to lack of practice. At the moment, I can only use my hands to pinch Mama and to pull Papa's beard. Now and again, I put one hand completely into my mouth. When I do that, everyone is pleased because it appears that my solo practice sessions for the next

Eurovision Song Festival are not very much appreciated.

I am writing this on the l0th day after my birth. Do you know that I played a trick on my parents? You know that it was Mama's birthday on the 10th and Papa's birthday on the 20th, so they had hoped I'd be born on the 15th. And so I let them believe I'd come into this world on the 15th. But when my Mama stopped for a moment at five o'clock with her work in the workshop where she was cutting patterns, I thought, "Now she will lie down for a moment, and I will seize the opportunity." Indeed she lay down for a rest, and I broke the water. That went quite easily, just a pang, and I didn't even hurt her. Of course, she knew that Papa would not be home much after that. He'd gone to Athens to set up a sale for the products of the workshop and, although that wouldn't finish until eight o'clock, he felt so strongly drawn to return home, that he left the stall and drove back in his Morris. He arrived at half past five, listened calmly to what Mama had to report, and went to find a doctor who could do a home delivery. Neither parent felt like driving to the clinic in Piraeus. But it turned out that none of the Greek doctors was prepared to take on a home confinement. So to Piraeus we went.

First Mama was examined, then she had an enema, and then she told Papa that it was high time indeed. That was at ten minutes past eight. There was no pain which disturbed the doctor so he gave her some tablets to bring some on. Still the pain was hardly noticeable, and the doctor whistled with astonishment to find her so far on without much pain. Then at ten fifteen, he prescribed an injection. That took her to the labor ward, she on the table, Papa beside her since his nursing experience entitled him to remain. This pleased Mama because he was able to talk to the doctor and translate for her. Now and then the man wanted Mama to push and she did. Then I came out. Floop! That was at ten thirty. Mama was stiched up and walked on Papa's arm upstairs to our room while I was carried by the nurse. Now they are not the only Sagittarians. I am one too. That means that I am just as hard-headed and pushy as my parents and that I have my own will as well and will not give in.

By the way, the clinic was typically Greek. We were first class, but do not think that anyone came to wash Mama. They did not seem to do that in Greece. What they wanted to do was to throw away the three bouquets which Papa brought the next morning and were in our room. Flowers smell, the Greek said, and that smell is bad for the newborn. Papa protested. He argued that it was a Dutch custom to feed the newborn an extract from odoriferous flowers. They thought it strange, but gave in. For the first three days, I had camomile tea with sugar because Mama's milk hadn't come in yet. Now she overflows. It shows she grew up among Zuid Holland cows, and I cannot get enough of it. At birth I weighed 3,600 grams; but how much I weight now I do not know. You can't get baby scales here. You cannot get much in Greece. Papa had to go all over Athens for a breast pump and ended up with only a very small one. Mama is struggling with it all the time.

These first ten days have taught me that, if I choose to live abroad, it won't be in Greece. What people! When we wanted to leave the clinic after 5 days, the doctor insisted that Papa pay. Papa was quite surprised because they had already agreed about a price. (Even in clinics and hospitals one can bargain for it.) Yes, said the doctors, it's the Greek custom to pay on the first day, but because you are foreigners, we've waited until the last. Well, Papa thought, they could have told me that a bit sooner. The luggage was already in the car, and Mama and I were dressed for the trip. Papa only had 1,000 drachmas in his pocket, half of the agreed price, and he wanted to pay this first; but the doctor wouldn't have it. "You don't leave without paying the full amount...." To pay within a week was not good enough. "NO." My parents were both angry. The doctor went off to phone his partner to ask how to handle it, and we drove off in the Morris.

Since then, of course, the bill has been settled. A strange country, Greece, but perhaps later I might think it interesting to have been born so far from home. Because Papa and Mama will always call Holland "Home." They hope to be moving on soon. If the workshop continues to do as well as it is, they should be able to.

That's the way it is when you have a car. Papa has now officially bought his Greek driving licence, and so that is in order. I like being with Papa in the Morris. When we left the clinic for home, we bounced over a few holes in the road which helped rock me to sleep.

When we came home to Perama, Mama was helped into bed first. Afterwards, I was transferred to my new rocking cot which was rather roomy, but quite comfortable. And then Papa came in with a big surprise. For some time now, we have had two chickens.

They ate lots of feed without paying for the costs. Now when Papa went to take them some food, he suddenly saw two small eggs, the first from our own pen. Since then, we have had two eggs a day, one from Pietepiet and one from Agaga.

Our room is nicely heated with an Aladdin paraffin heater and on this a kettle is kept constantly boiling for my diapers and all the other things they wrap me in. I am also wrapped in a lot of love, not only from my parents, but also from you which I saw in your telegram.

Now, dear Opa and Oma, I have to finish this because it's my feeding time again. Like in the zoo, isn't it? I long for you because I know that you like little children. But don't be mistaken. I am not so little any more. From the moment my umbilical cord was cut and I looked into the world with big blue eyes and took everything in, my parents have agreed that I seem quite grown up for my age. My face looked a lot like my grandmother van Dieijen in the first few days, but Papa thinks I have improved a little. Now I look like his brother Bertie. I have seen his picture and the likeness is really striking.

To close let me send you many dear wishes for 1965. I hope we will be able to embrace each other soon.

Your loving grandson,

Alwin Aronson

Poortugaal
[February, 1965]

Dear Alan,

In a hurry. First of all, congratulations on passing your [Ph.D. qualifying] exam. You didn't write, but I just guessed from your note that you are in a jubilant mood.

(Eds. Alex's congratulations were premature, for the results of this examination were ambiguous. Alan was far from being in a jubilant

mood. At the end of the academic year, he left Brandeis University for the University of Chicago where he completed his doctoral studies.)

And so are we here in Holland. For just this week, we received notice that we may move into an old farmer's house just a 10-minute walk from here. It belongs to the municipality of Rotterdam and will probably be demolished in 5-10 years. In the meantime, however, we have been allowed to rent it, and we are right now in the process of painting and decorating it. Fortunately, my wife and I share the same ideas about what is aesthetic and what is not. Alwin Tsvi doesn't have anything to say in the matter as yet, though he lets his voice be heard from time to time. We have 5 rooms to furnish, a hall, a kitchen, a toilet, a shed, a chicken pen and a vegetable garden about twice the size of Fannari. Tomorrow we all go to raid the flea market of Amsterdam which will have to provide most of our furniture. The main sitting room will be Old Dutch, at least our vision of it. I hope you will be here to enjoy it. We move in on the 21st of March (with the spring). The house is a very lonely spot in the middle of a polder with windows on all four sides.

More about our return trip from Greece in my next letter which will be written after receipt of yours. Do write a lot.

Our new address is ELFTPLAAT 5 Poortugaaal (ZH) Holland. "ELFT" is a fish that used to let itself be caught in this polder when it was still under water.

Poortugaal
? April 1965 [sic]

Dear Alan,

Finally a quiet afternoon and I shall try to concentrate on this letter to you. Your latest epistle is full of news and remarks which I cannot leave unanswered. First of all, and this may seem cruel to you, I am almost happy that you failed [your examination] because of politics. (I can easily say this to you because I am certain that in the end you will overcome all obstacles and pass with honors.) You see, a philosopher has to overcome one very great danger, and that is to become so much attached to his ideas, to become so much involved in a world of past and future, that in order to "solve" all problems of the present, he resorts to formulating these problems in terms of "could have been's" and "should be's." Much like a postal clerk sorting letters into their reserved spaces. I do agree that this system is excellent for the chosen few who wish to live up to it, but we easily forget that this world, unfortunately, belongs 50% to the unfortunate and 49% to the greedy. Resulting in this politicking which you (and I with you) so much detest.

But perhaps it is for the good that we are sometimes confronted with this business now and then. It may help us to understand bigger politics which really is very easy to understand if one only compares it with the politicking necessary to remain at school. A few hundred trucks for a few thousand Jews, a few monopolies for the right of Negroes to register, some business contracts for the *de jure* recognition of a country, a few ship-loads of surplus for the right to build an army base. Boy, it's so simple. So SIMPLE even that when you come to look at it from a distance (as a philosopher must place himself in order to see the whole) you can only shake your head at yourself for not having seen and understood it from nearby.

Anyway, coming back to your situation, an M.A. may be an insignificant degree in the U.S., but I never heard of Socrates having even that. I quote your letter: "I just want to lead a quiet life — stimulating and being stimulated in turn by students...." Dear, dear Alan, do you think a Ph.D. will give you this? Sure, you will get a position in some school and teach BUT.... 1) You will have to teach your whole class and not only the few who stimulate and are stimulated. You even have to teach gold-diggers if they pay their tuition fees to the school-board. You may not show favoritism. 2) You are to teach what is required in the books. You may not select the things which to you seem most important. You may not contradict General Opinion. 3) You are not the only teacher at a school. There will be types who will try to make you out a fake if only for advancing their own cause. I could go on indefinitely, but I think you understand what I mean.

The only quiet life, in which you can select the students that interest you, where you can teach what interests you, is the unobserved life in one's own closet. There you can concentrate, meditate, and live in a rarefied atmosphere with those who are at the same time your students and your friends. And even then you may finally have to swallow the cup of poison. Knowledge is a sorrow, indeed, and the vanity is other people's recognition of it by degrees and honors. Which is why I am glad to have stopped my singing lessons in time to be able to still enjoy it. What does the Torah say: *al tishtamesh ba-Torah ka-hafirah lahpor bah.*

(Eds. The literal translation of this Hebrew sentence is, "Do not use the Torah as a trench in which to dig." Alex is warning against worldly use of spiritual goods. To support his case he refers to a passage "in the Torah." But the proof-text he picks is not from the Torah, but from the Ethics of the Fathers 4.7. *In fact, Alex's version bears only a slight similarity to the original.)*

Anything that is used professionally stops being a pleasure. The ideal and most creative life, as I see it, was that of the old-time rabbis who were shoe-makers, lived poorly on their handicrafts, and were still very much sought after and respected by young and old. This is the kind of life that I am after myself, and I think that now that I am getting settled in married life, I am very near reaching it.

My wife goes out to work as a headmistress in a nursery school and earns more than I could ever get as a male-nurse. Moreover, it is a job she had always resented having to give up when she married me. During the daytime, I look after Alwin Tsvi and do most of the household chores, including the cooking and the laundry. Next week I will start to work three nights a week at the post office, doing simple jobs at an amazingly good salary (night jobs pay 50% extra). The rest of the time I can devote to my reading and writing, and since I have reinstalled my room in this new house of ours, I am just doing nothing, so eager I am to start everything.

My room, as you can well imagine, is as it has been always and everywhere. Overlooking a beautiful landscape (window on my left) bureau with all kinds of bits and pieces, in front of me from left to right a piece of a wall from the ruined [Linnaeusstraat] Synagogue in which my grandfather (Tsvi) was *Gabbai* [Hebrew, warden], a newspaper picture of Gandhi, your picture between two large photographs of Fannari, a map of Israel and, on the right wall, the Map of Classical Lands with some Greek stamps on it depicting Homer, Alexander the Great, and some others. Also, against the right wall, a simple edifice of bricks and wood which is my bookshelf and everywhere (around and above) original handwritings and pictures of Gandhi, Tagore, Buber, Schweitzer etc. Recently, someone offered to sell me a letter written by your friend Brandeis. I didn't buy it because I don't know enough about him. I did think of you, though; maybe you could bribe a professor with it. But perhaps his autographs are so common in the U.S. that no one would bother with it.

(Eds. Alex assumes that Alan had an affinity to Justice Louis D. Brandeis {1856-1941} because he was a graduate student at Brandeis University. Actually, since Alan's father had argued a case before Justice Brandeis, he did have an affinity.)

Our sitting room downstairs (my room in which I now write is on the second floor) has as its main feature the open fire which I have been dreaming of all my life and which we had put in at great cost (not yet paid) instead of a very ordinary stove. The wooden floor of this room we painted brown and the interior is in "olde Dutch" as we wish to call it. The room contains all sorts of market-findings we "discovered" in Holland and abroad, including a very ancient confessional chair from some Catholic Church which we restored ourselves. This room receives light in daytime from three windows and at night from a gas-lamp, an oil- lamp and a sabbath-lamp. The total impression is the same as the "Good Hour" in Haarlem which we visited together and which I believe you found most aesthetic. We do not have electricity, yet I managed to buy a Television-set. Please don't be disgusted; I need it here in the polder. It works on the battery of our little Morris. Only yesterday I saw an episode from "The Defenders," an American T.V.-series. This particular one was most interesting, and I hope you had a chance to see it. It was called "Old Lady Ironsides" and treated the matter of an old suffragette defending the rights of a pregnant girl to finish her school.

That brings me to the matter of the Negroes in your South. I shall start with telling you something that will shock you: I personally don't like Negroes; nor do I (usually) sympathize with them. I know I must sound very much like the anti-semite who says he just loves the work of Mendelssohn and Meyerbeer, but I am proud to say that my likes and dislikes have never [influenced my actions].... I like Baldwin and love Harry Belafonte.... But I have been too long in Africa not to know one thing: I shall never be able to live close with a Negro. If my child would want to marry one, I should warn him against it (though God forbid I shall ever tell him what to do in such respects).

Let me reassure you — (and I think by now you must be dazed by my honesty — that I am AGAINST all sorts of racial oppression and discrimination. But I do believe that some integrationists are going much too far. The main thing they forget is that Negroes ARE different from whites, that Puerto Ricans ARE NOT Americans, that Italians are not Dutchmen, and that Turks are not Greeks. Also Jews are different from the rest. THE big mistake that is made by the fighters of discrimination is that THERE ARE DIFFERENCES between all those groups. God created men in many shades and colors, having many mental differences, and the great thing about it is that human beings are all incomparable. A black man cannot be compared to a white in the country of the whites; neither can a pale-face be compared to a Negro in Africa. In America, you struggle with the problem of having to live with blacks who don't belong there, YET HAVE ALL THE RIGHT TO BE THERE. Even more: the whites have a debt towards Negroes for having enslaved them in the past and having taken them away from their natural surroundings. This terrible controversy demands a remedy. They want, they have the right, BUT they don't belong. I am resolute in telling you that "they don't belong." From all I have seen and heard, I believe that it is true.

Some churches in Africa are out of bounds for blacks. Can you imagine why? Naturally, the idea of a house of God being prohibited to a creation of God is wholly incongruous. HOWEVER, how would you feel if a portion of your synagogue's visitors would start weeping loudly at the *Kaddish* because it is written in their *Siddur* [Hebrew, prayer book] *Hier weint man* [German, One cries here]. How would you feel if people started shouting "YEAH, YEAH" at every word during the rabbi's *drasha* [Hebrew, sermon]? Personally, I would leave the place and start a new synagogue of my own or try to get the board of the mentioned synagogue to sell seats to selected members only. I know it is VERY bad of me, but I am serious.

Why does every sect and nationality in Jerusalem have its own *shul* [Yiddish, synagogue]? Exactly for that same reason: people have a certain method of worshipping to which they are accustomed and a disturbance of that means an end to all loving worship. The same goes for restaurants, cinemas, etc. There is only one thing that prevents or remedies problems and that is what you rightly call class-consciousness. I would call it decentralization AND racial-consciousness. We must first of all be aware of our own factors (and, as Pearl S. Buck rightly wrote, one must be proud of ALL one is, and not just a part). Secondly, we must cohabitate with our equals (and I mean equals in the most general sense). And, thirdly, we must be aware that whenever we step out of our own surroundings to visit somebody else's, we must conform to all customs, habits, and wants of the world we step into AND be aware we are only visitors there. I hope that you see what I mean: in short, no segregation forced by law, but separation by free will, common sense, and PRIDE.

As for Vietnam, I wholly agree with you. It is again one of those instances where America is most successful in making itself unpopular. You ask what I DO about it? What exactly do you mean? If I were a politician, I would naturally condemn America openly, which is exactly why I shall never be one. If I were a communist, I would demonstrate in front of the American Embassy which would be useless because communists in Holland get only shrugs of the shoulder. And if I were to take part in such demonstrations, while not being a communist, I would be taken for one, which would make the participation worthless. There is freedom of speech in Holland, but where should I speak and to whom?

The same goes for writing. I wasn't even able to prevent our government from sending away our three-year-old Jean-Paul as an "unwanted foreigner." He is now back in France where he is again in the Albert Schweitzer Village in the good care of a young Dutch couple who have children of their own, and his brother is there, too, while his mother lives not very far from there and is allowed to visit them once a month. Do you think that in "this free world" an ordinary citizen can do anything about the politics of his government? Anyway, I suppose it is for the good, for if *I* would have been able to change government policy, *everybody* could, and we would live in as chaotic a democracy as the ancient Greeks did. The only thing that we "men in the street" can do is to concentrate on our own personal lives and try to give an example by charity of thought, speech, and action. And if we do succeed in getting all good elements to join such a movement for *dharma* [Hinduism, individual right conduct in conformity to the ultimate law of all things], I think the government will gradually be influenced by it.

Elisabeth, to answer your question, does not speak English,

though she understands it fairly well. At times, I try to teach her. Her French, though, is very fluent, and her German is not too bad either. Enclosed is a picture of our present little family to which Alwin has added a snap of his own for you to keep in your purse. I was glad to read that you accept his godfathership. Fortunately the duties as such are not at all what they still are in France. The only obligation attached to it is to be his living example in action and thought. The official order of names is first Alwin, then Tsvi; he is called Alwin. (Tsvi is rather foreign to the Dutch tongue.) "Noble friend" is the meaning of it in old Dutch. The name in the 16th century (and earlier) was Adelwijn or Latinized Alwinus. "Adel" is nobel, "Wijn" is friend. I shall be happy to teach him English as soon as I have taught him to write. Then he can correspond with you, and he shall be brought up with knowledge and love abroad so that he will never become too chauvinistic.

You wrote about Sharon's marriage in March, and I sent her a telegram with good wishes which I hope she received in time. I was very glad that you kept me in touch with happenings. Since you wrote that you see Laura daily, I shall not write to her separately, though I do like to keep in touch with her. Please give her my news when you deem it proper. Also you might remind her of her promise to ask her father to send me his series of books on the history of Labor Unionism in the U.S. I would be glad to pay for it. I read the first book of that series which was the only one available in the University Library, but I had to return it before I had dealt with it entirely (by which I mean, taking notes etc.). I found it VERY enlightening and sincerely wish to study it at my leisure. If he will send me these books (I don't know how many of them there are), it would please me greatly (for the reason you know) to have him autograph the first book.

About the records, I am sorry to tell you that they were stolen in Greece. My mother-in-law received the parcel and kept it till I wrote to her from Greece to forward it to me. She did, but waited too long, so that it must have arrived after we had left. And although we left our address, we didn't get anything forwarded from there. (I know that at least five parcels must have been sent to us there, to say nothing of a number of letters which might have been important.) Greek mail is, as the people are, VERY unreliable. I have come to dislike them greatly, though it doesn't detract from my love for the country and its history.

Reading over your letter to see if there is anything I forgot to answer. We didn't get to Israel, you know. Although we were promised our keep and some pocket-money while working in Perama, only two of the three months were provided for us and the third we had to fend for ourselves which was one of the reasons we left. I am not a charitable institution and, when I work, I expect at least my board and lodging. I wouldn't have reasoned thus as a bachelor, but having wife and children gives at least the obligation of providing enough for them so that in later life they don't have to depend on charity themselves. So, after no funds had arrived for the fourth month, we departed. By then our money had greatly diminished. What contributed to this was the bill for the clinic for Elisabeth. Perama [the refugee camp] had promised to pay for this, but we had to pay for it out of our own pockets. So we returned to Holland without going to Israel.

About the birth of Alwin Tsvi, the following: It was a Monday and as usual I had gone to Athens for some business while Bessy was in the workshop cutting some models for clothes that had to be made. She was at it till five o'clock in the afternoon when she felt tired and lay down on the bed. Then she felt the water break and just waited till I came back from a bazaar we had organized. I arrived at six o'clock and after I had unsuccessfully tried to get a doctor to come to us for the delivery, we went to a clinic we had visited previously. (In Greece, children are not usually delivered at home, as is usual in Holland, where only in emergencies do people go to the hospital or to a clinic.) But first there were Jean-Paul, the dog, the cat and the two chickens which had to be brought to temporary "homes." After that was done, we went to that clinic (in Piraeus, 8 miles away) and arrived there at eight o'clock. The doctor examined her and said she had to take four pills to start the pains (she hadn't had any yet). Only three pills were necessary for, after an hour and a half, the young man started to get out. It took him fifteen minutes more to free his way, and he then shouted, with open eyes, "Here I am," to his proud father. I had been with Elisabeth all the time and could keep the essential eye on the doings of doctor and nurse. They wouldn't have graduated in Holland, but I was satisfied.

Bess had to walk up to her room five minutes later, and five days later we left the place to return to our room in Perama, which, though not luxurious, was still to be preferred to the noise and dirt in the clinic where people received visitors till late at night, and each one seemed to have his own transistor radio and his own idea of what is nice. We returned to Holland in the Morris and had quite a job getting through Yugoslavia and Austria. Thrice we were snowed in and the trip lasted for a whole week whereas in summer I could have done it in two days. Back in Poortugaal, we were very happy to get a chance to move into this here house. And what a change to what both of us have been used to all our lives. At last, then, we can comfortably lodge six guests in real beds. And it is strange to see how many things we had already found a place in our new home. Today's "high-fashion" makes people change their furniture every five years. Even flea-marketeers don't buy anything anymore, but *have to be paid* to remove things to their market. Of course, being a Jew, I have managed some good deals with neighbors and relatives, with the result that we have nearly everything furnished to our taste and liking. And I hope that you will soon be here to enjoy it with us. About the two records you wanted to send to me, I shall be glad to get them here by ordinary mail or by air, as you think best. You have to write on the declaration that they are *second-hand*. It is a pity for the Caruso record; I do like him ever so much. I do have some original recordings of his from 1905 and 1918.

For your information about Cynics, etc., some small excerpts from my books... *Cynics*: Founded about 380 BC by Antisthenes. Main feature was the merit of a proud independence from all outward things. Diogenes is regarded by some as a representative of this school (though I classify him as a Socratic). The word "cynic" hails from the Greek *kyon*, dog, and I think it must have been derived from the story of Diogenes when he first came to Athens. The school is often called anti-Socratic, but wouldn't anti-Platonic be more proper? *Epicureans*: Materialistic; the thing I like about them is their accent on individual taste and the needs of every single being. Important about Epicurus was his improvement on the cosmological ideas of Democritus concerning atoms and their movements.

But I'll save you the rest, you probably have better books than I shall ever try to understand. You see, after all, I am not a scholar and just make philosophy my hobby. I probably enjoy it more than you do at the present, too. Alan, all my love and best wishes for a successful re-exam. And when you do marry your Ph.D. do make your honeymoon in Holland.

Yours ever and ever,

Alex

Poortugaal
16 August 1965

Dear Alan brother,

What a great distance there seems to be between wanting to write a letter and actually starting one. Today has been a day of great heat in the polder. We were really put out of action from midday till about four o'clock. Something that doesn't happen very often in the nether countries. But the main thing is that with Elisabeth still having a week's holiday, I was able to take an old-fashioned siesta. With the result that I am not as finished as usual at the the end of the day but, the light not having completely gone yet, I am starting this epistle full of energy.

To begin with, many thanks for the records. Alas, old man Caruso did not survive the hazards of the Greek mail. His belly was split and so he was neatly laid in his grave. "Orfeu Negro" [a record of the sound track of the film "Black Orpheus"], however, was still in great form and since we don't take to racial discrimination, he is lying in between Pete Seeger and his Weavers and Beethoven. The only long-playing records I have here are the ones I have recently acquired. The rest are in Fannari. My taste in music has been developing.

And here my energy was interrupted by the sudden and unexpected arrival of an Iraqi-Israeli friend of mine (1959) with his brother and a friend. They are now sleeping in our house. Three more names to be added to the guest book tomorrow. They will stay two days. So since guests in the house always give me quite a lot of pep, I got up this morning at half past one. At the moment it is four o'clock in the early morning. Meanwhile I have done the dishes from last night, prepared breakfast for seven o'clock, cooked a nice pot of soup, and peeled two kilograms of potatoes. Otherwise life would have been like hell for Elisabeth whose grandfather is turning eighty-eight and is giving a feast too, tomorrow, or rather today. In order not to wake up the whole house, I have removed myself to the Morris Minor and, I am writing to you now with the typewriter on my knees inside the car.

Continuing a few words on guests. Since we have lived here, there has hardly been a week in which we were really lonely. The world is coming to us. Next week two Indian friends and an English woman (of theirs?), the week thereafter, a German couple with two-year-old son. And so they were living on happily ever after. Having these people around us gives us much joy, for we can pass on a lot of the hospitality both my wife and I received in our bachelor days. Enough of this.

Your godson is getting on fine. With the help of his parents, he walks through the house, and he sits in his eighteenth-century model chair like a preacher in his pulpit. He dictates to everybody, through he doesn't speak yet; he is loved by every person who sees him. The good Lord has given us a great treasure to guard. He is eight months old by now, but looks as if he were a year at least. Most clothes that are presented to him have to be passed on to smaller-sized babies, for he really isn't a baby at all and actually he never was. Enclosed, a little snap taken by another guest of ours, a German press photographer.

I was glad to see that you are going on with your studies. I don't very well understand how a scholarship is obtained; nor can I fathom why it is given by capitalism. A Ph.D. can't do much to advertise cereals, or can he? But I am happy for you that you got it.

(Eds. Alan had written that he had been awarded a Fellowship for continuing post-graduate work by the Danforth Foundation and that the Danforth Foundation was supported chiefly by Ralston Purina, a breakfast cereal manufacturer.)

Maybe some day you can ask those cornflake people whether they can give you a trip to Europe. Just tell them you want to find out how cereals taste over here.

How many more years do you have till you finally get your degree? Here graduate study leads up to what we call a Doctorandus, an unofficial, but officially recognized degree given to to those who have finished their studies and who only need to write a thesis in order to be called Doctor. The thesis has to be about some subject the candidate himself chooses within the limits of his studies. The funny thing, though, is that the thesis has to end with three principles which have nothing to do with his study at all, but which he has to defend seriously at his installation. Thus a friend of mine, a candidate in Chemistry and a well-known cantor in Holland, ended his Chemistry doctorate with the principle that cantorial music should be composed around the prayers, but not the prayers set to already existing music. And when he had successfully explained this principle, he was made a doctor of chemistry. How are the usual proceedings over there?

21 August 1965

This same friend was made a full professor in chemistry last week.

I was glad to read that Laura is DOING something in the hot spots.

(Eds. Laura was a political activist. At this time, she went south with the anti-segregationists as a Freedom Rider.)

If after that, she hasn't changed still, I suppose she never will change and shall remain what she was, a dream child. That can be of use in this world of hard realities. I sincerely hope that she will write to me from Alabama about the "happenings". I didn't get an answer to a note of mine, sent to her about a month or so ago. But to give up one's studies and certainty, when you have a scholarship, is not doing the cause any good, I believe. You see, fighting for such a cause should not simply be the whim of idealistic students, but an outlet for pent-up forces that have gathered during student years and are used as a weapon by the fully matured and qualified finalist. It is very unfortunate that also here in Holland many demonstrations and actions are instituted by students alone. They are so easily denounced as the "leftist youth who with their beards and corduroys try to stir up something." Fortunately, more and more well-known grown- ups are joining. Preachers and pastors of name, professors and doctors are signing their names against South African policy and the like. The day will come that these protests can't be ignored any more. At least that is what I hope.

Last week I laid my hands on another of these new inventions, the tape recorder. It is a portable transistor Philips CASSETTE recorder, very handy and with beautiful sound. We acquired it mainly to record our son's first groping words and sounds, but this week I put it to another use. A friend of ours, a Bahai youngster who works in one of the biggest record shops, lent me a Folkway record (for the first time imported to the Continent). On it was the "March on Washington" with President Kennedy and Martin Luther King. I was to have the record for just two hours, but that proved sufficient for me to copy it on one cassette. A treasured thing it is, especially because at the time Laura had given me a beautiful report on the March.

I don't know what is the matter with me, but still I haven't finished this letter. Today already the 17th of September, and I don't have the slightest idea of what will become of this. But now I have decided, even if the letter won't get completed, to send it off to you. So if what you receive ends up without proper greetings, you will know that more is to come.

What happened is as follows. We got to know from friends that there was an unmarried mother of twenty whose child was born in the Albert Schweitzer Village in France. She wanted to get rid of it by "selling" it off to an orphange which has dealings with adoptive parents. Somehow she was made to change her mind, but still didn't know what to do with the child. Her fiancé, however, agreed to accept the baby when they would get married, which is at least two years away. So we offered ourselves to take care of the child (which is at present six weeks old). It is against the law to do this as long as the mother is under 21 and the baby under 6 months. But when the Dutch authorities get their nose in it, the chances are a thousand to one that the girl's village will find out. (At this point, the couple does not want the village to know anything; the worry is that the boy's parents will object to their marriage.) So we keep everything as unofficial as possible. So last week, at two o'clock in the morning, I went off with the mother to France to fetch the baby and found her after a long and difficult search. We returned with it on Sunday afternoon, the total distance we had covered being 2,000 miles. The baby was terribly cared for, stinking skin, totally underfed, but already we have booked great success. Her weight has gone up a pound and a half, and her skin is getting better every day.

Besides this we are also getting, from some semi-official organization, a twenty-one-year-old mother to be (unmarried of course) who has to stay under cover until the baby is born. The idea is that, after her, others will be sent to our house to "recover." You know, we have always wanted to start something of our own, and the chance that we will finally succeed in doing what we want is improving.

Meanwhile old "Appy," as we insiders used to call Le Grand Docteur, has gone to join his forefathers. And it was just about time. He lived too long.

(Eds. Alex is referring here to Dr. Albert Schweitzer who died on 4 September 1965, at the age of ninety. Alex had worked with him four years earlier at Lambaréné and had reservations about the cult of personality which had grown up around him by then. Alex's misgivings do not alter the fact that he thought of Schweitzer as one of his guiding lights.)

Your reflections on him [Schweitzer] were absolutely right. My reply cannot possibly be made on paper. My thoughts and opinions concerning both him and the Africa of today are so uncommonly paradoxical — I realize that very well — that it can only be pronounced person to person. Can't you take one of those student ships? I get crazy when I think of having to put everything on paper.

I do wish to reply to your accusation that I am a racist. Well, maybe I am at that, but not a racist in the sense that it is generally used. You, on the contrary, make the big mistake (always made by the opponents of segregation) of saying that I decide any issues from the color of a man's skin. I do not. The only thing is that this difference in color COINCIDES with other differences between the White man and the Black man. I certainly do hope that you don't take LAW as being decisive in saying who is an American and who isn't. If law says Puerto Ricans are American, I emphatically refuse to accept them as such (until maybe the second or third generation). On the other hand, I have an acquaintance in Switzerland who is trying his best to get rid of the label "American." He married a Latin woman, became an anarchist, settled on some land in Switzerland, and is a hopeless nuisance to the authorities. He returned his passport. Still I will always see him as an American. Now what is the decisive thing about a person being what he is? Einstein to me will always remain a German as will all the other naturalized German scientists. I myself will always remain a Dutchman even though I possess the Israeli nationality and even if I eventually decide to live in Israel.

I don't know, perhaps it is just a sentimental sort of feeling about a person; certainly it is some sort of experience in my life of dealing with all sorts of people. By the way, writing that Italian cooking is all the Italian culture that remains in America is not complete. Unfortunately, it is all the culture that the Italians in Italy have succeeded in preserving. The fact that Dante is still sold in Italian bookshops doesn't mean that their culture still envelopes him. History, my dear fellow, nothing but past history. If he were still taught in Italian schools, if Italian television would regularly broadcast his works, he might have been part of today's culture. Still. But I don't think that this is done.

In these respects, Rembrandt IS STILL a part of Dutch culture today. And here again arises the question: when does a particular genius of the past leave the culture of his country? Generally speaking, I would say, when he isn't discussed anymore by the common people. Of course, this is a broad generalization, but what else do you want? For that matter, I must point out that Verdi's operas are still a very live part of Italian culture today.

(Eds. Of course, Alex's last observation undercut his previous argument.)

I doubt whether you understood my example of a person coming in to yell "Yeah" in the synagogue. I fully approve of him, as I do with your example of the mute man who whistled before the altar.

(Eds. This is a reference to the story of a mute man who could only express his devotion to God by whistling. In this Jewish tale, the mute man's mode of expression is put on a par with the prayers of his co-religionists. There are other similar stories, like the boy who played his flute at the Concluding (Nillah) Service on Yom Kippur because he did not know how to pray, and his playing helped the others' prayers reach the gates of heaven. This story is connected with the figure of the Baal Shem Tov.)

But, or rather BUT, I wouldn't want to pray in a synagogue where the majority of the devotees were mute. Finally, concerning your attacking my principle of separation by PRIDE, I don't think you understand — and how could you? For paper is such a terrible patient. It just lies there staring at one without answering. So let me try this personal illustration.

Although I married a *shiksa* [Yiddish, a non-Jewish woman], I am a JEW, I am proud to be a Jew, and I always intend to remain a Jew. Incidentally, this has not always been. There was a time when I would have loved to creep into a gentile skin; fortunately I couldn't. When people tell me, "You are just as good as we gentiles are," I straighten my back and say, " No, I am better in some ways." When people say that we are all equal, I absolutely deny this. I am a Jew and a Jew is not the same as a Greek, or an Italian, or a gentile Dutchman. OF COURSE we are equal as human beings, but we are certainly not equal in the way that some proponents of integration think. They wish to interpret the word "equal" to mean "the same." I am not "the same" as anyone, and the knowledge of this makes me try to enlarge the little I have of "my own" to show the world what it is that makes me different. I know this sounds silly and egotistical, but I can't express it differently.

Sitting on the floor now, by the side of my son's box, just to keep him quiet. Just fed and washed the little baby upstairs, and she is back to sleep. Elisabeth will be back from school in about an hour. I think I have written everything there was to say. Except perhaps this, no discussion on paper will ever be satisfactory to either of us. So, convince the University of Chicago to send you over to make a study of Rembrandt and his thoughts, or perhaps a study of "present-day Dutch philosofools." Then you can include me. But for heaven's sake, let's meet somewhere soon.

By the way, you will be interested to hear that I have at last realized my idea to form an organization of international meeting-places. It is called "The Group" and the idea is to establish lodges throughout the world in which people can meet and discuss, or just retire. Naturally, our place in Fannari has been included in the plan, and it is the first lodge of the group. Right now we are trying to lay our hands on a similar home in France and an old farmhouse in the North of Holland. Membership is limited to 52 as yet and, since I would love to include you amongst the first, I am sending you a membership card in the hope that it is something to your taste. Membership fee is US$3 per annum. That is for the Fannari lodge. Membershop of the Dutch lodge, when that is realized, will be more. If you have friends who you think will be interested, please let me know. Of course, the ultimate idea is to have at least one lodge in every country in the world. Perhaps a fantastic idea, but still I believe it can be done.

Well, I finally did come to the end of this letter. Not that it has been an unpleasant job, for writing to you has become one of my most beloved pastimes. The past few months I have hardly ever been able to listen to good music or to have a good discussion with anyone, so our correspondence is a light spot in the daily ploughing through life. Yet don't misunderstand me. I do love the ploughing, and so does Elisabeth. In fact, I doubt whether we could ever do again without it. But still, time to reflect and meditate are essential to me. Once again, do visit us soon. Let's hear from you regularly, even though my letters are most irregular. Send me a recent snap of yours.

Love to America with the exception of its lousy politicians. Greetings to Messrs. Corn-Flakes [Ralston-Purina],

Alex

(Eds. Enclosed in this letter was a copy of a Swiss newsletter called "Equality." In it Alex announces the formation of "The Group," which he describes as an "international cooperative society.")

Poortugaal, Holland
1 November 1965

My dear Alan,

This crazy household is going to my head one of these days. At present both Elisabeth and I are working. My wife is still at school although she has asked to resign. But no one else can be found to take her place, and it would be a shame to have the school close down just because of a whim of ours. I myself have taken the first step to becoming a millionaire. At least, if what they write of some millionaires is true — that they started off as newspaper vendors. For that is what I am doing these days. Or rather, since a system of selling of newspapers is not known in Holland, I am a deliverer of newspapers. For everybody has one or more subscriptions to papers in this country, and every morning or evening, depending on what newspapers they read, these papers are delivered into their mailboxes. (You know, there is a mail-box in every door to the street.) So my job is to fetch the papers and bring them from one door to the next. At present, I have one morning paper to deliver and two evening papers plus three weeklies. It doesn't pay too well (I make about 60 guilders a week), but I am trying to make a good job of it and to enlarge my rounds. So I am en route from five till eight a.m. Elisabeth leaves as soon as I arrive. She returns at four-thirty p.m., and then I immediately take off until eight o'clock p.m. So you can imagine what becomes of our house and food. Fortunately Elisabeth has a week's vacation now, and we can take a deep breath. This Wednesday I am starting a newspaper round with a motor-carry, and I hope that this will save me a lot of time (just now I am still using my wife's bike). When eventually Elisabeth will be able to quit teaching school, I hope to be able to earn enough for the lot of us.

By the way, you asked in your letter who pays for our "charity work." Well, nobody does. We are just happy to be able to add our little piece towards the completion of a just society. And it doesn't cost us much, really. If three are already eating, I don't think the addition of a few more mouths makes much difference. And neither of us has ever believed in saving, though I do fear the seven meagre years that are to come someday in each generation.

People in Holland are very well-off nowadays, no one wanting for work and everyone getting his or her share of the general welfare. Exceptions there are, naturally, the sufferers being mostly the aged who are still very badly cared for in some over- populated homes. (Children don't want to lodge their own parents anymore, partly because of the lack of living space, partly because family ties are not so strong as they used to be.) I suppose that you yourself get your fill of misery in your slum.

(Eds. In 1965-1966, Alan lived in a black neighborhood in Chicago.)

That you have chosen a slum to live in is quite what I had expected of you but I am very anxious to know how you will react towards it. Of my own experience, I know that feeling of "wanting to do something about it." The first feeling you experience is little short of hatred for the luxury you have been used to up to the moment you met poverty. Everything which is not really essential in this life becomes an accusation. Every penny spent on comfort points its finger at you saying, as it were, "You know where I really belong." So I am trying to find a little souvenir to send you which will be rare and costly and absolutely useless. I shall want you to regard it as a symbol of the beautiful things that riches can afford to have produced. Never blame riches themselves or possessions per se. Knowing you, or at least thinking so, I believe that you might get very strongly involved in the poverty around you. If so, please try to remember that the only way to do something about it is to stand aloof. NOT aloof in the social worker's way. I have recently had my fill of that, too. I mean aloof in the Olympian way, looking down and seeing everything from the top of the mountain and sometimes, when necessary, descending to earth to reason with man and to LEAD him to victory.

I hope you will agree that the majority of man needs a "Führer," however detestable this idea is to our democratic minds. But what is democracy anyway? I have thought a lot about the men whose plight you described in your letter. I have met the same conditions elsewhere, of course, but I have had reason to look up hopefully to my new great Guru, the little Abbé Pierre of whom you must have heard. Three weeks ago, I had the honor of working with him for two whole weeks, organizing a campaign in Hilversum to raise funds for some orphanages in Algeria. It was wonderful to speak with him, to exchange ideas and, very important, to get that much-needed injection of enthusiasm that he alone is capable of injecting into people today.

After the death of "Old Appy" I had been looking forward to meeting the Abbé again. (I had met him once in 1961.) I wanted to see whether he could take up the place that Schweitzer left vacant. For, however much can be said against Schweitzer, to those who have worked with him, he was and will always remain a great inspiration. A friend and co-worker from Lambaréné said to me recently that the greatest thing Schweitzer had achieved was to make people unfit for normal society.

But to return to Abbé Pierre. He made his name in his struggle for the *clochards* [French, vagrants] of Paris and after that organized communites of garbarge collectors — the so-called Emmaüs and Swallow communities — throughout the world. The fund-raising in Hilversum, the first of its kind here in Holland, was nothing more or less than the collecting of garbage: old paper and metals. We had the help of about five hundred volunteers (mostly school children), and we toured the city all Saturday with a hundred and twenty trucks. Statistics had proved that the largest gift from Hilversum's population had been fifteen thousand guilders to the Red Cross. In one day, we collected over thirty thousand. The paper and metal were sold that same day to a wholesaler. No money-gifts were taken. We had warned against so-called "cheque book charity."

Now what I wanted to ask you, isn't there scope for such a community in Chicago? It needs: A) unemployed men of all ages who do *want* to work and don't care what it is B) a large city which has much to offer by way of second-hand clothes, old paper, old metals, worthless textiles C)textiles and paper mills not too far off D) an acre of land with storage facilities nearby E) a cooperative city council. (This last, though, is very rarely found and therefore not absolutely essential.)

Do write to me what you think about possibilities, and I shall take it up with the Abbé. A total revolution would be needed in government as well as in mental capacities. I doubt whether man will ever grow up sufficiently to overcome his own natural urges of possession and power. Read *The Shipwrecks of Jonathan* by Jules Verne if you can get it. I read it once fifteen years ago, but haven't been able to locate the book in the five years that I have been looking for it.

(Eds. Alex is referring to Verne's Les Naufragés du "Jonathan," *published posthumously in 1909.)*

You write about a course in New Testament and Septuagint Greek. I hope you can persuade your professors that the New Testament was orginally written in Hebrew-Aramaic. In fact, this has helped me a lot in the understanding of the historical Jesus, a study guided by Albert Schweitzer, the great authority in this field. Just take the term "Son of Man" which Jesus so often uses for himself... Translate it into Greek and what do you know?...nothing! Translate it into Hebrew... *ben adam* and you have two possibilities. The first is just ordinary "man"; the second, however, the literal translation "son of Adam," may explain how Jesus felt himself related to the first man and how he felt himself responsible for the loss of Eden to such an extent that Jesus offered himself up so that paradise would instantly return. (There are many phrases pointing to this explanation. For example his telling the disciples that their next meal would be in "heaven.") Remember that the idea of human sacrifice descended from Persia just around those days. But

I am rambling on again as ever. Perhaps you're interested in just the Greek side and not the New Testament at all.

I tried to locate Chicago on one of my maps. I have Gulf touring maps of several of the States, but Chicago was not there. On my globe, however, I did find it. A small point not too far away from Detroit and on the waterfront near Canada. Am I right? Do send me some more details about your whereabouts so that I can picture you rightly. How I long for the U.S. with you as my guide. I wanted to mail you some little gift for your room, but my wife tells me I should wait till I could bring it to you in person. That was a very nice thing of her to say, if only I could see the opportunity of stowing away or maybe I can ask President Johnson to accept me as an aeronaut. (What is the matter with those people, anyway? Don't they want to live anymore?)

I am beginning to like those Ralston Purina Cereal people of yours. In Holland, too, money given to charity over two per cent of one's income may be deducted from the taxable amount. I think the system is O.K.

At the moment, I am not in a mood to talk about Formal Education as it is here in Holland. I had some very unpleasant experiences the other day. I wanted to enter a course on social welfare (child psychology, etc.). The course goes together with a job in that particular field. I applied for precisely that sort of job in a home for difficult-to-manage boys. Was turned down because I had not followed the course. And so one turns around and around. And permits, permits, permits. For everything one needs a paper. I have not given up yet, but I think I will throw education to the dogs and just go on with my newspapers. How I would love to start some sort of a school for myself and appoint the craziest characters as teachers. Would YOU care to be on the staff? Not that I regard you as a crazy character, but I believe you would be in good company then.

If I remember well, there is in Chicago the so-called World University Roundtable of a Dr. Howard Fast with whom I used to have a more or less regular correspondence a few years ago. (I am a member of that club, or at least I used to be.) Please look him and say hello for me, though I doubt whether he would remember my name. But he might be interesting for you to know.

Talking about the study of Divinity, I suppose that term is wrong. It should be Deities (unless your friend is Roman Catholic).

What is divine anyway? I used to have a girlfriend who thought Corelli was divine and Bach heavenly. I do like the term "History of Ideas." That's just to the point and more exact than "Philosophy" in general. So I come to the paragraph in your letter where you write (I quote), "I [Alan] keep telling myself that I must finish my own schooling. Perhaps this is a real concern... But perhaps it is also a rationalization...."

(Eds. By the time he wrote these lines to Alex, Alan had had student deferments from military service for at least five years. This situation caused Alan and like-minded students to examine and re-examine their motives for staying in school. As the years of increasing involvement in Vietnam passed, these students effectively avoided the draft, but they often did so with bad consciences because poorer, less advantaged eighteen-year-olds were being sent to Vietnam.)

You see what I mean? Here is where the History of Ideas starts: with man's reasoning to himself TO JUSTIFY IN ADVANCE WHAT HE IS GOING TO DO (which is also what he wants to do most). I don't think that there is any act a man may do for which he cannot find some sort of excuse. And it is the reasoning to make this excuse plausible which makes up philosopy. So the History of Ideas should start with desires (AND hopes) of a single person or a generation. The classical example is the plight of Arjuna in the first chapters of the *Bhagavad Gita*.

Back to your letter. How should the authorities know that the child [whom Alex and Elisabeth were protecting] isn't simply of a friend staying with us? Because the very peculiar Mr. Aronson, who is known to be a bit queer on the official records and who needs to be watched, had the fortune of marrying the daughter of Mrs. van Dieijen, known in the village as The Little Peacewoman, who has the same reputation (both mother, father, and daughter) for doing things to help others even where the law says explicitly NO. So, double attention for the couple Muktidas which simply refuses to accept "the reality" that the letter of the law must be followed before the call of the heart.

As you know, there are two ways of keeping a thing a secret. (This is originally my own discovery.) Either let nobody know, or let everyone know what is going on. In this case, it was the wisest to keep everyone in the dark. The Law says (and I am stuffing myself with one Law every day after meals) that no child under the age of six months may be cared for by others than the parent. The Law says also that mothers under the age of twenty-one and unwed are not mothers really.... No, Alan, don't laugh. This is just the beginning.

I am at the moment engaged in a fight to keep a fifteen- year-old boy out of an institution. He lost both his parents recently and spent a year at a youth camp after he had finished the primary school for the mentally weak. His guardian in that camp had selected us as a suitable home for him to stay. (We have opened our house to some cases like this.) The boy came for a weekend to see whether we'd fit well together; both he and we were enthusiastic about each other. Now as soon as the boy leaves the youth camp, he comes under guardianship of an organization which has to approve of us, too. And now the social worker has disapproved of our home because WE HAVE NO RUNNING WATER IN THE TOILET. Everything would be all right if there were many homes to be found for such cases, and they could simply select the best. But no such thing. There is no alternative home, only an institution. According to us, this will be fatal for him because he would be a number; what he needs most at the moment is to find his individuality. So I have started to fight again and, if need be, I shall take it to court. Not that I have any chance legally, but my credentials stand up well with the news-people, and there is a chance that I can make public scandal out of it.

Well, you see that I am what you would call "trigger happy" at present. There are many things that I would like to try a shot at. And then to think that I am a pacifist. Another item that we are fighting for right now concerns the forthcoming wedding of our Crown-Princess to the German soldier Claus von Amsberg. A slap in the face of all Dutch Jews and the gentiles who lost relatives and fought desperately against the Germans in the last war. A lost battle, but still we are trying to get the princess to release her claims to the throne (which she will never do). Yet, politics are unreliable. Something may turn up that will turn the tide, a picture, a letter, a word....

(Eds. On 10 March 1966, Crown Princess Beatrix and German diplomat Claus George Wilhelm Otto Friedrich Gerd von Amsberg were married. The new Prince of the Netherlands had been a member of the Hitler Youth and had served in the German Army for two months at the end of World War Two.)

Alan-my-lad, do write to me more about your struggles in Chicago and your observations of slum life. Don't get involved with an unwed mother of fourteen and take a course in first aid so you can help in case of a fight in front of your house. When you do your shopping and return home with your load, keep a small tin of biscuits in one hand ready to drop on the street when drunken loafers come too near. Don't give money to people who ask your help, but never refuse a sandwich. Read *God's Men* by Pearl S. Buck. Write to me again.

Greetings to your younger brother and love to you from

Alex

28 January 1966
[Rotterdam Harbor]

Dear Alan,

Midnight and five minutes; writing to you in the middle of my "work." I wish I'd know what holiday you are referring to when you wished me "good holiday" in your last letter twice. I don't remember having had one [a holiday, by which Alex means a vacation] last year. Elisabeth worked at the school until December (1965), and I started carrying those blooming newspapers around in October.

(Eds. Knowing that Alex attached a private religious significance to Christmas, Alan had wished Alex a "good holiday" in December. This was less awkward for Alan than saying "Merry Christmas" to a Jew. Alex simply misunderstood Alan's indirect greetings.)

My last newspaper found its way this morning. I suddenly got very fed up with it. It was a thankless job, people always grumbling even when the weather was at its worst. Moreover, my wife and I have had to endure a few nasty bumps from official child-care institutions, and we are just about to lose heart. So I got myself this new job as a watchman on ships and yards, which leaves me plenty of freedom. And then, too, I did get my contract with American Express as a "Top Tour Manager". (The English word for it is "courier.") This sheep herding starts about June, and I had to fill the gap. So I shall be doing a week's watching, then we hope to go down to Provence for about three weeks, and then we return to this watching business until we are requested to start with the tours.

Naturally what I am aiming at with American Express is an invitation to come to the U.S. to visit you and other, less important individuals. I even said as much to the boss when he interviewed me and asked for my reason for applying to American Express; so there might be a chance. This interview was more than just comical. On paper, I was asked the following question, "How is your nose?" My reply, "clean," evoked the boss's remark, "That's a stupid answer." To which I said, "It's a very foolish question." Tell me please, Alan, what would an American have replied and are those silly queries normal in the U.S.?

(Eds. Of course, the interviewer was asking Alex how good his sense of direction was.)

The news has come here that Martin Luther King is moving into the Chicago slums... to stay there until something is done about them. Is this true? Will he be staying near to your place and do you agree with this action of his? I was most happy with the photostat of his letter.

(Eds. Alex had asked Alan to give Martin Luther King, Jr., a small gift by hand. When Alan realized that it would be difficult for him to present it in person, he sent it by mail. Alan sent Alex a copy of Dr. King's letter of acknowledgement. Alex then wrote to Dr. King himself and received a reply, which we reproduce at the end of this section. Alex had had no previous contact with Dr. King.)

I wrote to Martin Luther King, hoping to get a reply, too. My letter included just a little bit of criticism which his presence here in Holland evoked in people like myself. For example, he stayed here in the Hilton Hotel — of all the hotels in Holland, the one that always systematically refused cooperation with spontaneous relief-projects.

(Eds. Sister Marlo, mentioned below, was a Black Spiritualist Advisor living in Chicago. Alan had sent Alex her calling card which had been slipped under his door.)

Sister Marlo's ad found a place on my wallpaper. Maybe I'll even look her up some day. In India, I found many of her kindred, and I can't say that I found them very harmful. In their way, they provide an antidote to many troubles of people who can't afford other narcotics. Separately, I am sending some wall ornaments to your home address. Also a paper written by a Prof. Dr. Krauss whom we had as our guest for a few days. Have you ever heard of him? He wrote a few words for you on the first page. I myself got a copy, too. This man travels around handing out his literature for free in the hope (vain hope, I am afraid) that justice will be done to him.

The booklet I sent you was the manuscript of a projected publication [of my own] which never was realized. They are the recorded replies I gave once (in 1960) to a Bahai girl whose guest I was in Poona (India). I used to have another copy, but I lost it somewhere. So I would appreciate your returning it when you are done. Before you give your criticism (which, of course, will be most welcome), you should know that in the meantime I have changed a few points, though, on the whole, I still hold to what I wrote then....

Neither Johan Huizinga nor his book, *The Waning of the Middle Ages*, is known to me, but I am trying to get hold of it. Right now, I am enjoying a delicious book by Hans Warner called *Through Greece on an Ass.* If one has described present-day Hellas as it really is, it is this adventurer. If you want me to translate it, please say so, though it will lose much of its meaning in translation. Some passages are to be felt, rather than understood.

[The following night.] I ordered Huizinga's book today. Was told in the bookshop that it is rather well-known and regarded as his best. Tonight watching on a ship with a lot of walking around and organizing to do. Therefore not much time to continue this letter and will mail it right now.

Do write again soon, also about your neighborhood and observations.

Yours ever,

Alex

(Eds. The following is the letter from Martin Luther King to Alex. It was written on stationery of the Southern Christian Leadership Conference, 334 Auburn Ave., N.E., Alanta, Georgia. The officers of the organization are listed as Martin Luther King, Jr., President; Ralph Abernathy, Treasurer; and Andrew J. Young, Executive Director.)

4 April 1966

Dear Mr. Aronson,

Thank you for your very informative letter to me. I can see that you have been involved significantly in the work of bettering the lot of mankind. I envy you your experiences with Vinoba Bhave, Dr. Schweitzer and Abbé Pierre.

I trust Mirabehn's work on Beethoven is coming along well. I shall be eternally grateful to her for her gift to me of the Gandhi booklet. Do communicate my regards to all your friends who have sought to meet with me during my Holland sojourns. I am terribly sorry that a meeting was not effectuated, as I am sure that I stood to gain much just from meeting those who are so kindred to you in spirit. Also, please extend my warmest sentiments to your wife and Alwin.

May our mutual work toward a world community of peace and brotherhood ever prosper.

Fraternally yours,

Martin Luther King, Jr.

Southern Christian Leadership Conference

S C L C

334 Auburn Ave., N.E.
Atlanta, Georgia 30303
Telephone 522-1420

Martin Luther King Jr., *President* Ralph Abernathy, *Treasurer* Andrew J. Young, *Executive Director*

November 22, 1965

Mr. Alan Mendelson
3838 Fulton Street, N. W.
Washington, D. C.

Dear Alan:

I send my deepest appreciation with these lines in consequence of your heartwarming consideration of me and that of your friend, Alex in Holland. I shall always cherish Mirabehn's 'Digest" of Gandhi's thoughts and am humbled and honored that the "Digest" should find its way to me at Mirabhen's request, via Alex and you.

I have already been inspired by Gandhi's life, work and thought and that he should now affect me through the compilations of his dear friend and secretary of twenty-five years is all the more inspiring to me. It goes without saying that Gandhi's philosophy and practice of "soul force" has been the key to the door-opening determination and deeds which have characterized the nonviolent warriors of the civil rights army, with which I have had the good fortune to be identified.

Do, please, excuse the belatedness of my response to your appreciated letter and gift of the "Digest." My prayers for you and Alex go with my thanks.

Sincerely yours,

Martin Luther King Jr.

Martin Luther King, Jr.

Kg

A copy of Dr. Martin Luther King's acknowledgement of Alex's gift. It was addressed to Alan because he acted as intermediary. (Cf. Alex's letter of 28 January, 1966.)

Section Four

Restlessness

April 1966 - November 1968

(Eds. The following letter was typed on stationery headed "Alexander L. Aronson, tourmanger and interpreter.")

Poortugaal
April [?] 1966

Dear Alan,

Writing to you for the first time under this new letter head. I have changed quite a bit in the past few months. Beard is off, too, and my stomach is about the size of the Michelin-man. In short, I have become a real old-fashioned house-father... from the outside. Inwardly, I still feel the same, although I do realize (my wife makes me realize it all the time) that my outlook on many things has changed. Still I often disagree with society, and I am continuously quarrelling with my boss, Mr. Harry Rubin of American Express. I take that as a good sign. But I haven't told you yet that I am working for this illustrious company as a Tour-Escort. I am herding Americans around in Europe, and doing it with pleasure, too. Though I was only accepted as temporary help for ninety days, I seem to fit into their program, for I have already Tours assigned to me till October. (I have done two 20-day tours so far.) And it is not laying any wind-eggs either.

Fortunately, for now I have been able to do my heart's wish: i.e., buy a little farm in France with the ruins of an old house on it which I intend to restore so that we can really live there. It is near a small village called Le Monastier in the Haute Loire, four miles from Le Puy [45°N, 4°E]. We have our own nightingale singing in our own trees. Isn't that something! Both Elisabeth and I are raving about it to everyone who cares to listen. The land around it measures one and a quarter acre, enough to do some farming and to keep a cow. Will you come and help us build???

The music I am listening to at the moment is *hazanut* [Hebrew, cantorial music], sung by my dear friend Hans Bloemendal, the Amsterdam cantor who has recently been made full professor of Chemistry at a Dutch University. It makes me feel a bit sad inside. I used to sing with him in the synagogues (sometimes a duet, sometimes a choir of four or six). Somehow Elisabeth and I are missing something. Not religion, for we have our stomachs full of that, both of us, but a certain atmosphere we used to live in, when single, which we lost in the quest for oneness....

I now agree that the man who has questioned and found his own answer has a happiness which is one of consciousness and not of blindness. The question I now feel popping up is whether blind love is worth more than reasoned liking. The first certainly is much nearer to nature. It is well known that knowledge and all that clings to it does not increase happiness. On the contrary. What is it really to know an answer? But what bewilders me is the question what can be done for a man who has an answer (not THE answer, AN answer) and who knows, but has decided he would much rather return to his former ignorance. For that is the way I sometimes feel myself. Knowledge can't be undone; and one will always continue to search; and when one knows, to teach, even when one believes that his teaching doesn't do anything to improve happiness. All this is, indeed, abstract. But concrete facts, too, pose the same questions. Negroes in slums. I am sure many of them feel very happy there. I am not talking about those who compare themselves with the rest of the world and become dissatisfied. I am talking about those poor bastards who take everything for granted. What if we do mix in their world and take them out of their slums in which they unconsciously vegetate. Will they be happy in our modern way of life? Aren't we, then, playing the part of those missionaries in India and elsewhere who teach what they believe is the One Way to live and who insist on a woman wearing at least a Mother Hubbard. We are continually talking about a solution, but I am now questioning our right (yours and mine) to help find one. As to our own existence... we ARE, and I don't think that it is any use to try to find out WHY we are and what we are doing here. The FACT that we ARE is there. It should be enough for us to realize it and make "the most of it" — whatever that may mean to each individual.

I am more and more inclined to believe that we have grown too far from nature to be able to be happy without questioning. You, for example, ask, "Why aren't you a vegetarian? Why do you eat chicken?" But isn't this the way NATURE is? Isn't that same chicken eating worms and killing some form of life itself?

Well, you should know from your studies how often all these questions have been asked and what kind of answers they evoked. Personally, I have reached the point of wanting just to exist and enjoy myself. The one concession I am making to my "reformative instinct" is that I try to let as many people as possible participate in my enjoyment. I may be wrong. I may be just getting too lousy average, but I have quit fighting the odds. My wife would be laughing loudy at this because she thinks I am fighting something or someone all the time.

In fact, as a tour-escort, I am quite extraordinary, always taking the herd to places that are not on the program and changing it whenever it suits me. It is true, though, that I don't hate the crowd as much as I used to. Also I am beginning to be quite tolerant with the stupidity of the plebs. Is that the beginning of true wisdom? My beloved Socrates might have an answer to that.

Alan, I started this letter after another letter sent to some girl in Chicago to whom you gave my name. I hope I replied to her well and that you agree with what I told her. She may be coming back to you since I told her to. Send as many people over here as you like. They are always welcome. From here onward they may get introduced around, but I can't give addresses to those I don't know personally. It's just one of those things.

By the way you should know that I was reported to the president of American Express as being ANTI/AMERICAN. The reply I gave (in a report) was as follows: "My best friend and godfather of my son is an American. I have many relatives working and living in the U.S.A. and I was made a distinguished fellow of the Columbus Association for special merit in the field of creating better understanding between America and the countries of Western Europe. Yet I am a Tour-Escort and, as such, have to explain anti-American slogans such as YANKEE GO HOME which the people see en route. I am sometimes obliged to explain sentiments which are not my own. This happened in France while I was on tour. After all, tour-members are, without my knowledge usually, confronted with these things. I fully realize that my clients are on vacation and should not be troubled with controversies, but when they do meet antagonism, I feel it my duty to explain. And maybe some other Tour-Escort will do the same for the **Russian** Express Company tours.... Anyway, although I do think that American Express is a bit over organized, I like working for your company. But I do wish to say that when the complaints of one single excited woman are taken so seriously as to invite all sorts of lengthy reports and letters, there is something lacking in coöperation between Company and Escort."

So you see, dear Alan, that though I try to be moderate because part of my French farm is still unpaid, I shall *never* betray my true self. I still believe that it pays to be honest and not just write, or say, what sounds like perfume and roses. And so far, my clients have liked me for it. If I don't get thrown out, I will surely get invited to America. If so, I hope to look you up. It will be my main point of interest in your country.

Do write to me again when you can spare a moment, but don't expect my answers soon. It's a mad world, this touring business.

Yours ever,

Alex

(Eds. Although this letter was written in October, 1966, it was not sent for several weeks. Alex explains what happened on a small slip of paper: "Sorry, but the first envelope got lost and turned up after two weeks, spoiled by the car battery. Hope you don't blame me for not copying the letter over. Happy Christmas. Alex." The envelope was not all that was spoiled by the car battery. The letter itself arrived in an advanced state of disintegration. In some spots, it has been impossible to reconstruct, so we have inserted asterisks to indicate an actual loss of text.)

On board the "Chateau Margaux"
[Rotterdam Harbor]
25 October 1966

Dear Alan,

Or rather, cher Alain, for after an interval of a month I am again at my watching business. Yesterday Elisabeth, Alwin, and my mother-in-law returned from a month's holiday in France. I don't know whether I ever wrote to you that I had bought a parcel of land in the Haute Loire, but that's what I did a few months ago. I was not pleased with the land I'd already got in the Dordogne. (Before finishing the sale there, the agent messed about with some trees so I refused to go on with the bargain, and it's up for sale again now.) * * * The land itself, however, far exceeded our expectations. Beautiful trees and meadows, interesting population. The few weeks we stayed on it were well occupied. Cleaning out the stable so that we could move in there after having lived the first week * * * then starting repairs on the one room of the building which was not completely ruined. And we did quite a job there, too, considering the soft nails and wood of bad quality we had to work with.

Old William, 76, father of my cherished woman, did his share to add to the liveability of the stable. (He is as hard-headed as his daughter so I just let him do whatever he pleased.) You can imagine that there was no time to do any letter-writing. Yet, you have been foremost in my mind. I would have loved to show you the place. You are probably aware of the fact that I am (and always was) somewhat obsessed by the possession of *LAND*, to my belief man's greatest resource and stable riches. Though I haven't been back to Fannari in Greece, many friends have been able to spend a few pleasant weeks there.

Le Monastier, the village nearest to my "French Farm," is nearer to Holland [than Fannari], and we expect to be there more and more often and longer as time passes. Next letter will contain some pictures, if they turn out well. * * * My American Express employment, in the end, proved not to be satisfactory enough for my bosses. I haven't been sacked exactly, but I wasn't given more than the 90-day contractual engagement. That means 3 tours, the last of which was a nightmare. Imagine 30 people in the same narrow bus for 40 days, all the time travelling and having to absorb new impressions. Moreover, except 3 nurses, all were teachers and have you ever met more difficult people than those? Except for one fortunate circumstance, this last trip was a complete failure. The one thing that saved my happiness was the presence of a lovely young girl, Florence, sent on this trip by her great-aunt. I can't explain to you how our relationship came about. Elisabeth met her, too, and felt about her as I did. So after the tour (which ended in Paris), she stayed in our home for 3 days. Were it not that she has a boyfriend back home in Virginia, I would have insisted on her meeting you. What a lovely pair you would have made. She is natural blonde, big on all sides, 19 years young, and virgin in body as well as mind. She helped me plow through 40 days * * * Incidentally, I named my new car after her. But don't think that by "new" I am describing a 1967 model Mercedes. My great new treasure is a 1955 Diesel London taxi-cab as heavy as a lorry, as old and shaky as the Paris elevators, but a darling. She withstood 2,000 miles (to our French home and back) as well as a Mercedes would have. She is slow but oh, so reliable. And she cost (with repairs and all that) only $500. I brought her to Holland myself, having saved her from a dump in London. So much for our material existence.

Our spirtual life has also been enriched by many experiences. We had, of course, several children to care for, the last time two Mongolians (I hope you know the expression). Those children were in our care for a month (Mother in hospital). They are very hard on the housewife, for they give a lot of work, but are ever so nice and good-natured. Alex Aronson himself is in politics once again. The pacifist-socialist party opened a new seat near my home. I joined and now serve as secretary and lecturer on pacifism. The chances are good for me to be elected as town-councillor, next elections, and oh-boy, will the big blockheads have to kneel, that stand behind Johnson's dirty politics and our own stupid monarchy. * * *

I believe it's time for me to * * * act * * * instead of standing helplessly on the outside * * * I hate politics, but doesn't one have to tackle the imbeciles on their own ground? However, I don't think the pacifist-party leaders approve of me. I steadfastly refuse to preach what they teach in their rules and regulations. But I act and speak as my conscience dictates, and that is supposed to be irregular. You see, as with many in the same fix, I am looking for a loudspeaker with which to voice my opinions. And I am not at all satisfied; not with the world, not with myself. I am still young, not yet ripe for retiring in a monastery (which I intend to do at old age, when my wife is gone), and too old to be satisfied by club life, idealistic pamphlets or even "dedicating" myself to some cause or other.

It's funny, really, but after having worked with people like Vinoba in India, Schweitzer in Africa, Abbé Pierre in Europe, I am still (or, it would be more truthful to say AGAIN) "searching." What I am really looking for, perhaps, is a CAUSE, in which *both* Elisabeth and I can believe without scepticism. For with us it has gotten to the point where if one of us is in doubt both of us are unable to work. There is one thing, though, in which we both continue to believe — children. And if we find an opportunity to serve them in any part of the world, we'll not hesitate * * *

brotherlove,

Alex

N.B. Your godson, Alwin, is growing fast. Starts to speak and has a will of his own that is difficult to please. Loves animals, travelling, and is afraid of no one. He has strong sympathies and antipathies, looks like his grandmother (on his mother's side) when he cries, and like me and my father when he laughs. Also speaks two words of French: *bonjour — au revoir*.

Poortugaal
[Early 1967]

Dear Alan,

Your letter in front of me is dated 11 December, and I think it is the last one you wrote and I still left unanswered. Here it goes, the first few lines of an epistle which has to bring you up-to-date on our spiritual and worldly welfare. Life on the Elftplaat has been shockingly unshocking. Both Elisabeth and myself are aware that something drastic has to be done in order to bring some life into the brewery, as the saying goes in Holland. Which brings me to the final remark of your letter...that the people you live with are unconscious. I know exactly what you mean by that, but I think that a little tolerance should be shown to the unconscious. We should always remind ourselves that we are working for them and, mostly, with them. If it were not for my work with the Int. Civil Service (which is a continual fight against easy living rich-people's-kids and their ridiculous notions of how an organization should be run), I might have joined the unconscious myself. The fact that I have struggled myself out of financial debt (notary costs of our French place) and am continously on the lookout for a new job, helps too. American Express, naturally, doesn't want me anymore and earning my daily bread is going to be very hard this summer. (The rate of unemployment is growing fast in Holland.) I am doing my best to earn my daily salad, by working our garden every spare moment. It should provide us with a full year's supply of vegetables if weather permits. Mother Earth... how I long for Greece and France to make my little loan of hers there profitable, too. I just received a report about Fannari from an English friend; she and her sister were there for three days. It seems that Sophia and her parents keep the place quite nicely in order. As for our "monastery" in France, we do hope to get there again some time soon.

Just now, while I was writing this, your letter arrived, confirming the receipt of Rembrandt. Another parcel of souvenirs (printed matter) is on its way; just little nothings, but I have a feeling that they belong to you. As for your friend (Laurie) in Paris, I will write to her that she is welcome in case she is too shy to take the initiative. No, I doubt whether there will be much travelling for me this year. Business is very slack, so I am just working when there is some "watching" to do in Rotterdam harbor.

I have no Haiku book; neither do I know what a Haiku is. So I very much look forward to your parcel. I was glad you found that *Dictionary of Classical Antiquities.* And I hope it is what I expect. If you find a BLIND MAP OF GREECE in a large schoolroom size, it will be a great help. Here nothing can be found like it, and it seems that in Greece they don't work with blind maps in the schools. (In case you wonder what a blind map is, since I don't know whether it is used in the US, a blind map is a large scale map of a country on which major points are the only indications of some city and no names are printed on it. In other words, just the outlines of a country on blank paper, with dòts for towns or cities and lines for rivers.) I intend to fill it up myself like the National Geographic's Map of Classical Lands of the Mediterrean, but more complete.

Do write some time about your studies and what practical use they can be put to. From a philosophical point of view, I imagine, nothing is really practical to the world at large. Compared to the universe, all our attempts are small and futile. From a PRACTICAL point of view, however, I see that what we get out of it ourselves. Practical is the building up of one's personality. As Earl Stanley Gardener wrote in one of his early (good) books "in all fields where the goal is financial success, there is a lot of competition. When the ultimate aim of one's thriving is spiritual success, one is absolutely unique, there will be no competition, and usually the end becomes a financial success as well." All this from an intriguing murder story, just imagine!!!

Well, Alan, my brother, our love to you and yours. Do let us know something about your new surroundings [a different neighborhood in Chicago's South Side].

Yours as ever,

Alex

(Eds. The following letter had to be returned to Alex by the post office because the address was insufficient. As an address, Alex had written simply "Chicago, Illinois, U.S.A." Attached to the letter was a note: "Dear Alan, Here is the letter that went astray. It came back because you are not too well-known in Chicago. Try to send a letter to Alex Aronson - Holland, and it would reach me sooner, I think." The letter is written on Alex's "tourmanager and interpreter" stationery. Next to those words, Alex scrawled a large question mark.)

[Rotterdam Harbor]
16 June 1967

Dear Alan,

Night duty at my new job: porter in one of the ports of Rotterdam. Doing this now for four weeks. "Doing" and "work" are rather big words, "being" would express it better really. I have to *be* around, attend the telephone in the porter's lodge, and sit there watching the gate and the people who pass through it. When ships are expected, I have to see to it that they are moored in their proper places. On night duty, my main concern is that they don't catch me sleeping. They pay rather well. As for the watching, this I do a few nights a week, just in order to have a little more spending money. This porter's job may be a temporary one only, and there is a chance that either my employers or I myself may refuse to make it "permanent" after the first two months. The last expression, of course, in quotation marks, for how many things are really "permanent?" Jobs certainly not, at least not for me. And when it is decided that I am not going to stay on, I thus may go back to "watching ships" all the more easily.

Today an emergency telephone call from some organization which wants us to be camp parents in a 6 week summer camp for handicapped children. Right along our path, but how the hell can I do it when I just entered this new job? I told them to speak to my employer. Maybe they will give me special furlough, though I doubt this very strongly. A lot of people take their vacations right at this time.

Talking about holidays, Elisabeth and I are planning to go to our place in France during the month of September, the best time of year in those parts. If this summer-camp deal is accepted, I don't think we'll have that vacation; we'll have to wait until next year. Meanwhile, we bought a secondhand mini- caravan, rather like a double-bed on wheels, with just room enough to stand in, and I am now fixing it with some cooking facilities (gas) and light (car battery). A small item for these luxuries is bought every week. The whole set-up is rather common-place and out of our line, but it fits well behind the Morris and will eventually help us to escape everyday life even when funds are low. Its major advantage is that it makes us independent of hotels and restaurants on the way.

When, oh when, will I see Fannari again? An English girlfriend of mine spent a week there with her sister a few months ago; they loved it. The neighbors keep it very tidy. Electricity seems to have reached it too. I sent a letter to these neighbors with a few drachmas enclosed, but so far they have failed to reply. I don't think the change of govenment will affect life in such a small village. On the whole, Greek history has shown that changes take place only in Athens. The idea you express in your letter of Fannari being a cherished place, a sort of terminal of the flight from sordid life, is just what it has become to me. You know that throughout these past years I have stocked it with the best books, the most beautiful records, and pictures. However small the cabin is and primitive to spoiled modern man, I do think it adequate for a hermit with ideals which, I think, we both are at heart. Music and literature are bread and wine for me, even now when I sometimes seem to sink into bourgois unconsciousness.

Your gift of two Indian records gave me a big lift. I am not going to thank you either for the lovely records or for the *Classical Dictionary*, both being exactly what I had dreamed them to be. The thanks I could express would be words only and not befitting the spirit in which you sent your gifts. I only hope that my thoughts and feelings of gratitude will reach you somehow in the spirit of soul-embracing. I do believe something like that happens somewhere in the stratosphere when two people *think* about each other simultaneously. For your information, the time is now 01.45 on 17 June (18.45 on 16 June, Chicago time).

Laurie was a nice guest to have although personally, if I would have anything to say in the matter which I have not, I wouldn't choose her for your wife. Typical old world way of thinking, but that's the way I am. Critical comment: She has lots to learn about housekeeping. Positive comment: she's really nice and absolutely good with children. (Your godson Alwin is a difficult one in his choice of friends, but I am glad to say that she made the grade after one day.) I am afraid that the impression she must have had of me is not too beautifying. I had worked nights for weeks on end, and my humor was not too good. Tiredness makes me into an impatient and shouting moron, very hard to please. I do hope she will return in summer to see our home in the happy peace it usually is.

An important thing she mentioned was your getting your Ph.D. next year and your subsequent vacation, possibly in Europe. I COUNT ON IT... having you with us then. According to Laurie, the picture of you nailed to my wall (over the statue of Socrates) is a little out of date. She said you have changed a little. So please send me a new photograph of Alan Mendelson today.

So far I haven't written a word about Israel and its friendly neighbors. Thanks be to God that this time they have again beaten their foe. The question is what will be the outcome of the UN General Assembly which convenes tomorrow. Holland has been marvellous with its moral and financial support. I believe it is the one country that put itself spontaneously on Israel's side, government and people alike!!!

(Eds. The previous paragraph was prompted by the 1967 Six-Day War.)

Alan-me-lad, do write to me about your studies and your life in the city of Al Capone and Martin Luther King. Give my regards to your parents and receive all our love.

Yours ever,

Alex

(Ed. The return address on the following letter is the "therapeutic summer camp" at Oisterwijk, Holland.)

15 July 1967

My dear Alan,

I received your letter dated 7 July yesterday night. So it appears that you haven't yet received mine which I wrote at night while on night duty in the porter's lodge. To me that was a very important letter, for in it I thanked you for all your good gifts, the marvellous *Classical Dictionary*, the two beautiful records and more. I wrote something about Laurie's visit as well as about Israel. About the latter, I did not write as explicitly as you would have liked.

I shall continue on the topic which, to me, was NOT so disconcerting as it seems to have been to you. For, first of all, I do not see a particular ASCENT of "military thought" in Israel. The country has always been, from the very start, when the Keren Kayemeth [Jewish National Fund] bought land from the Arabs, through its act of independence (via a United Nations simple-majority decision) and its maintenance against mighty opponents and continued insurgency, until its last military act, a stage for violent fighting. A struggle for life which, in view of non-recognition by its opponents, could only be fought on the military field.

As for Israel's right of existence, I do not believe myself (or you) capable of an objective view. How far does a people have to go back in history to assert its right to a territory? And what decides their right? Their majority? Their achievements? I do not think that an answer to these questions can be given.

Rhodesian whites, though a minority, base their independence on achievements. Algerians, fully colonized by the French, based their independence on majority. Greeks, when struggling for independence against Turks, had (at the time of the struggle) neither a majority in their own country, nor any achievement to show. The Turks had ruled their country for a full 400 years and Greece had only history to show for its right to the country. (There remains the factor of church; but then in Western Turkey, as well as in Southern Yugoslavia, there were as many Orthodox as in Greece.)

If I have to define the right of Israelis to their country, I should start with history. Though one has to go back very far, I do not doubt this right. Then there is the factor of achievements, both by the first immigrants as well as by the present-day Israeli. If, as I see it, the land that God gave to mankind, has to be exploited as well as possible (like I believe that anything that is given us is to be used), one should give that land to the farmer who raises the best crop. There is also no doubt that the Israeli is the better farmer. One should not count the majority question. If one compares the number of Jews at the minute of independence (1948) to the number of Arabs present at that time in Palestine, I am sure there were more Arabs. (If one counts the Jews in the Diaspora as possible future Israelis, so one should also count all Arabs in the world.)

However, there is one right that the Jews have to Israel that is undeniable: the right based in NEED. The Second World War has proved that beyond questioning. This right, together with achievements and history, is more than enough for me to say that the Jewish people has a right to Israel. From here we can go on to post-independence warfare.

The pacifist, after whom all pacifists are modeled, of course, was Mahatma Gandhi. I regard myself as a staunch pupil of this great Master. His greatness was based on the fact that, though a man of very strict principles and severity towards himself, he knew where to draw the line and how to compromise in his dealings with the outer world. Though he regarded fighting as a great evil, he thought it worse to be regarded as a coward. And he realized that men who started fighting for possession would not stop with the capture of material possessions. They would continue to fight till they possessed body and soul of the captured. And the soul should be preserved at all costs, for it is God given. Therefore, when you recognize Israel's existence, you HAVE to allow it its right to fight for its soul.

I do not know whether you, when studying in Jerusalem, saw much of Israel's military soul. I did, for I participated in its army for a year and also voluntered in the first Sinai campaign (1956). Throughout I noticed the people's determination NOT to capture, but to gain security. And I am sure that this security is the only thing they want now. But then do they have the right to keep the captured parts? I believe that they may and will. They will keep the Gaza strip because it shortens the border by so many kilometers; they will keep the old part of Jerusalem because Israel's ties with it are too strong and also because it solves the problem of the Scopus enclave. The rest (Sinai, Jordan) will be returned to their former owners on condition of permanent U.N. supervision and (probably) de jure recognition of Israel by the countries concerned. Once this recognition is a fact, there are more ways towards peace than just the military which, though disgusting, has been the only point of contact between the parties. And it was NOT Israel that wished it thus. I am with Israel when she denies the right to lost territories to opponents who do not recognize its existence and still speak of the *Memshelet Tel Aviv* as if Israel were naughty rebels.

(Eds. Alex is alluding to one of the circumlocutions used by certain Arab governments in referring to Israel. "Memshelet Tel Aviv" *means "the government in Tel Aviv." It is similar to the phrase "the Zionist entity," which also indicates a refusal to recognize the State of Israel.)*

I am with Israel when she wars in the open and "according to rules" against the vermin who continuously try to enter in the dark. I am with Israel when she says, "I am here for keeps."

I hope that this may help you find where you stand. Please realize that, when at war, no neutral position is possible. The question is to find the source of evil and kill it.

Greece and its people finally got what they deserved. Please forgive me for being rather bitter about it. But having come to know the Greek very well, I cannot but rejoice at their getting a lesson; a punishment for their weakness in not being able to shake off empty customs and in not taking a firm stand in their desire for mental modernization.

(Eds. On 21 April 1967, a military junta overthrew the interim government of Premier Panayotis Kanellopoulos. Among others, ex-Premier George Papandreou, a leader of the leftist Center Union Party, was arrested. King Constantine, then 27 years old, attempted a countercoup on 13 December; it failed, and the king went into exile.)

I believe that this new Greek miliary government is the apex of a crisis in the struggle between foolhardy and blind traditionalism, on the one hand, and modern thought without backbone, on the other. I hope this government will be strong. For if they are, the force that overthrows it will be strong enough to overcome evils such as *prika* (dowry), slavery, and egoism.

About Vietnam, I may write more in my next letter. I am sure it will keep on till then. I share your feeling of involvement. Yet I am beginning to doubt the wisdom of continued demonstrations. Help me look for another way to influence world politics.

Against all probabilities, I got special leave from my new boss to go with Elisabeth as camp parents for the six-week summer camp for asthmatic children. We are feeling very good about doing it. I got a three-week leave. The other three weeks I will travel up and down from my work to the camp, and I am going to have a busy time earning money in Rotterdam and being Papa to twenty sick children here in Oisterwijk. (Look on the map near Tilburg.)

Well, Alan brother, do write again soon, and let me know when we can expect you here. And if you come, don't be "an American *doing* a country," but stay with us for a few months. That will give me the chance to teach you Dutch and you the chance to read Frederick van Eden and Ruysbroeck. Lots of love to you and your family.

Yours ever,

Alex

tourmanager and interpreter...

Poortugaal
5 January 1968

Dearest Alan,

After a very long time without writing a single letter to anyone, you're the first to benefit from a moment of sanity in my hectic life. I really don't know when I wrote to you last, or what I wrote then. As matters stand today — just to bring you up to date — I am a porter in the port of Rotterdam. I have had this job for a year now. I am earning fine and have a lot of spare time. My wife is still Elisabeth (no Taylor). I say this to prevent you from making the mistake that I have become modernized and changed wives with someone. We still have only one SUN who shines brightly in our home, but who evidently is not a pacifist. We still live at Elftplaat

5 in Poortugaal, but have acquired meanwhile a ruined farm in France with two acres of land and another farm in better condition in the north of the Netherlands, Friesland. We hope to move to Friesland within another year and a half, by which time the new buildings that are approaching our house here will have shut us in amongst the most profane plebs a port produces.

We are all healthy, including our fifteen-year-old French stepson who is staying with us to learn a trade in Holland. This summer, we will again act as camp parents in a six-week camp for asthmatic children, as we did in 1967. So far the Aronsons today.

And now, how are you getting on with your studies? Laurie predicted that you'd be able to come to Europe in 1969. Will this prediction become true? I most sincerely hope so. We heard again from Laurie last month. She sent the most beautiful pictures of our son we'd ever had.

About the [Palestinian] "refugees" who don't *want* to return to Israel, did you know that most of them live on the earnings of relatives working in Kuwait and that they don't want to return because of the impossibility of transfering money from Kuwait to Israel. Besides, I really *believe* that better understanding and more willingness on the part of the Arab *leaders* would influence the condition of the refugees greatly.

About Greece, you may find me cruel, but I really rejoice in the failure of its king. Playboy would be a better name for his function. If any amelioration for the Greek will come, it will be by *revolution of the people only*. Believe me, I know them. I repeat what I said before, they have earned the government they got. People like Theodorakis and Louisa Vlachos are, like Gandhi in India, exceptions. This also goes for all those centerists who are kept prisoner. You don't know it, but I do... All their so-called "reforming" was to be for their **own good only**. Do come here and let's discuss this. Do live in Greece for three months, and you will agree.

Alan, I want you so much to go, see, and get to know this lovely girl called Florence. Though she is going steady, I really feel you should at last meet her. Please, Alan, do go and visit her for my sake; her address, in case you lost it, is... c/o Searcy's Drive-in, Onley, Virginia. Please do drive in just once.

(Eds. Alan did not drive in to meet Florence.)

To return to your last statement on the cover of your letter...

survival of the fittest = Darwinism = for the animal world. Don't you think the animal world is more sane and healthier than our "human" world? Who was it that said he wished people were still cannibals who killed only to eat?

Enclosed is an article on a Chinese Haggada [book for the Passover ceremonial meal] issued in New York. If you have the chance, please phone and ask whether they are still available and whether they issue catalogues of their other Hagadoth.

Do write soon. I long to hear from you. Love from us all, and a very happy 1968.

Alex

tourmanager and interpreter...

Poortugaal
6 April 1968

Dear Alan,

Your letter arrived yesterday just before the very shocking news of Martin Luther King's assassination. Of course, here, as I imagine everywhere else in Europe and the world, it is the talk of the day. The "long hot summer," which was predicted some weeks ago and of which you also spoke in your letter, will be very hot indeed. And the reaction for which I have been waiting for two days now has not come. King's death, making a martyr of him, could have been turned into a very good thing if his "managers" would have taken it in hand immediately, and pushed forward another great personality. The possibilities I have been thinking of are Roland Hayes, if he is still alive, or better still, Marian Anderson. These should have capitalized on his death and on his ideas of non-violence, drowning the market of sensation with his ideals, and suppressing the voices of people [militants] like Stokeley Carmichael and his likes. These, the greatest danger in the U.S., may well turn King's death into a tragedy which it need NOT become. Believe it or not, Alan, but your letter as well as the news have made me very jumpy. If I got the chance, I would run into the first aeroplane going your way to work and DO something. And here I am, sitting quietly on my fat arse and getting paid just for reading detective stories. Being far away and safely removed from Vietnam and the U.S. does give me the advantage of being able to see more clearly what is going on, but, oh, the impotence one feels.

I have broken with the Dutch pacifist party. Boy, it is so easy to be a pacifist in peace-time. I would welcome just a tiny war in Holland, if only to test all pacifists. Not half of them, I am sure, would remain true to their ideals. Just looking at all those demonstrations for Vietnam and integration makes me SICK.

(Eds. Alan participated in the very demonstrations which Alex found so impalatable; he also belonged to organizations similar to those described below.)

Perhaps they all mean well, but just get into one of their numerous committee meetings. (The Dutch are great at committees and all sorts of clubs.) Not ONE organization has a top that functions well and without inside struggles. If I ever get into a meeting again, it must be with a whip in my hands. And since "democracy" (how I have come to hate the very word) does not permit this kind of ruling, I probably will never get into one, ever again. This all may sound bitter to you, but have you ever had an important issue in a conference turned down because the secretary bought too many printed letterheads, and the whole conference just kept to that subject?

There is one thing Elisabeth and I are going to do again this summer: the six-week camp for asthmatic children. It gave a lot of satisfaction, both to us and to those kids who went home better than ever.

Today I am at my "work" as gatekeeper in one of the ports of Rotterdam. Two weekends out of seven I am on duty, working an average of 40 hours a week, which leaves me quite a bit of spare time. Most of my spare time is used to earn extra to finance the construction that is being done on our farm in Friesland. We may have to move there earlier than we expected, for just this week we received news (still not officially confirmed) that our home in Poortugaal may have to be pulled down within three months.

During our Easter vacation we will go to friends in France for four days. Not as far south as our own lovely spot there, but at least far enough to breathe some fresh air, and I hope to get gloriously drunk at least one night on its wine. No work being done in the port today or tomorrow, I have the whole place to myself. I am enjoying the rare beautiful weather, writing to you, to Laurie, and to Florence and reading Emil Ludwig's (Cohn's) biography of Heinrich Schliemann. On the one hand, I cannot say I like the man [Schliemann {1822 - 1890}; discoverer and, some might say, destroyer of the site of ancient Troy]. On the other hand, I know myself and know also that I have much in common with the person described.

Someone has very thoughtfully given me anonymously a subscription to the *National Geographic Magazine*. I cannot think of anyone doing such a thing, but you or Florence. And unless I am greatly mistaken, you would not choose the *National Geographic* yourself. Personally, after reading four issues, the only thing I can say is that I like their subjects, but cannot exactly love the way they are treated. So, if I owe thanks to you, I hope I am not offending you instead. It would be just like Florence to remind me in this way that I haven't written to her for such a long time. Anyway, the photographs in this magazine are truly beautiful.

(Eds. Alan had not sent Alex the subscription.)

Sunday

Last night the news came through of Ralph Abernathy being pointed at as King's successor. If ever a butcher became priest it is him, so to speak. I do not know him personally, but on the first sight, I cannot say I admire the choice. No personality. No pep. Please let me know your thoughts on the subject.

Finishing now because there really is nothing to be said besides the issues that govern man's mind today. I am with you and yours in prayer and thought.

Love from us all,

Alex

De Wilp, Holland
[November, 1968]

Dear Alan,

It seems your letter has been the sign for some very pleasant things to start happening. But let me begin first by thanking you for your pamphlet. It was readable and made me feel very sorry not to have known this Dr. Goodenough or to have studied under him.

> *(Eds. Alan had written a memoir which was published in* Religions in Antiquity: Essays in Memory of Erwin Ramsdell Goodenough. *Alex is referring to a reprint of this article. Dr. Goodenough, who died in 1965, was a leading scholar in the field of Hellenistic Judaism.)*

I forgot when my last letter to you was written and what I wrote in it. I think I mentioned that we moved from Poortugaal. Or perhaps not, for your last letter was still addressed there. Anyway, I am sure I wrote to you about buying this old farm (can one say, "farmlet"?) and, after finishing our summer camp for asthmatic children, we moved to permanent residence here. A nice job was offered me (Head of a department in an institution for mentally retarded children), but after four (4) days, I was given the sack. Nothing special had happened, but, as I was given to understand that in my new department I was allowed to do some PIONEERING, I forthwith started to do so; probably a little too vigorously. At least the nuns (it was an RC institution) did not take to my new approach.

Fortunately, we have a very good nationalized social security system, so I just stepped into my No-Labor-Pension [unemployment money]. In the province of Friesland, where we are now living, it is very hard to get a job at all, especially when one is limited to one certain field of work. (Which I am not, really, but I lose my rights to this pension when I take up something else. It is all very strange and confusing, I know.) Looking around for a job, I got in touch with some Americans in Europoort (Rotterdam area) who are part of the Start-Up Team of Esso Chemicals. There is a new plant here which, when it runs smoothly, will be taken over by the Dutch. They produce FERTILIZERS. And the manager of this team needed a secretarial assistant, so this is what I am at present. It will last for a few weeks only, but I accepted it, for I was intrigued. And my curiosity, though I don't know a damn about technique, gets very satisfied indeed. Did you know that a FERTILIZER plant can be converted INTO AN EXPLOSIVES FACTORY within a day? So that is why so many countries are interested in having a fertilizer plant of their own, and why both the U.S. and the U.S.S.R. are so eager to help them.

The day your letter arrived, we got some very interesting visitors — a group of Dutch boys and girls who are going to start a sort of community very near to where we live. Our house is going to be the starting point for some of them. It is hard to explain the whole set-up, but the idea has much in common with *kevutsa* [Hebrew, cooperative] living, mixed with a few Bellamy ideals, and a lot of healthy realism.... This is one of the happy events your letter brought. The second one was that, on the same day, I got invited by a study center to give two series of lectures starting in January on Development-Aid (on which subject I am beginning to become some sort of authority) and on Gandhian Thought and Action.

The third and most important event happened last night when I thought of starting my reply to you. I received a wire from Terre Des Hommes (a very important Swiss organization) asking whether I am prepared to head a group of International Red Cross to Libreville in Gabon and to organize and lead the transport of children from Biafra to Gabon and Cote d'Ivoire. I am to leave next Tuesday (another three days to go) by plane. AT LAST, AT LAST, AT LAST. Alan, am I going **TO DO** something. Believe me, this is going to save my life.

Gabon is, as you know, the country of the Albert Schweitzer Hospital (whose present leader is the Swiss Dr. Munz, a good friend of mine whom I talked to on the phone only two weeks ago; he married in Holland with a Dutch girl). Naturally, I do intend to go there when in Libreville. God, how I shall love running around again and building up something. Fortunately, the job will not have to be on an entirely voluntary basis, so my wife will have something to eat even when I am away. You see, Alan, that is the worst part of being married. (Mind you, I love wife and child.) You are not free from financial obligations and, therefore, not free to do as your philosophy preaches. I do hope that this (first) assignment will lead to something. I hear your question: if I would have to start all over again, would I marry again or not? At times I think I wouldn't; at times I think I would. As it is, I married a very good woman who stands fully behind my ideals, who agrees to every job I undertake, and who doesn't grumble when her household budget is rather small. I could ask for better?

Back to your letter. So Nixon is president. Personally, I doubt whether it will be any worse than if Humphrey had been chosen. It may be a good thing that an American president is limited by a Senate that is opposed to him. It may also be good for the prospect of a change in the two party system. Will [Eugene] McCarthy start a new party? The chances are ten to one that he would succeed. This election has at least proved that your system is wrong.

Your reaction of "escaping" I can understand and appreciate. First of all, your presence in a confused situation (as it was in Chicago) would not have altered the facts in the least. Secondly, too much involvement would have biased your attitude as a philospher (which you are going to be). Thirdly, being beaten up for the sake of your friends does not help your friends. Someone HAS TO stand at a safe distance.

(Eds. In August, 1968, just prior to the National Democratic Convention, Alan "escaped" from Chicago. He had participated in demonstrations in Chicago earlier in the year, experiencing first-hand the hostility of the Chicago police. When a friend offered him a ride to California, he happily accepted. They had a radio with such poor reception that the broadcast might have been coming from another country. In this way, lying under the stars somewhere in Montana, Alan learned about heads being bashed in Chicago. He felt guilty for having run away. Alex turns this into a position of principle, which, Alan says, it was not.)

On the expedition I am about to undertake, I may find a lot of opposition, both from governments (independent Africa is not easy to deal with) and from Africans who disagree with steps I may take. Though in a way I am going to take a risk (the job may bring me into frontier territory in Nigeria), I am assured of the "prayers" (ridiculous, but I can't find another word) of my wife who is also not involved herself, but who I shall always know is "behind" me. That is worth a great deal.

I hope soon to be able to write to you more of what the situation really is. Though Biafra seems very sympathetic to me, I have so far hesitated to take sides either for Biafra or for Nigeria which I have also known to be inhabited by VERY nice (Moslem) people. The Haussas are a nation apart, and very lovable, too, while the Biafran Ibos have, with their Christianity, acquired a certain unnaturalness and insincereity.

So, to end this letter, a large question mark should be fitting. Please give my regards to all those who are dear to you and understanding,

all my love and friendship,

Yours ever,

Alex

Section Five

Professional Parenting

February 1969 - July 1974

(Eds. On 30 May 1967, the Eastern Region of Nigeria declared itself the independent Republic of Biafra. At that time, Biafra had a population of 14 million; the majority tribe was Ibo. Civil war broke out on 6 July 1967. The Biafran troops were under the command of Col. Odumegwu Ojukwu. Few countries recognized Biafra. Tanzania did, and then on 8 May 1968, Gabon recognized Biafra as an "independent sovereign entity." To aid the victims of the Nigerian civil war, Alex went to Gabon.)

Gabon
24 February 1969

Dear Alan,
A very hectic three months have gone by since I wrote to you last. I believe that was just one or two days before I left Holland to go to Africa. Where I still am now. My initial contract of three months (for the Terre des Hommes organization) has just been renewed for another three months. Which means that, for the time being, Elisabeth and Alwin shall have to do without me, I being at present the guardian angel of about six hundred Biafran children here in Gabon. Finally some action again, and I am revelling in it. Of course, being now a husband and father, I cannot do this work as a volunteer any longer, so the organization is paying me regular wages. I am the only "paid" man in our team of two doctors, eight nurses, two house managers and myself. Though officially registered as a male nurse, my work has nothing to do with nursing. I am acting as deputy to our Terre des Hommes delegate which means I have to look after the official contacts, make new ones, talk to people, and try to get our organization as good a deal as possible.

Besides, I am in charge of about twenty native workmen who build latrines and wash-places and schools under my guidance. On the whole, a very satisfactory job, especially when you see the kids running to the toilets you have built and being taught in schools you have put up.

Next week we are starting with a new program which consists of building four permanent houses that are to lodge 800 more children in the near future. Biafran children are still being evacuated, even now, at a rate of about fifty each week. You can imagine that there is quite a lot to be done. For it does not seem that this dirty war in Nigeria will end soon. Only last week I was there myself, accompanying a Red Cross flight of food and medicines that had to be handed personally to our people over there. (If that is not done, it gets lost somehow.) I stayed in Biafra for two days and enjoyed every minute of it. The Ibos are a very industrious and intelligent people, quite different from the rest of Africa's Negro population. Which is probably the reason for this war in the first place. I am honestly glad to be able to DO something. The kids here are marvellous, and I wished I could adopt some of them. But that, alas, is quite impossible.

Please, Alan, forgive me for not writing more or more often. I am really very busy, but thinking of you often and wishing you were here to share the joy of DOING something with me. I know how you long for action yourself. Terre des Hommes might start something for South American children (Peru) in the near future, and there may be a possibility that I shall be invited to give a hand there when my job here is over. If so, we shall surely meet each other. Once this Great Ocean is crossed, nothing shall stop me coming to your United States. Please write to me care of Poste Restante, Libreville, Gabon. At least if you write within the next three months. After that I may be elsewhere.

Greetings to all and love,

Yours ever,

Alex

(Eds. Alex speaks rather casually about going on a flight containing food and medicine. In fact, these flights attracted Nigerian gun-fire. For instance, on 5 June 1969, the Nigerians shot down a relief flight sent by the International Committee of the Red Cross to Biafra. By August, 1969, twenty fliers in emergency airlift operations had been killed in airplane crashes. The Red Cross actually suspended operations for a time because of the danger.)

Libreville, Gabon
20 March 1969

Dear Alan,

I was most happy to get your letter. Don't think that receiving letters is just a pastime. It is much more important than that. It helps to keep up one's spirit at moments when our spirits are very low and, you can believe me, here in Africa there are many such moments. Right at the moment I am getting desparate at the thought of having to cooperate with a German pastor who arrived here to replace the man with whom I had been working up until now. So far the cooperation has been excellent, but I am afraid that I shall have a fight on my hands within the next three days. The man has never been to Africa and has ideas that he can do the management here as it can be done in Germany. *Befehl ist Befehl.* [German, An order is an order.] Anyway, I shall try to make the best of it.

On Saturday, I am going for a day to Biafra (the second time) to accompany the flight of a DC-6 carrying ten tons of food and medicine for our team over there. If I don't go, the chances are ten to one that more than half of what we send will disappear. And we don't want that to happen. A lot can be said about Terre des Hommes organization here, but one thing is certain: there is nothing cleaving to the fiddlestick. A Dutch saying which I hope you understand. Whatever is given to us reaches its destination.

Many of us here have some kind of support actions going on in their hometowns; these are organized by friends who stayed behind. The usual procedure is for the collected money to be sent to the team-member personally. That team-member then consults with the others, and it is then decided what the money is going to be spent on. Usually it enables us to buy something for the children or the Biafran teachers, which cannot be bought from the general federation funds; like shoes, swimmming-suits, some games or anything else that the federation considers not "immediately necessary," but which we here on the spot think extremely useful. This method has the advantage that we can write home exactly what the money has bought us so that the donors know their money has DONE something and is not lost in the big heap. So if you too want to send something that shall naturally be very welcome. Maybe you can interest some friends or relatives? Anyway, the best way to send money is to write out a cheque and to send it by airmail. Please address the cheque to me in person. Perferably a cheque on the Chase Manhattan Bank which has a correspondent here. That facilitates payment. If you cannot write a cheque on that bank, any other LARGE bank will do as well (not any of those family banks, please).

If you have any preference as to how you want the money spent, please write so. If you leave it to my own discretion to decide what is most essential, please write that too, and I shall subsequently give you an account of how the money was spent. So far my happy thoughts on your kind offer which, incidentally, I do certainly NOT regard as a gesture of American Chequebook Charity. I know just how you feel with regard to your own inability to ACT, and I appreciate it.

By the way, your running away from difficulties, as you call it, is a typical Chinese reaction. Did you know that? Confucius said: of the seventy-nine methods to solve a problem, by far the easiest one is to run away from it. I think he has something there.

And then there is something else. Do you think that I could do whatever I am doing here without the legacy of a "few Jewish Alexandrians of 2,000 years ago?" This Alexandrian Aronson here is very much a product of his wandering forefathers, and, although I am not a "practicing orthodox" Jew — how could I be? — I do feel VERY CLOSE to (my) religion. I am not the praying kind of Jew, but God, do I identify myself!!!

(Eds. At this time, Alan was working on his doctoral thesis on Philo of Alexandria {ca. 20 bce to 40 ce}. Alex enjoyed making puns on the coincidence of his own name and the birthplace of Philo.)

What I want to say is this: your studies of the "history of ideas," or whatever you want to call the knowledge of what motivated our forefathers, is very much essential to keep my kind of active human being at it. Without people like you discovering the mistakes that have been made in the past and the good examples that have been set in the past, without scholars capable of conveying this science to present-day humanity, without students keeping up our knowledge of the past, WE ARE NOTHING. So, please remember, your duty is to keep up with your science. By holding on to that, you are by far more effective than in whatever other capacity you might wish to work.... So much for that inferiority complex of yours. Enclosed find me as I am now, with three children on my knees. From right to left: Antonio, oldest of our children and more or less their leader; Suzanna, my favorite, whom I would have liked to adopt (impossible); and her sister.

All my love and regards,

Alex

N.B. Please send a picture of yourself. I have no idea whom I am writing to.

Ibusa, Nigeria
16 July 1969

Dear Alan,

Reading the first pages of Henry Miller's *Colossus of Maroussi,* I have to stop, following an urge to write to you.

(Eds. The subtitle of Miller's book, written in 1950, is On a Visit to Greece.*)*

As usual your Chicago address is lost so this letter will again go to Washington's Fulton Street, which is imprinted in my memory. Yes Sir, look at the stamps on the envelope. I am in Africa again, this time the other side of the fence, Nigeria. After half-a-year in Gabon, and part of that time in the homeland of the children I was looking after there, and a month's vacation in Europe. (Of which a week-and-a-half at home with darling son and wife and three weeks roaming through the South of France and Greece!!! with a nursing collegue of mine.) The work in Gabon was finished due to improvement in health of the children. Back home, a sudden phone call from International Red Cross, calling me to duty in Nigeria. Though I had hoped to stay at home a little longer, the chance was too good to miss.

It may, at the end of half-a-year, enable me to finally come to the U.S.A. Moreover, it is always an improvement of one's mind to learn what is behind propaganda. For I now know that the pro-Biafra feeling in Holland especially is mainly due to a finely manipulated propaganda in which I, for one, was sometimes caught up too. The truth, as usual, is somewhere in the middle. One thing I am now convinced of: there is no question of genocide — it is NOT a religious or a racial war. The bandits, as usual I presume, are mainly the financial interests of a few. I do not wish to go into political discussions. Let it suffice that I am glad I came here for my own conscience. The work I am doing for the Red Cross is mainly medical. I started off as team-leader in a three-man team, consisting of myself, my Dutch colleague, with whom I had travelled previously, and a Swiss doctor. At the beginning, we had a dispensary in one village, Ibusa (12,000 inhabitants), with a few beds for the seriously ill.

(Eds. It is significant that Alex addresses the issue of the alleged genocide of the Ibo people. In June, 1969 — that is, not long before this letter was written — a neutral team had investigated allegations of Nigerian genocide in Biafra. The team found no evidence of mass killings. Reference: Facts on File, *1969.)*

In the one-and-a-half months that we have been here, we have expanded our activities considerably — with the result that I am now in charge of a 34-bed hospital and dispensary in Ibusa as well as dispensaries in 5 more villages, including a leper-settlement we discovered in the bush, abandoned by all medical personal and care. Our Swiss doctor is a complete non- entity as a medical man as well as a person. He leaves all real treatment to me and can hardly make a diagnosis without consulting me. Well, so far so good. My medical (nursing) training which had gone rusty since my Israeli-army period is up-to-date thanks to intuition rather than knowledge.

(Eds. As an Israeli citizen, Alex would have been subject to the draft. It is probable that he served in the Israeli army as a medical orderly.)

Yesterday, a memorable event. The town council of Ibusa notified me that I was nominated to be made a traditional chief, a rather dubious honor since the 5 present chiefs of the town have all got their office by donating high sums of Nigerian pounds to the town. However, I am going to get it for free and for a Jew that is always attractive. One good thing about being a chief, it gives me a seat in the town council and the opportunity to do something for my hospital and the refugees who are still being kept huddled together in a school instead of being incorporated into town-life.

Well, I could go on again with all my impressions, daily occurences, and experiences. It would fill a bible (another one), but time is short. Please let me know how you are faring and what your plans are. Loving you as ever,

Your,

Alex

Asaba, Nigeria
16 August 1969

Dear Alan,

Thanks very much for your lovely letter. It is good to know that someone loves me so much to worry when I don't write. In fact, life is rather primitive out here, and I am writing you by candlelight. First about THE MONEY. (How I hate it and want to dispense with it.) Since my work here also is with Ibo children, only by change of fortune NOT under Biafran rule, I have taken the liberty of advancing from my own account the equivalent of your $115 to provide for one irreparably blind child (out of the village in which I was made chief) to be brought up in a Lagos institute for the blind, the only one of its kind. It will probably cost more later on, but I have more or less adopted the child (named Augustin, 7 years old, see picture). If the project is satisfactory to the people who donated the money, you can pay it into my account by sending a personal cheque in my name to the Amsterdam Rotterdam Bank, Rokin 43, Amsterdam.

I prefer to use the money this way than to send it on to a place where I cannot keep an eye on it. Hope you agree.

The Red Cross is having a hard time with Nigerian government at the moment, and we may have to pull out after one month. If not, I hope to stick it out a little longer, though God knows that living conditions are rather maddening. One good thing about it. I am losing weight rapidly. Reason for my leaving Gabon before the end of the contract was that no more children were arriving there; the ones who were there already were *well* provided for.

The project I worried about when I wrote to you was financially and fully adopted by omnipresent Germany. Well, so far, so good. What is the subject of your thesis? If I know it, I want you to give me the honor of adding one sentence to it. A foolish request, maybe, but that's the way I am.

(Eds. Alan did not accord Alex this particular honor.)

as ever yours,

Alex

(Eds. The following is a feature which appeared in "Algemeen Dagblad" on 16 January 1970. Alex had returned from Biafra and was seeking funds to support a trip to Nigeria so he could work with the homeless and injured there. The civil war had come to an end just four days before this article was published. The Biafran surrender of 15 January ended a 31-month civil war which left millions of people, most of them Ibos, in dire need. Reference: Facts on File, *1970.)*

ALEX ARONSON AND HARRY VAN DEN ENDEN WOULD RATHER LEAVE TODAY THAN TOMORROW

A dyed-in-the-wool helper and organizer in Asia and Africa, a man who has returned from a Biafra where he spent six months working with refugees, Alex Aronson is ready to leave for Nigeria. But there is no one who can pay for his trip.

No one, despite the millions of guilders which the Dutch have given for war victims in that country. I can hardly understand this.

Who is he? Alex Aronson from De Wilp, 12 kilometres from

Drachten. He is thirty-five-years old and has fifteen years' experience in refugee work — setting up camps, dealing with epidemics, and treating war victims.

In 1961, Alex Aronson worked with Albert Schweitzer. Before that, he was in India and Algeria with Development Aid. With his wife, he set up a refugee camp in Greece. He worked with the Israeli Red Cross at one time. Only last month he returned from Nigeria. He had been working in the former Biafran district where he had been sent by the Red Cross. You could say that wherever there was trouble, danger, and despair, Aronson was there to help.

Are we talking about "danger money?" He laughs, "If I walk through Amsterdam, I am in greater danger than in Nigeria."

I met nurse Alex in Swolle. Open collar, thick jumper, moustache, big hat. Development Aid is no charity, he says. It is a profession, and it is an economic necessity. You have to have a wage because, afterall, you and your wife need to eat. You could call me a professional volunteer.

This "professional volunteer" has also been to Gabon with Terre des Hommes to set up camps for children. In short, you could say about a man like Aronson that he knows what it's like. "Yes," he laughs, "I do know a bit." In the last six months, they've set up five jungle clinics and a forty- bed hospital in what was the Biafran section of Nigeria. They held a polio clinic at the hospital and, once a fortnight, a Swiss doctor arrived to see the most serious cases. Once a week, the Aronson group visited their bush clinics. They did everything — combatted malaria, distributed vitamins and food, identified the most seriously ill, and transported them 300 kilometers to the hospital.

In Alex's passport, there is a visa for Nigeria, valid for twelve months. But if he does not arrive before 26 February, the visa will expire. The same is true for Harry van den Enden, also from De Wilp, 25, married with one child; a youth worker.

Aronson says he has spent 200 guilders telephoning people in Holland to solicit money. You can imagine how many phone calls he has made. No one is prepared to pay for their trip to Nigeria. No one. The Biafran Committee cannot not do it, despite the 17 million guilders received on giro account 400. The World Council of Churches cannot do anything either, and they did not even know that you could fly direct from Amsterdam to Lagos. Alex has worked for the Terre des Hommes, but they cannot do anything either, they say. The Red Cross cannot do anything because the International Red Cross does not work in Nigeria any more. So they sit, Aronson and ven der Enden, waiting.

It is only 25,000 guilders, says Aronson. For that, we can cover our return trip, work in the bush for three months, and keep our wives in housekeeping money.... Everyone keeps saying to Aronson that he will have to wait awhile. They want to see how the situation will develop.

"Wait! Wait! Wait!" shouts Aronson. "My work is waiting there. We built something important in six months. The people need us... There are people whose lives are at risk. I know from experience. I am twiddling my thumbs here."

The hospital where Aronson worked is situated near the Niger, in what was Biafran territory. Lots of false stories have been told, says the man who has been given the title of Chief.... It is not true that people in the jungles die of starvation. They eat plants and lizards and find nourishment from many things we don't know about. I've seen them with their food collections. They looked healthy.

I've also seen Biafran prisoners of war. They are treated reasonably. The idea of dropping food by air is nonsensical. Of course, they kill one another for a parcel. So if you want to do something, you should do it through the Nigerian Red Cross. One should not use the name Biafra any more; it hurts Lagos. What is important is to help people. This is MOST IMPORTANT. So, if you've been there and you know the way to do it, then you have to go that way and quickly because within a month, the weak are dead.... That is why Aronson and van der Enden want to leave NOW. But the Minister of Aid to Developing Countries says that they should present him with a petition....

25,000 guilders is a joke if you put it next to the millions which the country has put into the bank for Nigeria. Yet it seems impossible to get 25,000. Why? Because Aronson dares to say that he does not believe in the so-called mass murder in Nigeria? Yes, of course, heads will roll. But mass murder? Not at all. Because Aronson dares to say that during the autumn the Red Cross was allowed to buy food in Biafra for the population, but it had to pay its funds into a bank in Geneva? Because Aronson dares to say that Col. Ojukwu has a villa in Geneva?

Aronson says, "Look, in Geneva there is a 73-year-old Swiss

gentleman who has a beautiful flat. He represents the Red Cross there, and says, 'If you need me, come and see me.' But that is no way to work," says Aronson. "You work on a one-to-one basis. You work as a man to a man. You don't go with haughtiness. You don't say, 'We'll just go and help those blackies.' Or, if you do, then you'd better stay at home."

(Eds. To elaborate slightly on Alex's point here, we can turn to an article in Facts on File, *1970. According to that source, when the Biafrans surrendered, Ojukwu fled with "three tons of luggage and a Mercedes-Benz saloon car with him on the aircraft." After the war, the population of Biafra was estimated at 3 million, down from 14 million.)*

(Eds. On 23 January 1970, Alex sent Alan the following telegram. In it were instructions as to how Alan might facilitate Alex's entry into the United States.)

MENDELSON 1455 EAST 54TH PLACE CHICAGO ILLINOIS PLEASE CABLE ME THE FOLLOWING TEXT IMMEDIATELY... FRIENDS MARTIN LUTHER KING INVITE YOU TOUR STATES FOR LECTURES. TRAVEL EXPENSES YOURS. LODGING ARRANGEMENT OURS. STOP. WILL COME FEBRUARY. QUESTIONS CAN YOU FETCH ME NEW YORK OR SHOULD I FLY CHICAGO? LECTURES OF COURSE HOAX BUT COULD IT BE MADE TRUE? ARONSON DEWILP

(Eds. Alan sent the telegram of invitation which Alex needed.)

29 January 1970
De Wilp

Dear Alan,

First of all, thanks for the prompt telegraphic reply. It was essential, for some local complications threatened my coming to U.S. I was expected to return to Nigeria and the only way out of this was to show that I had an alternative engagement. So we came to a compromise. I would fly to the U.S., passing through Lagos and Dahomey. A little round about, but it is being paid by the people who want me to go there; till Lagos anyway. The rest is on my own savings.

Separately, I sent you today a registered package which you will please keep till my arrival. In it are a number of lists of members of an organization to which I have belonged for a long time. People who show hospitality by offering bed and lodging to passing idealists. Experience tells me it is better not to have these lists on one's person when passing immigration authorities anywhere. I have a non-immigrant visa valid till 1974 on which I may enter or leave the States multiple times. Anyway finally, finally I am coming.

I am very much looking forward to meeting you first of all and getting to know that country of which every well-meaning person has so much criticism. Fortunately, I have learned not to judge till I have seen with my own eyes. With, of course, the consequence that I have to keep on travelling to see everything. How fortunate I am to have a wife who never minds where I go and for how long!

In the package also some maps of the U.S. which I already possessed. They are Arkansas, Louisiana, Mississippi, Utah, Idaho, Atlanta, Montana, Delaware, Maryland, West Virginia and Virginia, Kentucky and Tennesse. Could you meantime try to buy maps of the remaining States? Also please look around for any possibilities to lecture. One of the reasons for my coming is to try to collect money for a very interesting experiment of which you will hear more on arrival. See you soon. Will cable arriving plane as soon as I know more.

Alex

(Eds. Less than a week after Alex wrote the preceding letter, he sent Alan a telegram: "ARRIVING THIS SUNDAY PANAM 1640 HOURS." When Alex arrived in Chicago, he looked as if he were dressed for an African safari. Carrying a tall ebony chieftain's staff, he set off almost immediately to collect money for his latest humanitarian venture, the establishment of what he called the International Emergency Brigade. Shrugging off any suggestion that some neighborhoods in the South Side of Chicago might be dangerous to the uninitiated, Alex set off on foot to raise money. He stayed with Alan in Chicago for about two weeks. Then he cut himself free from those moorings and went to seek his fortune elsewhere in the United States. At one point, Alan learned that Alex was washing dishes in Baltimore. All told, he remained in North America for three months during the spring of 1970. He made no contact with Sharon or any of the other women who had been his guests in Holland.

Difficulties arose from his endeavors. It never occurred to Alex that he could not simply go out on the streets of Chicago and solicit funds for an unregistered charity. Before long, complaints were received, and the Attorney General for the State of Illinois began to investigate. By that time, Alex was back in Holland. To explain his role in the affair, Alan wrote the following official letter.)

July 14, 1970

Attorney General's Office
Charitable Trust and Solicitations Division
160 North LaSalle Street
Chicago, Illinois

Dear Sirs:

Today I signed for a certified letter which was sent to my residence for the International Emergency Brigade (IEB). I signed for this letter because I have been receiving, sifting out, and forwarding the mail of the IEB ever since the IEB's founder, Alex L. Aronson, returned to his native Holland several months ago. Upon reading your letter (to see if it required his attention), I immediately called your office at which time I was requested to explain my relationship to IEB.

I met Mr. Aronson in Europe in 1962. When he informed me in January of this year that he was coming to this country, I invited him to stay with me. This he did for a period of two weeks in February, 1970. Since he had no other fixed address, he used my address for personal and business mail. During his stay, I did not open any of the IEB's mail. Nor did I have any idea of its contents.

My knowledge of the IEB is minimal. I do know that Mr. Aronson decided not to incorporate in Illinois because he felt that the fee was too high. He thought it would be less expensive to incorporate elsewhere. Whether he actually incorporated in the United States is not known to me. I know, further, that the IEB is chartered in Holland. It has about ten members, all of whom are European medical or social work personnel. Needless to say, I am not one of these members — a fact which could be established by your obtaining a copy of the original charter. I do not now have in my possession, nor did I ever have, a copy of that charter since I never was linked in any formal way with IEB and since I cannot read Dutch.

When Mr. Aronson left Chicago, I periodically sent him his bank statements which he had Continental Bank send to my address. I am enclosing in this letter the last one which arrived. As you can see, it closes out the account. These items are the only papers concerning the IEB that I have in my possession. For further records, and cancelled checks on the Continental account, I can only refer you to Mr. Aronson himself, since as far as the IEB is concerned, he did not take me into his confidence. Mr. Aronson's address in Holland is.... Although I doubt that I can be of further help to you, please feel free to contact me. Since I understand that there are complaints about the IEB, I am sorry that I cannot provide you with more information.

Sincerely yours,

Alan Mendelson

(Eds. When the Attorney General's Office began to look into the International Emergency Brigade, Alan naturally wrote to Alex. Alex responded by writing two letters, a personal one to his hosts in Chicago and an official one to the Attorney General's Office. These two letters follow.)

[July, 1970]

Dear Alan and Sara,

First, let me tell you how sorry I am to get you in all this trouble. All because of my rashness and hardheadedness in not having wanted to conform to "the American way." I have sent my letter [to the Attorney General] as you instructed, right away, and enclose a copy. I hope it releases you from any blame they may have wanted to shove into your shoes. Still, if they try anything, do contact that friendly lawyer in Woodstock, Illinois. I will write to him without too many details, explaining how the International Emergency Brigade did and does. The IEB is not out of the world yet, though it may still take some time before it will actually start *de facto*.

I myself have been extremely occupied. First, a two-week vacation in France with Elisabeth and Alwin, a period during which we were more busy and "doing" than usual. For we discovered a children's home, tended by nuns, not aided by the government of France, and in great need of help. So home we went with the purpose of collecting clothes (of which we have by now sufficient) and money to buy a cow so that they can supply their own milk. I have already raised half the amount necessary. We also collected tinned or powdered milk to help them while the money for the cow is being collected. I brought a little boy home with us for a three-week vacation. Also we have an old woman who is fully crippled by rheumatism and needs to be lifted and washed and everything (three weeks also). Tomorrow, I leave again for France to return the boy and, at the same time, bring the clothes and milk-products to the home of 40 needy children.

At the same time, I have been preparing to go to India. A Dutch priest is leading a large refugee project in Madras (30,000 Indians who were chased out of Burma). He has an organization here that furnishes him with funds and goods. This organization wants me to go there to take over the lead, for it is growing too fast for the priest to lead (together with his church duties). So here I go again, "off to the war" against misery.

Sorry I was delayed in sending you this letter. Things have been going rather fast. The IEB is, as you can read in your copy of my letter to the Attorney General, "legalized." I do not handle its mail any longer, but we have a real secretary and a post-office box (no. 123, Drachten). So please send everything concerned with IEB to that box number. My function is now "chairman" though you know I am not in the habit of sitting down very long. I had the charter changed (one reason it took so long to register) so that we do not only act in medical, but in social emergencies. Reason for this being that for the latter we can do more, with less money (of which we have none). I'll send you a photostat copy of charter as soon as I get it.

Love,

Alex

International Emergency
Brigade Inc.
Post Office Box 123
Drachten (Fr.)
The Netherlands
19 July 1970

The Attorney General's Office
Charitable Trust and Solicitations Division
160 North La Salle Street
Chicago, Illinois U.S.A.

Dear Sir,

With reference to your letter WJS-MSA/gt dd. 6 July 1970 which I received today, I would like to inform you of the following.

I entered the U.S. on 8 February, this year. The purposes of my visit were (1) to try to raise funds for the IEB, an organization founded by me last year; (2) to locate people willing to form a local committee backing this organization in the U.S.

When I left Holland, papers had been filed to register the IEB in this country. I left here under the impression that the act of registration was a matter of days only. Not awaiting the final confirmation, I opened with my own funds, a bank account with the Continental Illinois Bank, and I had a paper printed stating the purposes of the IEB. As I was staying with Mr. A. Mendelson at 5454 S. Harper Ave, a personal friend, I gave as my forwarding address his address, however without having previously consulted him about this. Mr. Mendelson, moreover, had no contact with or knowledge of my doings. I also mentioned that address as being the location of the Registered Agent, firmly believing that finding someone to fill this post would be easy. To register, however, I had to wait until papers from Holland had come through. After a month, I learned that my presence here was necessary to sign the registration and that, contrary to what I had thought, the IEB was not registered here yet. It had, therefore, no legal existence as yet, and I immediately stopped raising funds (which I had already started). I remained another two months in the U.S. for tourist purposes and then returned to Holland. Registration here has by now been confirmed.

Since I had stopped any fundraising or other activities by the time your first letter reached me, I saw no point in filling out your form until the time I could legally start anew. Hoping that this letter answers any questions that may have been raised, I remain,

Sincerely yours,

Chief Alex L. Aronson,
Chairman IEB

(Eds. "Chief" here refers to the honor conferred on Alex when he was made a traditional chief in Nigeria in July, 1969.)

De Wilp
3 February 1971

Dear Alan and Sara,

Today we received the announcement of your wedding. If we would have gotten it earlier, you would certainly have received congratulations by cable. As it is too late now anyway, just this short letter; as usual in a hurry. I myself only recently returned from a 3-month trip to India where I visited some relief-projects. The intention was orginally to join one of them, but many things combined to make me change my mind. Non-cooperation of the government, the aspect of the project on which I had set my mind (it proved to be purely a missionary affair, contrary to what it was supposed to be) and, last but not least, the realization that my house and family had become more dear and indispensable to me than I had ever thought possible.

The tour, however, was not entirely wasted. I managed to smuggle a fourteen-year-old orphan boy whom I had picked off the street, back across all borders, home to Holland. Of course, it is against all law and order. People in this country have the habit of soothing their consciences by putting a quarter in the weekly collection boxes. Not so the Aronsons. Somehow our conscience costs us more than a mere quarter. So far no reaction from officials, but, one of these days, I will have to answer for my illegal action. Six-month prison maximum which is not much considered a lifetime may be improved because of it.

I am working in the port of Rotterdam as a guardian (semi-police job). Same as I have done several times before, though I am trying to enter the Academy for Social Work. Back to the schoolroom again, which will not be easy. A roll of adhesive tape will have to accompany me, to be stuck on that open mouth of mine, if I feel the compulsion to criticize my teachers.

To both Sara and you, my friend Alan, my wishes for a long and happy life together. *ad me'ah ve-esrim* [Hebrew, may you live for 120 years]. Send us some pictures of the wedding. And do show yourselves in the house of your friends which, as you know, is yours, too.

As ever, yours,

Alex

(Eds. This letter was written to Alan in Israel where he taught Hellenistic Judaism at the School for Overseas Students, Hebrew University of Jerusalem, during the academic years 1971-1973. When Alex asks him to call on his brother, he is referring to his half-brother.)

De Wilp
20 May 1971

Dear Alan and Sara,

I was very happy to get your letter. All the more so since I don't get much mail anymore which is mainly my own fault. I stopped writing. No more time which really isn't meant as a joke. After coming back from India, I worked for a short time in the port of Rotterdam to cover a laborless period, then finally got into the work which I had coveted for a long time, "child protection".... Of course, I am joining the forces that war against the establishment. Fortunately, we are getting more and more of what we want. Also

I have returned to the school benches to study for the necessary papers that will make me a qualified "protector." The course I am following is quite stiff, a one- year concentration of a course which originally took 2 1/2 years.

My work at present is in an "observation" home. However, because of my difficult personality, I was sacked already twice in 3 months (and taken back again). My third release from duties should be in one more month, but I must get my way again, this time concerning the authoratative way our children are being treated. I keep telling them that love is a much better cure. Of course, it is much more involved, but that would take too long to explain in one letter.

One thing I have to tell you: both the work and the study obsess me to such an extent that all desire to travel has vanished. Believe me, this trip into psychology and applied love is a journey that makes all my travels obsolete. Elisabeth and I have, moreover, joined some voluntary organization which brings poor children from abroad into homes for vacation. So we are kept really busy. As for my Indian son, he is proving himself a brilliant boy. Since my study also covers child-law (it is a special department in our jurisdiction), I learned that jail is not for me. Holland has no punishment for the smuggling of persons. The risk of Velu getting sent back to India is also getting smaller. He is in an English/Dutch school that costs a lot of money (paid by a considerable number of friends here in Holland). But next year he might get a scholarship from the Society of Friends.

When you get to Beersheba [Israel], please call on my brother. He'll be glad to see you and is a lot like me.... If you go there fast, you may also meet my father, who is on vacation there at present.

Meanwhile do write again some time soon, but don't expect too fast an answer. Have you been wailing at the wall already? My love to everyone you meet.

Yours ever,

Alex

De Wilp
24 February 1972

Dear Alan and Sara,

For a change an immediate reply to your letter which was rather unexpected, but not the less welcome. It is evening and I am relaxing after having written all day long — a lecture on observation and reporting. And I am doing this relaxation under the beautiful tones of a concert by Theodorakis. He happened to give a concert here in Groningen (30 kilometers from home). His own music played by his own six-man orchestra and conducted by himself. Of course, I went!! A beautiful new contraption, a Japanese micro-cassette recorder in my coat pocket. The recording turned out fine and, at least once a week, I re-live the fastastic happening.

When I last wrote, I suppose that I was still working as an assistant house-parent in a home for bad boys. I was thrown out after a heavy disagreement with the management board. Since then, I only had one other job, as a house-parent/observer in a home for affection-lacking children (7 to 13-year-olds). Very interesting because of the guidance there is by a very specialized professor (Hart de Ruiter). In this country, he is on an equal footing with your Redl and Wineman. In Fannari, I decided I had learned what I could in that house. At the same time, I got my first child-protection diploma (A). Then, I applied for and got the job of head house-parent in another house, this time blind and retarded kids, 6 to 18-year-olds. A fantastic "rise in power" considering my short time in this branch. (The head house-parent is the man right after the director.) Three weeks ago, I also passed an exam enabling me to skip a third-year course (child-protection B) and to enroll right in a fourth-year course in ortho-paedagogic and institutional management. The first three lessons (one day and evening a week) have passed, and I feel right at home. As I believe I wrote before, I am so intrigued by the subjects (child law and deliquency, psychology, psychiatry, pedagogy, etc.) that it is verily a "journey of mind" and the urge to travel has more or less completely passed.

In the present capacity, I intend to last the duration of the course, 4 years. *Oi veh's mir!* [Yiddish, Woe is me.] I myself give weekly lectures on child problems to the house- parents, give them supervision, jobs our psychologist has turned over to me as "I am better equipped." I have the overall management of daily affairs and have invented some dealings with the children for my own benefit, giving them what I call a "father hour" twice a week, since there are only female "house- parents."

That is all about Alex. Elisabeth and Alwin are fine. So is Velu, the Indian boy for whom I managed to scrounge a scholarship at the English-speaking Quaker school. We had another great victory in fighting the official apparatus for adoption with their own weapons, which are mine now too. We have been recognized as a "therapeutic foster-home." The result is that two step-sons have entered our house and two more are to follow soon. Elisabeth gets help twice a week. When the other two children come, it will be daily. And we get a great kick out of looking after these children and giving them what no institution can ever give any child. We abhor and loathe HOMES (my motivation in working in one) and believe a house, a real nest, should be found for every kid. Elisabeth, too, sends you her greetings and she hopes some day to welcome you here.

Write again soon.

Yours ever,

Alex

N.B. If you see Zwi in Jerusalem, give him my friendly greetings. (He is a full professor, I believe.) He is a good friend of my school days, used to be my teacher, and he may be helpful in your getting university jobs. Good old Zwiebel (his nickname, don't use it) knows me as Lex Aronson, my given name at the age of 18. Since then I haven't been law-abiding enough, so my name has been A-Lex.

(Eds. Two points should be noted about names. Alan was warned not to use the nickname Zwiebel—and probably for good reason. ***Zwiebel*** *means onion in German. As for the name Lex, that means law in Latin.*

Alan continued to teach in Jerusalem for more than a year after the receipt of this letter. In July, 1973, the Mendelsons left Israel to settle in Oxford, England, where Sara began work on her D.Phil. In the Spring of 1974, only months before Alex departed on his last journey, Alan travelled to Amsterdam, took the train to Friesland, and spent a day with Alex. Alex gave Alan several gifts: an old Dutch guilder made, as Alex proudly pointed out, from "real" silver; two old, cracked Dutch tiles dating from the 18th or 19th century, which Alan carefully restored; and a soapstone carving of the head of an African woman.)

De Wilp
25 July 1974

Dear Alan and Sara,

Time for a few words in the midst of preparations for a new trip. Yes siree, at the end of August, I will be on my way again... to Kurdistan! You may know that they are in a war for independence from Iraq, and what is better for a Jew than to help the enemies of enemies of Israel? Although I don't know yet how long I will be going to stay, the original plan is for me to set up my own hospital there, mainly for the benefit of the many refugees, but I imagine that quite a few wounded "military" will come my way as well. All this is going to be private enterprise. Terre des Hommes didn't want to back me. But I found a nurse who shares my wish for travel and adventure and who will accompany me.

I suppose I will be gone for a long time, [that is] if I don't get hit by a Tupolev [Soviet bomber] or other such fine Russian specimen the Iraqis work with. I might not be back for a few years.

If you are interested, I will write to you extensively about the Kurds who seem to me a very friendly people. I have met two of their ministers and their representative in Holland, a 26- year-old student of sociology. Their main representation is in London, and I may have to go and see them before I leave. In that case I will naturally come to see you [in Oxford] as well. So far no interesting tiles found, though I do watch out for them.

Please give my love and scorn to ye olde England and kiss the Irish for me.

Yours ever,

Alex

Alex in the early 1970's.

Section Six

Kurdistan And Baghdad

September 1974 - December 1975

(Eds. The history of the Kurdish rebellion against Iraq is a long one. In 1943, Mullah Mustapha Barzani organized an uprising against the Iraqis. Between 1961 and 1969, he continued his armed resistance. Then in 1974, after a period of relative quiet, the Kurds (encouraged by support from Iran and still led by Barzani) renewed their struggle. In response, between March and September, 1974, the Iraqis conducted a military offensive against the rebel Kurds. One of the results of this offensive was the dislocation of 100,000 Kurdish civilians. {Reference: Facts on File, *1974.} Their plight, depicted on Dutch television, induced Alex to take on their cause.*

Late in August, 1974, Alex began his journey to Kurdistan. This series of letters, sent to his wife in Holland, chronicles his trip eastward. It has been translated from Dutch.)

Istanbul
6-7 September 1974

Dearest Betje,

After a trip which has gone much more quickly than I had planned, I arrived here last night, parked the car, and decided to stay at least until Sunday. I'm desperately in need of a day's rest. I drove through the night on Monday. By Tuesday afternoon, I was already in Zagreb. There I slept from 5:00 in the afternoon until 3:00 a.m. on Wednesday. I then drove to Vita's in Rataje [Yugoslavia] and stayed there until after lunch. At 10:00 p.m., I passed the Greek border. By then I didn't have enough energy to visit Sophia and her husband and decided to go straight to Fannari [Greece]. Panajatis and wife received the television with lots of "ohs" and "ahs." It didn't suffer at all from the trip and worked right away. Then I crossed the border with record breaking speed — just five minutes.

They didn't even look at the car. Istanbul has not changed at all. It is still very busy and active.

It is a pity that Frans van Hasselt has just left for Athens. I had hoped to pay him a visit. Except for a single, lonely hitchhiker yesterday, I've had the company of an old girlfriend for the whole trip. I thought I had lost her, but three days ago she re-appeared from her corner again (top left, behind the windshield) to look at the world and to devour a Yugoslavian fly. It must be great to travel the world in this way as a Frisian spider.

I just sent my first card to Alwin and one to Oma of the Sultan Ahmed, in other words, the so-called Blue mosque. It is the only mosque in the world with six minarets. I'm parked directly in front of it between caravanettes with foreign number plates. A popular international meeting point.

Tehran, Iran
Wednesday night, 11 September 1974

After covering 6,000 kilometers in 9 days, I arrived here at two o'clock this afternoon. The Merc was fantastic all the way. He did not give me a bit of trouble. Not even a flat tire. Good boy. Tomorrow he will get an extra nice greasing from me. At the moment, I'm in a little hotel, two-star (if five is the most expensive), as a guest of the Kurdish government whose bureau I visited first thing upon arrival. I was received very hardily by their representative, Bep Udink, daughter of minister Udink and committee member of Terre des Hommes. She came to see things for herself.

A few Kurdish officials are in the hotel "on business," and tonight I had a taste of Kurdish hospitality. Everything was informal and friendly. Already I've mastered my first five Kurdish words. The formalities here (together with the Iranian authorities) will probably take a day or two, and I will take this opportunity to get my breath back. I don't have to do a thing. Everything is being arranged. I hope that your letter and the card sent to American Express arrive in the meantime. I'll wait until I have your news and know my next address before mailing this. Alwin should get another card from me tomorrow.

Tehran
Friday, 13 September 1974

Your letter has just been handed to me by Dr. Ahmadi, director of the Kurdish bureau. It arrived yesterday. Today is the Moslem Sunday so everything is closed. Tomorrow Ahmedi hopes to get my special travel pass, and then I should be able to leave. The American Express card has not arrived here yet. Will you send me the Merc [handbook?] with the bill please?

I always think a candle is a nice present, but don't send one because it might melt on the way; it is that hot here. How nice that Alwin signed the letter himself.

Lots of love from your bad, but still loving,

Papa

(Eds. Shortly after writing the previous letter, Alex left Tehran for Kurdistan, northern Iraq.)

Tuesday, 17 September 1974

Just returned home from work in the hospital, and so I can start to write you something real now. "Home" for the coming days is the information center of the Kurdish government; a block of houses halfway up a mountain where all the foreign guests (journalists, photographers, and so on) are received. Possibly I'll stay here 10-14 days until my definite work area has been settled. On my first evening, I had an interview with Dr. Mahmood, head of the medical department and one of the most politically powerful men in the country. We agreed that first I would work in the hospital for a few days to acclimatize and perhaps to give them a chance to try me out. After that, I would go (like a stick insect) to visit the remote villages in the mountains in order to establish a fixed route for the clinics.

The hospital is made up of about ten tents and a number of small huts of hardened mud spread in a rock cliff. Approximately a dozen doctors work here. (I can't get a definite number.) Some of these are specialists. One is a surgeon who does not operate, another is an orthopaedic surgeon who treats fractures in the strangest way; the third is a dermatologist who does small jobs. Along with these, there is a doctor in charge of public hygiene who does not know what a septic tank is. The chief doctor is a pediatrician. He has already discovered my preference for children. While he was away for a few days, he let me take over his practice.

It is a myth that there aren't any hospitals here. In fact, there are a number of these centers. In general, things seem to be well organized. There are ninety doctors distributed fairly evenly over the country. It is a big question as to where Lex Aronson can make himself most useful.

Alwin will find this funny. They call me Kak Askander which is not excreta, but our friend Alex. This is a compliment for my progress in their language of which I now speak between 30 and 50 words. Many Kurdish words are similar to Hindi only the accent is more like Arabic.

Friday, 20 September 1974

Today a German journalist headed home so I gave him a letter for Alwin plus a polaroid snapshot. Postcards are unobtainable here, and there is no postal service. Therefore, I'll give this letter to some Dutch TV people from NOS who have made a film. The enclosed photo is also for Alwin. Also there are some rolls of film which I'd like you to have developed and printed (matt, please) by the Chemist de Groot. Please save the negatives and mail me the prints. I've enclosed money to cover it. You won't have much left, and I have no expenses here. By the way, I haven't even spent 300 guilders yet. This morning I went with a companion, or perhaps I should say escort, to the tailor. It was decided that I should dress as a Kurd, and so I have been offered Kurdish dress. The pictures should show you. What do you think? Do I look the part?

We are about 34 kilometres from the Persian [Iranian] border, not much of a distance, but, due to the roads, it's nearly a two-hour drive. You don't notice the war much, only occasionally the sound of anti-aircraft guns aimed at a passing Iraqi Tupolev. About a four-hour drive from here, fighting is going on on three fronts. This will stop, however, within another month because of the winter.

Saturday, 21 September 1974

Before I forget to ask: will you have two prints made of any photos which have people in them and mail them to me? I might please somebody with one sometime. This morning again it was quiet in the hospital. I'm amazed that everyone who works here doesn't suffer from calcification of the arse. How any self-respecting doctor can be satisfied to see only fifteen patients a day is beyond me. More and more, I wonder whether I can be of any use at all. I'm sure there must be areas in need of medical help, but nobody will mention them. Keeping up appearances is a very important occupation in these parts. I've resolved to give it one more week, then move on.

Tuesday, 24 September 1974

The Dutch club is ready to leave, and so this must go. No decision yet. I've had two days' work alone in the clinic in the mountains, but things remain uncertain. Heavy storms and tornados last night and this morning. Sun still shining.

Lots of love,

Papa

Wednesday, 25 September 1974

Although it has not yet been made official by Dr. Mahmood, the decision has been taken that I won't stay in Kurdistan. The three French doctors from Medecins sans Frontieres, sent to assess the situation for their organization, have come to the same conclusion. There is a fourth Frenchman, who has been here since March, a post-graduate student researching Kurdish culture. The five of us had a long talk last night. We agreed that medical services are well organized here. We can contribute what we like; we feel that it still is not enough. This is a result, no doubt, of our Western education. Also it is not for us to say that MORE has to be done.

I already knew one of the French doctors from Biafra; a hard worker. The primary reason that help from abroad is welcomed is that foreigners can interest their governments in the situation. There is less of a need for doctors, nurses, and medical supplies than for political gestures. It is the political gesture that stands. Also foreigners serve as show pieces for the press. Only with difficulty have I kept my face out of the TV film made by our photographers.

I stopped working in the hospital two days ago. Instead, with the help of a Kurdish doctor who translates, I've been trying to reorganize a neglected clinic I discovered ten kilometres from here. We emptied the building completely, scrubbed it clean, and put everything back in order, creating a better arrangement. There we see about fifty patients a day. I'll remain in this neglected corner until Dr. Mahmood returns from the front, which I hope will be this coming Friday.

So my stay is not completely in vain. I say that for myself in contrast to the French team — a surgeon, an internist, and an ear, nose, and throat specialist. The organization here sends as many sick refugees as they can to the camps in Iran... to fill the eyes of the world with pity. Am I becoming cynical? I have pity for the refugees, but, as for the governments (Egypt, Jordan, Lebanon), they are all the same. I shit on them.

Friday, 26 September 1974

Yesterday was my last working day in Galalah [35°N, 45°E]. While I was going about my business, a Kurdish suit was being tailored for me. Now, after many alterations, it fits perfectly. My business included having a long talk with Dara Togiq, the minister of information and education. The minister of health, Mahmood, is returning today. Tomorrow, I might make a trip to the so-called Badinan district where the need for medical staff seems to be greater. Before committing myself I said I would have to see the place for myself. If you want to know where it is, look in the northwest of Iraq on the Turkish and Syrian borders (which are strictly closed) where you should find the towns of Amadiyah [37°N, 43°E] and Barzan [36°N, 44°E]. It is said to be paradise there.

Monday 30 September 1974, 8:00

Arrived in Amadiyah yesterday morning after a nightmare-like trip over rock paths, past ravines, and similar terrors. We could only travel at night because of the airplanes, creeping along at 17 kilometres per hour. We were on our way for fourteen hours. I'm over the horrors now, but there were moments when I asked myself if I was in my right mind to have started such a trip. And to think that I've got to travel the route back in a few days. The Merc would never have survived it. Only jeeps and landrovers can get through here. So I was offered a jeep with a chauffeur and a translator. The translator was about as useful as my Mercedes. All the same, it's worth the cold sweat. It is paradise.

At the moment I'm a guest of the hospital of Amadiyah. There is a hardworking and enthusiastic young doctor here. And they can cope very well without me. Great!

Friday 4 October, 1974, 15:00

I've been in the Zakhu district (in the mountains near the Turkish border) because the town of Zakhu itself [37°N, 42°E] is in the hands of government troops. The hospital is in a large cave which divides into two storeys. Men are on the ground floor, ladies on the upper. It's like something out of a fairy tale.

Yesterday I took a "walking" trip for twelve hours past some mountain villages, a distance of some forty kilometres of which 3 kilometers are straight up. My heart went rikketikketik because there are no roads and everything goes over rock. I managed to cross two rivers by jumping from one rock to another. Papa the mountain goat. Arrived home dead tired and a few kilos lighter. But it's been worth it. Look at the photographs in the third roll. I can certainly make myself useful in this area, but, because of the predicted three meters of snow, not before March. My job would be to pay regular visits to the surrounding villages.

I've arranged with the local authorities to leave now and to return at the end of the winter season. I am still awaiting permission from Uncle Mahmood. Tonight, I am having a farewell dinner with the governor of the Zakhu district. Tomorrow I'll travel back to Amadiyah.

Namperdam [?]
Friday, 11 October 1974

Yesterday after a return journey lasting three nights and two days, I arrived in the capital shattered. The farewell dinner turned out to be an invitation to an extended stay. Believe me, I would have liked to have stayed even longer. The winter still seems so far off. I've travelled and seen a lot and finally felt settled. So I have written an extensive report about medical provisions. This I handed to Dr. Mahmood last night. He plans to read it immediately. At ten o'clock tomorrow morning, I'm to meet with him and his two under-ministers to discuss my future here. My report is quite critical. If he accepts my criticisms, he might ask me to remain to make some changes. The more likely response is, however, that he will merely thank me for my interest and let me go. Then I scram.

I won't be able to report on this immediately because I have to let this letter go within the hour. French journalists are taking it with them to Tehran, and they are about to leave.

I received a book and letter from Alwin and a letter giro yesterday. I'm writing to Alwin separately.

(Eds. The following letter was addressed to Alex's mother and step-father in Amsterdam.)

20 December 1974

Dear Mother and Uncle Sam,

For the first time since leaving De Wilp, I slept in a proper bed. I have just woken up, flooded in tears, because of an awful dream. Normally, I have only pleasant dreams. Anyway, a good, quiet moment to write to you. (Isn't it odd, at unpleasant moments, one always thinks first of mother.)

Contrary to expectations, my stay in Kurdistan lasted only four weeks. I travelled widely, visiting all kinds of medical centers; hospitals in tents and caves and clinics in remote villages....

With the approach of winter, when heavy fighting and bombardments will cease (so no wounded) and the snows cut off the villages (so no patients), there is no point in my staying on. I have, however, been asked to return in March to set up a new hospital, and I have promised to do this. It is quite nice, especially in the Badinan area at the borders of Syria and Turkey where national health can do with some improvement.

I'll stay here a week, then travel around in Pakistan, India, and perhaps Bangledesh. I hope this letter reaches you in good health.

Your loving son,

Lex

Saiyidan [33°N, 72°E]
Swat [Pakistan]
Friday 21 February 1975

Dear Betjeme,

Thank God, it seems my torture is over. This trip will be with me for the rest of my life because never have I dealt so much with the police. I wrote to you before about former "meetings" with the Hermandad. This time, returning from India, I fell right into it.

I still had a week left before I had to agree to the through passage to Kurdistan. So I decided to visit some friends in Swat. At the moment, Pakistan is in great political unrest. Because of the general unrest and because the tourist season has not started, I received an invitation to visit the police station. That was on February sixth. My visit to the station (I was "just visiting") turned out to be three days' detention. Fortunately, my friend Wali was able to save me from spending the nights in jail. Instead, placed under two official guards, I was given a bungalow of my own.

I was less fortunate when they transported me to Peshawar for further investigations. This time I was interrogated for five days while checks were being made on my friends and acquaintances. For this little operation, I was favored with a cell. It was a beauty, a bare cold room 4 by 5 meters, a concrete floor, a shit bucket in the corner which got scooped out once a day with a tin. There I slept crowded in with half-a- dozen thieves and murderers. On the sixth day, they told me that were satisfied. I was "clean."

Back I went to Swat under guard while a report was being prepared. And then, alas, another "high uncle" appeared on the scene. He wanted to start a third investigation just to make sure. Up until this point, I was left completely in the dark, but now Wali arranged for me to speak with a solicitor. Thanks to him, I was allowed to walk about on bail.

As it turned out, I didn't get much of an opportunity to walk about, but my good friend Tasnim, receptionist in the Swat hotel, offered me hospitality and stood by me along with all his friends and relations. I was in a terrible depression. Even though I knew I had nothing to hide, the situation was so uncertain that I didn't know at all where I stood. The worst is no knowing how long it will take. And I'm expected in Kurdistan already.

What I hope will be the last report came in yesterday and is being discussed. The solicitor chosen for me said that they cannot accuse me of anything. Meanwhile Wali and his son Arviangzeb (an MP) have requested continually that I be treated with velvet gloves.

To make waiting a bit more agreeable, Wali sent me cigarettes and whiskey regularly, an unknown luxury here. Finally, with suggestions from all sides to hasten the settlement, I hope to be free tomorrow and back on my route. I shall go straight to Tehran where I hope to receive mail from you. My weekly card to Alwin has gone by the board this time. But I hope he received all the others. Tasnim has a little brother his age so homesickness has not been one of my least sufferings.

Perhaps they won't need me in Kurdistan anymore. I have no idea what the situation is. In the meantime, lots of love. I spent our wedding anniversary in a cell, but thought of you. You have not enjoyed me much during these ll years. Only lots of worries and ups and downs. For me you have meant a lot and still do. I am mentally supported by you. Once back in Holland, may I come for coffee again?

Your loving,

(Eds. This is the last letter Alex wrote to his mother and step-father before his arrest on 24 March 1975.)

Sideka [36°N, 44°E]
Kurdistan
13 March 1975

Dear Mother and Uncle Sam,

It is once more your turn to receive a letter from me. And it looks as if I shall have all day today to write, for my donkey and luggage are gone. But I will tell you about that later. Last week I arrived in Kurdistan (Iraq) with the intention of going to Badinan. Badinan is near the Syrian and Turkish border. Amadiyah is the biggest of the towns in that area.

They need doctors and nurses urgently. That's a fact, but, because the border between Iraq and Iran is very likely to be closed, the political bosses here have decided that all foreigners should be evacuated. By foreigners, they are referring to a few press photographers, the team of five English from "Save the Children," and yours truly. The hospitality is so extensive here that at the first sign of a threat, they are stepping out of their way to secure the safety of their guests. The local bosses mean well. However, what daddy has in his head, he doesn't have in his arse... by which I mean that whatever I have set my mind to, I don't give up easily.

I was determined to go to Badinan. I went from one political office to another, pestering all the leaders save for Barzani himself. Finally, I was rewarded with a letter of introduction to all the Kurdish military commanders requesting that they give me the help necessary for me to reach my goal....

(Eds. On Mullah Mustapha Barzani, see the note at the beginning of this section. The headquarters of General Barzani were in Galalah, a village mentioned several times by Alex.)

There is a road, but it's a passage blocked by snow and bombardments. There are villages on the way, but they have been abandoned. Anyway, I got a lift by car to Galalah.

I forgot to tell you that by the time I returned to Tehran, the old Merc was at the end of its life and hardly worth a tuppence. I sold it for the pittance it was due, Hfl 2500!!

From Galalah onwards, we moved on foot. For a guide, the local commander gave me a Pesh Merga (Kurdish Freedom Fighter). The first day was very hard going so I had my eye out for a donkey. On the second day, I succeeded in buying one from the people we met. After that all my luggage, medicines, papers and duffelcoat were transferred to that beast of burden. Meanwhile I had to congratulate myself on the sense I had had to start out in my new walking boots instead of sandals. The route runs along stony and muddy paths less than a foot wide, and through streamlets themselves as it rose and fell steeply. Every thirty minutes or so, we had to duck to avoid the bombers flying over head. Now we are so close to the front we can hear bombs which they let loose every now and then to scare off any local people who have stayed behind.

Yesterday we reached Rost [36°N, 44°E]. There my guide left me. I was welcomed by the local "doctor," a nurse who is the only medical person in the area. After a few hours, a small group of patrolling Pesh Merga came by. I reached an agreement with them about guiding me to Sideka since they were continuing on to the village. We set out with the donkey, but after less than an hour, we met some people who told us that the snow along the path we were following was too icy and deep for the animals. We then divided into two groups, my Pesh Merga and I continuing along the treacherous shorter path, the other two Pesh Merga taking the longer route with their donkey and mine. So far they haven't reached Sideka....

After an exhausting treck through the mountains, I reached Sidakan alone at five o'clock in the evening. I went directly to the hospital and received a very warm welcome from the doctor who, for once, turned out to be a real one.

If my donkey arrives today, I expect to continue on my journey tomorrow. There is only one more day of trekking by foot. After that, I should be in Shamanawa [36°N, 43°E]. I've been told that there is a real road there, and I should be able to hitch a ride in a vehicle.

The bombardments, which have been steady, have at last stopped. It's strange how quiet everything is. I can hear birds for the first time this week, birds which up until now have been outnumbered by flying Migs and Tupolevs. For the sake of the civilians, we count this as a blessing.

Am I going to remain here? That is still a question. If I should have to leave, I'll return by the Bombay-to-London bus.

Anyway, all best wishes and lots of love to everybody.

Yours

Lex.

(Eds. A week after this letter was written, the passport application Alex had arranged for a crippled Indian girl was stamped in the Embassy of the Netherlands in Tehran. He had found her sitting on a road on his trip to Calcutta to collect medical supplies for the Kurds. Her adoption had gone through in three months whereas the normal procedure takes five years. Not long afterwards, this child, named Whilhelmina Aronson in honor of the Dutch Queen, arrived safely in Friesland. There, thanks to Elisabeth's efforts and help from the De Wilp community, the child was given the medical care she needed and was sent to a special school. Of similar age to Alwin, she remained in the family as an adopted daughter.)

(Eds. The following letter was written on 1 February 1976 to Alex's father, Mr. Leo Aronson, who was then living in Amsterdam. The author of the letter is Dr. David Nabarro of the Save the Children Fund. The events mentioned in the letter follow almost directly from Alex's last letter to his parents. The letter portrays Alex's situation and concerns shortly before his arrest. Aside from Sideka and Amadiyah, whose co-ordinates we gave earlier, it has been impossible to locate the villages mentioned in this letter.)

Dear Mr. Aronson,

I saw your son on 20 March 1975. He was breakfasting with me at the home of the leader of the Barzan community, Sheikh Abdullah, in preparation for a journey to Badinan. He was taking medicine and other equipment with him so that he could set up a surgery to treat the inhabitants of a single community somewhere in that area. He had bought a donkey to convey these items, but unfortunately this had got lost between Senidan and Sideka, over the pass to the east of Hassanbeg Mountain with the snow so deep that no donkey could traverse it.

The donkey was under the control of two Pesh Merga (Kurdish Freedom Fighters). Apparently they became separated from your son and he had no idea of the [whereabouts of?] this medicine or his passport and money. He was travelling against the advice of the Kurds in the border area who were keen (at that time) that all foreigners should get out as quickly as possible. For this reason, he retraced his steps to try to find the donkey, yet wanted to press on towards Amadiyah. He had spent a day or so looking. He asked me to look for the animal. I made inquiries in both Sideka and Semilan, but I could not find it. However, as at that stage there was total chaos in these villages, it was not at all surprising that I was so unsuccessful. I must explain that he was in danger, as he had no identification papers with him when I saw him.

Yours,

David Nabarro

(Eds. The author of this letter speaks of chaos in the villages of Kurdistan. On 7 March 1975, the Iraqis launched a drive against the Kurds "along the entire front with a force of six divisions." The Iraqis were able to do this because the Shah of Iran had reached an agreement

with Iraq and had withdrawn his support from the Kurds. By 11 March, Baghdad's forces "had pushed deep into insurgent [Kurdish] territory." Eleven days later, General Barzani conceded that his forces had been overwhelmed and that the fighting was over. A report of 30 March states that Barzani and his two sons fled to Iran. Reference: Facts on File, *1975.)*

* *

(Eds. The documents which follow contain some contradictory information. This derives from the way news about Alex's arrest, imprisonment, trial, and ultimate execution reached the Western press. For more than half a year after his arrest, there was virtually no news. During this period, Alex's parents tried to obtain information themselves; they also attempted (unsuccessfully) to have Alex visited by a member of the Dutch Foreign Ministry. At the same time, support groups formed in De Wilp and Amsterdam.

On 3 November 1975, Dutch radio and European newspapers carried the story that an Israeli citizen by the name of Alexander Haroun had been hanged in Baghdad for spying. The source of this story was the Iraqi News Agency (INA). Confusion resulted from conflicting reports about the date of the execution and the name of the condemned. Three days later the Iraqi Chargé d'Affaires in the Hague announced that the original story was false; he was not dead, but faced execution. Still, no independent party was able to attest to these facts.

In the ensuing months, efforts to secure Alex's release continued. Unknown even to Dutch officials at that time, there was evidence Alex was still alive. For Alex had written messages on the underside of the silver foil of cigarette packages. These he managed to have smuggled out of prison. The messages travelled at irregular speeds via Switzerland or Germany. Basing their hopes in the continued arrival of these messages, Alex's parents continued to work for his freedom. Then, on 15 March 1976, Alex's mother received a telephone call from the Iraqi Embassy in the Hague. She could stop wondering about Alex's fate, she was told by the official on the other end of the line. He was dead. Alex's parents have determined that at that time he had actually been dead for more than three months.

The documents we have been able to procure which relate to the months of Alex's imprisonment and the uncertainty about his fate (March 1975 - March 1976) include press reports, formal letters of appeal, letters about his case, and letters written by Alex. What is most striking about Alex's letters is that, for the most part, they were written without access to information about his own situation. There is only one incident in which Alex appears to respond to information available to the outside world. Ironically, this response is based on a wrongly heard or misinterpreted report. After spending six months in a Baghdad prison, in mid-October, 1975, Alex was transferred to a prison twenty miles to the south. There he found a cell-mate with a transistor radio. A BBC World News bulletin led Alex and his cell-mates to surmise that the Dutch government had requested his release. The truth, however, was that the Dutch goverment was responding to the false information leaked by the Iraqi News Agency. In fact, the Dutch authorities were not requesting his release; they were asking for his remains.

Since Alex was writing from inside the prison, without knowledge of the efforts which were being made on his behalf, it would be misleading to present Alex's final messages together with other documents within one chronological frame. In no sense should we think of Alex's last words as part of a dialogue. The smuggled letters were not made public until 17 March 1976, only when Alex's parents were convinced that there was no more hope.

The newspaper articles, reproduced below, contain odd mixtures of error and truth or adjustments in the truth. Alex's family name first appears as "Haroun." This is later corrected. He is said to be an Israeli. That was promptly denied by the Israelis. Yet as is clear from comments made in letters written to Alan, including Alex's insistence on travelling to the United States on his Israeli passport, that he had an Israeli passport and had been in the Israeli army. Again there is an error when Alex is credited with having participated in the Six-Day War; his letters show that in June, 1967, he was at home in Poortugaal, Holland, planning for a summer job at a Dutch camp for asthmatic children.

The clippings from the Daily News Bulletin of the Jewish Telegraphic Agency were compiled by the Middle East Research Department of Amnesty International, London. The editors wish to thank both the Jewish Telegraphic Agency and Amnesty International for their permission to re-print these documents. Material from other newspapers and Dutch petitions and letters were given to us by Alex's family or friends in Holland.)

DOCTOR'S ENCOUNTER WITH MAN HANGED BY IRAQIS
from the English newspaper, "The Guardian"

Baghdad, 3 November. A Jew of Dutch origin has been hanged in Baghdad on charges of spying for Israel, the Iraq news agency reported today. He was identified as Leon Aaronson and was said to have taken the name Alexander Haroun after emigrating to Israel in 1954.

The agency said he was arrested on 24 March in possession of political and military reports to his "Zionist superiors." Mr. Haroun was condemned to death on 11 October (Agence France-Presse).

Edward Mortimer writes: Speaking by telephone from Amsterdam last night, Mr. Aaronson's father told a British doctor that his son, a 38-year old male nurse, was neither Jewish nor Israeli. He had visited Israel only once for a two-week holiday in 1953.

The doctor, Dr. David Nabarro, had met the executed man in Iraq on March 20, this year. Dr. Nabarro, who was working for the Save the Children Fund, was on his way back to Iran from Iraqi Kurdistan, where the revolt led by General Mustafa Barzani was about to collapse. He met Mr. Aaronson travelling in the opposite direction, dressed in Kurdish costume and carrying a pistol and a letter from General Barzani explaining who he was.

(Eds. From the very beginning, the authorities in Iraq raise the specter of Alex's having spied for Israel. As we have stated earlier in this volume, we do not believe that this was the case. Iraq's concern about Israel may have been related to the fact, admitted by Kurdish sources at the time, that Israel had supplied the Kurds with some financial support and had given the rebels "several medium-range artillery pieces." Reference: Facts on File, *1974.)*

Jewish Telegraphic Agency
Volume 56, Number 197
5 November 1975

IRAQIS HANG DUTCH JEW
by Yitzhak Shargil

Tel Aviv, 4 November. Iraq's official news agency has announced that the "Israeli citizen Alexander Haroun" has been hanged in Baghdad for spying, following his conviction by a military tribunal last month.

The agency alleged that the hanged man had worked as an adviser to the rebel Kurdish leader Mullah Mustapha Barzani.

Vicious lies

Relatives of Alexander Leendert Aronson — not "Haroun" — in Israel described the allegations as "vicious blood libel." They told the JTA in detail the tragic life story of Alexander Aronson, a Dutch, not an Israeli, Jew and a survivor of the Bergen-Belsen death camp.

Born in 1934 in Holland to an assimilated family, the Bergen-Belsen experience marked the young Alexander for life. After the liberation Alexander dedicated himself to helping people in need and worked for some time at the Albert Schweitzer Hospital in Africa where he became a qualified male nurse. After that he went on an aid mission to India and Pakistan, volunteered to help the hungry and the sick in Biafra, and spent some time in the Virgin Islands where he was apparently stranded. [sic!]

Visits to Israel

Between 1954 and 1958 he visited Israel twice for longer periods as tourist and worked as a male nurse. But he could not settle down and returned to Holland where he married and raised a family. He never took out Israeli citizenship and his step-father, who is now living in Amsterdam with Alexander's mother, told the JTA that the young Aronson was the holder of a Dutch passport.

Family Life and More Travels

After their marriage, the Aronsons settled in a small village near the northern Dutch town of Groningen. By that time, they had four children — one of their own and three adopted boys and girls, one of them the son of a Palestinian Arab refugee.

But again Alexander found no rest. In the middle of last year he converted a trailer into a medical aid station and left for the journey from which he would never return.

He reached India with his car and his mobile medical aid unit, but decided that his services were more needed by the Kurds, at that time engaged in a life-and-death struggle against the Baathist regime.

Refuses to Leave

Via Iran he reached the Kurdish frontline outposts where he tended the wounded and famished survivors of the bloody Iraqi onslaught. When Mustapha Barzani's forces were on the verge of collapse, all the foreign medical aid volunteers left the area.

But Alexander refused to leave. When the last bus carrying doctors and nurses departed for safer destinations, he was persuaded to board it, but a few minutes later was seen leaving the bus and disappearing.

Where is Our Son?

Alexander's mother, his wife, and his step-father started to look for him. They approached the Dutch Foreign Office, but the latter was unable to obtain any information from Baghdad.

A direct approach was then made to the Iraqi Embassy in the Hague, but again to no avail.

There were rumors of a pending trial, but the Iraqis would neither confirm nor refute them. There was no information about any charges.

The report on his execution on the gallows by the murderous Iraqi regime with its long record of public hangings and other atrocities stunned his family in Holland and in Israel.

The "Angel of Mercy," as he was called by those whom he helped in their need, the man whose destiny took him from the Bergen-Belsen death camp to an ignominious execution in Baghdad, who never served in any army and could never settle down, was now found in possession (we quote the Iraqi official communique) of "classified military and political information for the Israeli intelligence."

(Eds. This article also appeared on 5 November 1975. It has been translated from the Dutch regional daily, the "Leeuwarder Courant.")

HE WAS DEVOTED / ARONSON WORKED AS A S.O.S. TELEPHONIST

De Wilp. The nurse from the Wilp (executed in Bagdad) worked for ten months for the S.O.S. (helpline/lifeline) telephone service in Leeuwarden. This statement comes from the chairman of the S.O.S., Rev. Ype Schaaf. Mr. Aronson had read an article in the "Leeunwarder Courant" about the need for volunteers. He applied and was sent to Rev. Schaaf whom he already knew, since they had been in Cameroon at the same time. In fact, Schaaf had visited Aronson there in prison. Aronson had been imprisoned for entering and travelling in Cameroon without a passport. At the time, he had been on his way to visit Dr. Schweitzer in Gabon. According to Rev. Schaaf, Aronson had hitch-hiked through Africa. "I like that kind of person," Schaaf said, and so he offered his help.

Mr. Aronson reached Schweitzer and his hospital at Lambaréré. He also turned up in Nigeria during the revolt of the Biafrans, though by then he was working for two help organizations, Terre des Hommes and the Red Cross. Aronson was deputy-project leader of the S.O.S line and did a fantastic job, said Schaaf. Aronson was an excellent organizer as well as a very dedicated worker.

Rev. Schaaf wasn't surprised when Aronson told him that he wanted to go to Kurdistan. But he warned him that, as a son of the Old Nation, the Jews, he would have to be careful. "It won't be that bad," said Aronson. "I'm only going to set up a medical service." Kurdistan appealed to him because he had seen a television program about the situation there. As soon as the program ended, Aronson telephoned the Kurdish spokesman at his hotel and told him, "I'm coming." And Aronson went.

After a while, Rev. Schaaf received a letter from Aronson asking for twenty thousand guilders to help him establish medical treatment sites. Word was circulated around the churches, and the sum was sent.

Schaaf says that suddenly everything in Kurdistan went wrong. Aronson's wife and father asked him if he could use his connections to help get Aronson out. He did what he could, but his connections were limited to affiliates of the church. Rev. Schaaf believes that Aronson's father has been in contact with a friendly Iraqi ambassador. He is sure, however, that by the time this contact was made, Alex was already in prison in Baghdad.

One of two things must have happened. Either the ambassador lied to Aronson's father or the ambassador was not informed by his own government about Alex's predicament. Aronson's nature was restless, and he followed whims. He wanted to help where help was wanted.

His father denies that there is any truth to the rumors that during the Six-Day War Aronson served with the Red Cross as a soldier in Israel. According to Mr. Leo Aronson, he was here in Holland during some of that time and studying nursing in London. Aronson was not home in De Wilp very much because of his travelling. While he was travelling, however, he always kept his wife informed as to his whereabouts. Therefore, she was surprised when, after early March of this year, his letters stopped.

He is a clever man. He usually figures out a way to send a letter, she told the people of De Wilp.

The Aronsons are known to be hospitable. But their hospitality did not appeal to everyone. They tried holding a series of discussion evenings in their home, but this didn't suit the village, which put a stop to them. One time Aronson returned to the village driving an old Model T that belonged to the Red Cross. He'd welcome friends from all over the world, giving them a roof over their heads for a few days. One local is certain that Aronson was being watched. But he doesn't know how or in which way.

According to the Iraqi Information Service, the arrested inhabitant of De Wilp attended a PPR meeting. [Possible reference here to a meeting of the anti-government Kurdish group known as the Revolutionary Proletariat Party.]

(Eds. On the following day, 6 November 1975, this article was published in the English newspaper "The Guardian.")

EXECUTION OF DUTCHMAN DENIED BY IRAQ

The Hague. The execution of a Dutch male nurse, Mr. Leendert Alexander Aronson, aged 40, announced officially in Iraq on Monday, was denied today in a telephone call from the Iraq embassy in the Hague to the Dutch Foreign Ministry.

Iraq now says that Mr. Aronson, who, it claims, has Israel nationality and was spying for Israel when arrested in Kurdistan in March, has been sentenced to death, but the execution has not been carried out.

Mr. Aronson's parents in Amsterdam heard the report of their son's execution in a Dutch radio news bulletin.

Mr. Max van der Stoel, the Dutch Foreign Minister, summoned the Iraq ambassador on Monday to protest the secret trial and execution report.

Jewish Telegraphic Agency
Volume 56, Number 200
10 November 1975

The Iraqi Government claimed on Friday afternoon in an official statement to the Dutch Foreign Ministry that the Dutch-born Alexander Aronson was still alive, contrary to the report of the Iraqi News Agency that he had been executed as a "Zionist spy." The Dutch Foreign Ministry had demanded that his remains be transferred to Holland where his family lives. Iraqi Chargé d'Affaires, Said al-Khadi said the Dutch Jew still faced death, but had not been executed.

Jewish Telegraphic Agency
Volume 56, Number 203
13 November 1975

ARONSON'S FATE UNCLEAR

Den Hague, 12 November. The Dutch Foreign Ministry has announced that its Chargé d'Affaires in Baghdad has not been allowed to visit Alexander Aronson in prison, contrary to an Iraqi Government promise. No explanation was given.

Last week the official Iraqi News Agency announced that Aronson had been executed on a charge of espionage for Israel. He was a male nurse who tended wounded Kurdish soldiers during the uprising. A few days later, the Iraqi Embassy here said he was not dead, but faced execution for spying.

The Dutch Premier J.M. den Uyl told a press conference that Holland must do everything to prevent his execution. Aronson's mother told Dutch TV that her son's experiences as a child in Bergen-Belsen had brought him to help others' suffering.

A public campaign has been launched in the Friesland province, where the Aronsons live, to save his life. Letters and cables are flooding the Iraqi Embassy with appeals for clemency. Leading politicians have placed themselves at the head of this campaign.

(Eds. This letter was sent to the Iraqi Ambassador to the Hague by the Mayor and Councillors of the Municipality of Opsterland. It is clearly in response to the Iraqi decision not to treat Alex as a Dutch citizen. The letter is not reproduced in full because of the repetition of some details.)

14 November 1975

Excellency,

An inhabitant of the Municipality of Opsterland (Province of Friesland), Mr. Leendert Aronson, born 20 December 1934, has been sentenced to death by an Iraqi tribunal, according to announcements in the press. To give you more precise detail, we would like to add that Mr. Aronson lives in our municipality, a sizeable agricultural community of sixteen villages.... So as not to confuse it with the bordering "De Wilp" in the Province of Groningen, this part of the village is commonly known as "de Friese Wilp." Therefore Mr. Aronson, like his wife and son, is registered in in this municipality.

Since 21 August 1968, he has had his official residence here. He is of Dutch nationality. We should also like you to know that he has had a troubled life behind him. As a child, he was in two concentration camps. He survived and, after recovering from tuberculosis, he took up a course of study in nursing in England. He had a restless nature. He wanted to help, especially where help was most needed. According to our information, he has been to Gabon to visit Dr. Schweitzer, to the Cameroon, Nigeria (Biafra), Bangladesh, and Afghanistan. As far as we know, the last place he stayed was in Kurdistan where he offered medical aid. We declare emphatically that Leendert Aronson is a man deeply moved by his feelings and full of love for his fellow man. As an idealist who strived for a fairer world, he has alas become the victim of the circumstances in which he has fallen.

For these reasons, we sincerely plead for his life and appeal to you to use your influence to save it....

Burgemeester
[Dutch, Mayor]
of Opsterland

(Eds. The following letter was submitted on behalf of family and friends, including a psychologist, a doctor, and a social worker.)

To the Cabinet of Her Majesty
The Hague
16 November 1975

Majesty,

We would like to draw your attention to our concern about Lex Aronson's fate.

The latest messages which have reached us have been confused and contradictory. They leave us with hope that Lex is still alive, imprisoned in Iraq, sentenced by a military tribunal but.... Up to now, the Dutch Chargé d'Affaires has not succeeded in obtaining entrance to the prison so that he himself could see if Lex is still alive.

This refusal to grant entrance is based on the Iraqi government's protestation that they are not dealing with a Dutch subject, but with an Israeli. To prove his Dutch nationality, we have enclosed a brief life chronology.

Jewish Telegraphic Agency
Volume 56, Number 209
21 November 1975

IRAQ REFUSES DUTCH PLEA ON ARONSON

Amsterdam, 20 November. Iraq has once again refused Dutch Chargé d'Affaires Gerben Meihuizen permission to visit Alexander Aronson, who has been sentenced to death on charges of having spied for Israel and helped the Kurdish rebels.

The Dutch diplomat yesterday met the Iraqi Under Secretary of State for Foreign Affairs to renew this demand, but was turned down.

The Iraqis reportedly said Aronson is an Israeli national and Holland can therefore not intervene on his behalf. The Iraqis also say the entire matter is "an internal affair."

The Dutch authorities are now trying to obtain copies of the evidence brought against Aronson at his trial. They have also forwarded to the Baghdad Government a copy of his birth certificate showing he was born in a small village in northern Holland and is still a resident there.

Jewish Telegraphic Agency
Volume 56, Number 213
27 November 1975

RED CROSS ARONSON APPEAL UNHEEDED

Amsterdam, 26 November. The International Red Cross Committee have been trying for the past week to obtain permission to visit Alexander Aronson, the Dutch citizen sentenced to death by the Iraqi authorities. Red Cross sources here said today that no permission has as yet been granted for such a visit.

The Iraqi Embassy in the Hague even refused to accept a gift parcel from his mother. An Embassy spokesman said Aronson "is an enemy of Iraq" and as such is not entitled to any help or assistance.

The Dutch Foreign Minister has summoned the Iraqi Chargé d'Affaires for yet another meeting in Holland's efforts to clarify the situation and find out what Aronson's fate is. There was no statement following the meeting.

Jewish Telegraphic Agency
Volume 56, Number 217
3 December 1975

HOLLAND CONTINUES EFFORT ON BEHALF OF ARONSON

Amsterdam, 2 December. The Dutch Foreign Minstry has summoned Iraq's Chargé d'Affaires in the Hague and requested that the Dutch envoy in Baghdad be immediately granted permission to visit the Dutch national Alexander Aronson, imprisoned pending execution on a charge of espionage for Israel.

The Iraqi Chargé d'Affaires was told that the Dutch Government was "very dismayed" at what it regards as a "very unusual state of affairs." The reference was to the Baghdad authorities' refusal to allow visits to Aronson.

(Eds. The following letter was sent to Alan at Oxford by his cousin, Hanan Bar-On, then the Ambassador of Israel to the Hague. It was in reply to a letter of inquiry about Alex.)

Ambassador of Israel
Buitenhof 47
The Hague
12 December 1975

Dear Alan,

Thank you for your letter. I am afraid there is little doubt that Aronson who is in prison (hopefully) in Iraq is the man you know.

The facts of the case, as far as I know them, are the following. In late October, the Iraqi News Agency published a story that an Israeli spy by the name of Aronson, of Dutch origin, had been executed. As Mr. Aronson's parents lived in Holland (divorced for the last 30 years), the case naturally aroused a great deal of attention here, and the Dutch Government protested vigorously to the Iraqi Ambassador here. A few days later, the Iraqis announced that there had been a mistake and, even though Aronson has been condemned as a spy, he has as yet not been executed and is still alive. The Dutch authorities demanded to interview with Aronson in prison, but this has been until now denied to them. There is therefore no clarity at present whether he is alive or dead.

As far as I know, Aronson went to Kurdistan late in 1974 to work at a field hospital. I am not clear whether he went on his own or on behalf of the "Save the Children Fund." One thing is absolutely clear: he certainly had nothing to do with spying or working for Israel. I am sure that he was in Kurdistan purely on humanistic grounds. There is evidence by a Dr. Nabarro of the "Save the Children Fund" in London that he was last seen alive on 24 March 1975, and the same evidence said that he was actually killed (or executed) a few days later. But, at least I have not yet seen any confirmation of that.

I am sorry if all of this sounds a bit vague, but this in the meantime is the best I can do.

We are about to leave Holland and are being moved to Washington, which means that we will see the family, and I very much hope both of you as well.

Aliza sends her fondest greetings to you and Sara. All the best.

Shalom,

Hanan

Wolfson College
Oxford, England
20 December 1975

Mr. Hanan Bar-On
Ambassador of Israel
Buitenhof 47
The Hague

Dear Hanan,

Thank you very much for answering so quickly and in such detail. The additional facts you gave make it certain that the person involved is or was my friend. Along with the sadness, I cannot help feeling a sense of irony. As you probably know, in his early childhood, he was in a Nazi concentration camp; and now this, "payment" for a life devoted to his humanitarian concerns. After serving in the Israeli army (I believe), he travelled extensively in the Middle East. Though he had a deep commitment to Israel, he always extolled the virtues of the simple Arabs. Despite the facts and his own liberal attitudes, it is ironic that he should have been linked in the "minds" of the Iraqi authorities with Israel. What I am getting at is that, like the assimilated Jews of Germany before the War, he did not escape his past or his people.

I am not very optimistic. He could be very stubborn and was outspoken and principled, not one who would take imprisonment lying down. I think that, among other things, he may have miscalculated the nature of those who imprisoned him. At times I thought he courted martyrdom. In his own peculiar way, I don't think he would have considered Israel an unworthy cause to die for, though it must have troubled him that he hadn't helped bring peace in the process. (He always thought in cosmic terms.)

If, in your remaining time in Holland, you hear anything further about my friend, I'd be most appreciative if you made a mental note for me. If you are interested, I'll fill you in on other details when I see you next. Again, many thanks.

Yours truly,

Alan

(Eds. International interest in Alex's fate grew. Yet the authorities preferred a quiet approach, as is evident in this letter sent by Alex's mother to Alan.)

Amsterdam
19 January 1976

Dear Mr. Mendelson,

I am the mother of Leendert (I call him Lex) Aronson and remember your name quite well as one of Lex's friends. First of all, I wish to thank you very heartily for your gift on behalf of the special Committee called "Helpt Leendert Aronson." I got your letter from Elisabeth, who asked me to write to you because she has so very much to do with three children to take care of and not much help.

I am very sorry to have to inform you that there is no news about my son — except that the Dutch government is sure he is alive, but in prison. The Committee has done everything it could... cables to the United Nations, Amnesty International, publicity where possible, and so on... however without success.

I can tell you that the Dutch government has done its best to gain access to my son, but so far the answer has been no. Dutch newspapers, television, and radio have treated this matter often and in detail...so far with the same negative result.

So we have to wait and wait and wait, following the Dutch government's view that it is better to give no more publicity for the present.

Once again I thank you sincerely and remain faithfully,

(Mrs.) S. van Straten-
Cohen

(Eds. Like Alex before him, Leo Aronson wrote directly to the Queen of the Netherlands. The matter was referred to the Foreign Minister, who favored a "bilateral approach" and urged restraint. By the time these meetings took place and this advice was given, Alex was dead.)

Ministry of Foreign
Affairs
The Hague

12 February 1976

Dear Mr. Aronson,

Referring to your letter of 29 January 1976 to her Majesty the Queen which has been forwarded to me, I'd like to inform you of the following in connection with our 8 January meeting.

I seriously regret that the Iraqi authorities have still not reacted positively to the Dutch request for the release of your son and that the temporary Chargé d'Affaires has not been granted permission to see him.

In order to pursue these objectives, I prefer to take a bilateral rather than a unilateral approach.

One can lodge a complaint with the International Court of Justice or through the United Nations, as you suggest, but even if one is in the right, these organizations can but insist, without having the power to force an execution of their decision.

The publicity of one or the other would, in my opinion, not work in your son's favor. The only way we might succeed is through repeated approaches to the Iraqi authorities on a bilateral level.

As you must know, this procedure is under constant discussion, especially with the temporary Chargé d'Affaires in Baghdad.

I can assure you that this Ministry is doing everything possible to reach the hoped for solution and that I am personally attending to your situation.

Mr. Max van der Stoel
[Foreign Minister]

DUTCH PROTESTS IRAQI EXECUTION OF ALLEGED SPY
from the "International Herald Tribune"

The Hague, 16 March. The Netherlands recalled its chargé d'affaires from Baghdad today for consultations on Iraq's execution of a Dutch Jew accused of espionage. A Foreign Ministry spokesman said the Netherlands was not severing its diplomatic relations with Iraq.

Announcement of the recall of the chargé, Gerben Meihuizen, came hours after the ministry said Iraq had confirmed that it executed Leendert Aronson, 40, three months ago.

Iraq took the view that the matter did not concern the Dutch government. The Iraqi chargé d'affaires here, Ismail Said al-Khadi, told reporters, "It is proved that Leendert Aronson was an Israeli citizen. As a Zionist spy who caused much damage and suffering to our people, he was sentenced to death by an Iraqi court and was executed."

Mr. Aronson, a male nurse, was reported to have been arrested by Iraqi security forces last March in a Kurdish area of northern Iraq, and convicted of spying for Israel by a revolutionary tribunal in October.

In Jerusalem, officials said Mr. Aronson was neither an Israeli citizen nor a spy.

(Eds. This is a translation of a feature article by Jos van Noord which appeared in the Dutch national daily, the "Telegraaf," on 17 March 1976. Two days earlier, the Iraqi authorities had informed Alex's family that the execution had already taken place.)

ARONSON SENT HIS PARENTS NOTES FROM IRAQI PRISON

"What kept us going these last months was that we received several notes in December last year through contacts in Germany and Switzerland. These notes had been smuggled out of jail in Baghdad. Therefore we were certain that our son was still alive in December. We had signs of life.

"My ex-wife and I have kept this to ourselves. Even the Ministry of Foreign Affairs did not know that in December we still had proof of life. We didn't dare to talk about it because ex-prisoners passed on the letters.

"Nobody can imagine how we feel now. All hopes smashed at once. There is nothing left to fight for." So said the grieved, disraught father of the 40-year-old son who is no longer alive. The Iraqi authorities phoned through on Monday afternoon (15 March) informing his mother that he was executed on 15 December. Father Leo Aronson, a 67-year-old retired accountant from Amsterdam Sloderdijk, showed us the last of the smuggled letters of his executed son and revealed the deep secret which for months had held him and his wife in a tight grip. "Now we can only try not to get too depressed."

Deepest Secret

The letters which Alex had smuggled out of jail shortly before his execution via fellow prisoners are written on cigarette papers. Both parents recognized their son's handwriting. Also these letters contain certain details only Alex could know, his mother explained. She interprets the fact that he wrote [in the first letter to arrive, dated 21 November] about an inflammation of the ear as proof that the notes are from Alex himself. He suffered frequently with this ailment. The second letter to arrive is dated three days before his execution [on 12 December]. On 29 December, Father Aronson received a third and last letter via a Geneva contact. This one, 5 cigarette papers long, had been posted by a Kurd in Tehran. It appears to have been written (earlier than the other two), on 9 November which is six days after the false information leaked from the Iraqi press bureau (INA), and two days after the Dutch government, believing the execution had taken place, asked for the body.

Father Aronson: "I never even dared to inform our Chargé d'Affaires in Baghdad about these letters from my son. Twice I travelled to Germany and Switzerland to collect them from contacts who have to be kept unknown for their own safety. These small signs of life were my only hope for months. That is why I knew that my son was still alive in mid-December when the Iraqis had already spread news of his execution."

Lies

"For months, nothing but lies have been perpetrated by the Iraqis; but the Iraqi authorities did not know that I could prove their news wrong with Alex's letters. Now that Alex seems to have been murdered, afterall, I can reveal these lies. Alex was murdered in cold blood.

"The fact that he was a Jew was his death sentence. When he left for Kurdistan last year to work in refugee camps, a friendly minister from Leeuwarden [Rev. Schaaf] warned him that he was going to an enemy country. Alex replied, 'I am going to help other people, fellow men in despair. In spite of the fact that he spent his childhood in a Nazi concentration camp, Alex always trusted people...."

(Eds. Alex's final communications with the Dutch Embassy and his family are reproduced below. They have been placed in chronological order.)

Central Prison, Iraq
9 November 1975

To the Dutch Embassy:

My first worry is for my wife and child. Because I have not been able to send a testimonial to the *intkeringsread A'dam* [for war reparation income], I fear that my wife has not received any pay since August from the grant due for victims of the 1940-45 war. This is our only source of income. Please intervene in this matter.

As for myself, I am in need of reading material (English), a transistor radio, and money to buy food. I am living off the charity of my fellow prisoners at the moment. Apart from a big mental tiredness, I have no complaints. I am in good health. Treatment since my arrest has been favorable.

I would really appreciate a visit from you and information about what is going on.

* * * * *

(Eds. The following letter to Alex's family was also written on 9 November. It was mailed from Tehran to Geneva.)

This letter will be sent with a fellow prisoner who got out. Since my arrest on 24 March, I have been forbidden to make contact with anybody. Now, after six-and-a-half months in Baghdad prison, I've been transferred to a prison twenty miles to the south. I arrived here on 12 October. A fellow prisoner has a transistor radio, so we received a BBC report in the cell. From this we surmised that the Dutch government has asked for my release. I hope this is true because the mental torture is getting me down. I do not have to tell you that I am innocent of spying, but the tribunal judged otherwise. I am waiting my fate. I am fairly healthy, barring my mental state.

* * * * *

(Eds. This is the letter which was five cigarette papers long. As we received it, this letter was puzzling. Then we realized that in transmission the proper order of the papers must have been obscured. By reorganizing the paragraphs, we discovered a clear and touching document.)

21 November 1975

To the Dutch Embassy in Baghdad

Dear Sir,

There are many rumors about my possibly being freed. Officially, however, I haven't heard anything and I am still living (literally) in fear of death. A visit or some news from you would help a great deal. Are my wife and child well? I myself am suffering from middle ear infection. I am being treated by a specialist thanks to a fellow prisoner.

On 12 October, I was transferred to this place after six- and-a-half months in the prison of the Baghdadi Gestapo.... My fellow prisoners tell me that my name has been mentioned by the BBC and that my extradition has been requested. I hope this is true, for I am sick of the psychological hassling. That I am innocent of any kind of espionage needs no elaboration. The court, however, chose to decide otherwise, so here I am sitting in a death cell awaiting my lot.

I get treated well thanks to further treatment of my fellow prisoners. We are together in the cell. I have got inflammation of the middle ear. I would like to know how my wife and children are.

Alex....

For the attention of my wife, Mrs. E.C. Aronson:

Dear Betje and Alwin,

The death cell in this prison is hardly the place to write a congratulation. Even so I'd like to take this opportunity to wish you a very special day on the 10th and 14th of December [their birthdays]. In thought, I will certainly be with you. In fact, not a day passes that I'm not. I can't do much besides think here.

Fortunately I married a nursery school teacher who taught me to make use of useless materials. From cigarette boxes and silver paper, I make little toys for the children who come to visit my colleagues. This is a fitting task for a useless father and husband like me. Will I ever see you again? God grant that I will be able to be happy with you for a long time yet. If not, I will, together with my grandfather Herman [= Tsvi Cohen, who died in Bergen-Belsen], put in a good word for you with Our Good Lord. To both of you, with or without me, may lots of love be allotted.

Papa

* * * * *

3 December 1975

I am very cold and would like blankets. Have no writing paper. Sorry.

Alex

* * * * *

9 December 1975

To the Dutch Embassy

Dear Sirs,

I am in great need of
(1) News about my chances,
(2) A small transistor rado with short wave for use with round batteries,
(3) English newspapers and paperbacks.

Not immediately in need of money. Fellow prisoners looking after me very well. Would like, please, a warm woolly sweater and woolly socks. It's begining to turn very cold.

Thanks.

* * * * *

12 December 1975

In Kirkuk [35°N, 44°E], I was arrested through the betrayal of a Kurd, or first arrested and then betrayed. In the beginning, I had the help of a solicitor who raised as defense that I was no Israeli. From the first, I too have pointed this out to the Iraqi authorities.

Lately there haven't been any executions. Vice President Saddam Hussein seems to be against capital punishment. I have good faith.

Alex

Afterword

1976 and Beyond

(Ed. Months after the international efforts to release Alex began, Alan received word of his fate and wrote the following letter to Alex's mother.)

Oxford, England
23 March 1976

Dear Mrs. van Straten-Cohen,

Only today did I learn, to my great sorrow, of your dear son's fate. I cannot begin to tell you how grieved I am. Not since the tragedy of Martin Luther King in my native country have I felt so keenly the plight of those rare human beings who are ready to sacrifice themselves for higher principles. And indeed Alex was the rarest man I have had the privilege of knowing — principled, idealistic, and yet a man who was willing to put words into deeds.

People have said in these troubled times that it is not how long a man lives, but it is the quality of his life. I believe this; sadly, it has come to pass that this saying should apply to your beloved son. Yet I can tell you that my own life was changed as a result of knowing him and the thought of his many sacrifices shall remain with me always.

Many years ago I bought many of the great religious classics of the world for Alex's house in Greece. I bought the books from an old man who asked whether I really had the time to study the deep wisdom which those books contained. I said I did not have the time, but that they were for a friend who had a cabin in the mountains of Greece. I said that he had the time as well as the devotion. The old man thought a moment and said, "Then he is saved." I have always thought this was appropriate for Alex.

I would deeply appreciate your conveying these thoughts to

Alex's wife. I am sending this letter to you because I cannot write French; yet I would like her to realize that I am richer for having known her husband.

May you be consoled by the fact that the memory of Alex and the thought of his dedication and sacrifice and of his kindness will live on in me and in the hearts of people in many lands.

Very truly yours,

Alan Mendelson

(Eds. On 7 April 1976, Mrs. van Straten-Cohen arrived in Baghdad. During the following week, she kept a journal. Most of this journal seems to have been written within hours of the events recorded. The editors have made no attempt to free the text of small inconsistencies. Throughout these negotiations, the Iraqis maintained the fiction that Alex was not a Dutch citizen. They resented any connection which Mrs. van Straten-Cohen had with the Dutch Embassy.)

Baghdad
9 April 1976

Today is Friday. At the moment, I am sitting in the Dutch Embassy, and I'm taking advantage of an available typewriter to write the following report.

Wednesday's flight was very fine with excellent service. There were stop-overs in Istanbul (fine weather) and Damascus (partly cloudy). In Istanbul, I was allowed to stand out on the staircase for a breath of fresh air. Most of the passengers disembarked there. We arrived in Istanbul at 1:30 pm (local time) after departing from Amsterdam about 9:45 am. We then flew on over Cyprus and part of the eastern Mediterranean, over Beirut, which was visible although nothing could be discerned from our great height, and then across an inhospitable region of stone huts. In Damascus, we were allowed out of the plane for a brief half-hour. A glance around the airport revealed some poor and miserable folk. We were not allowed outside.

Arrival time in Damascus was approximately 4 o'clock; departure at 4:30. Sand and rocks, few people. We arrived in Baghdad at 7:10 pm (local time which is a two-hour time difference from the Netherlands). I had a pounding headache and actually I didn't get rid of it until today, after getting my first good sleep last night. In taking my leave from the plane, the whole crew wished me strength through friendly glances and gestures. Evidently they were completely aware of my situation although they did not let on. In the airport hall, not nearly as dreary as that of Damascus, our flight captain, Mr. Giessen, even stopped to apologize that it could not have been done for me sooner.

Waiting for me at the airport were Mr. Meihuizen (the Chargé d'Affaires), Ms. Verkuyten (the Embassy Chancellor), and Mr. van den Oord of K.L.M. [Royal Dutch Airlines] who took the responsibility for the declaration of my baggage. And that was no small task because in addition to my suitcase there also was an enormous quantity of [kosher] food which K.L.M. gave me to take along — thanks to the efforts of Rabbi Pereira — even including sandwiches for light meals. Because some of the packages were marked with the name "Israel" and all sorts of Hebrew letters, he had it all wrapped to be out of sight. He managed to get the whole business through customs at once.

Everyone was exceptionally obliging and helpful. First we were driven with Mr. Meihuizen by his chauffeur to an Embassy reception which was for him routine procedure. The Dutch flag was covered after he stepped out of the car. After that we were driven to the Residence, a fantastic house which according to Mr. Meihuizen would bring in a four-figure rent. By good fortune, in 1960 the Dutch government had bought a number of residences with all their amenities in several countries. The house was almost unimaginable, something out of the movies, with a round staircase that descends into the main hall and everything made of marble. It was decorated very tastefully, and there were many rooms, each having its own function. On the second floor, I was given a bedroom, a sitting room, and a bathroom. Unfortunately, Mrs. Meihuizen and the children were not in Iraq, but rather in Holland on matters of schooling. Nevertheless, the lovely little passover packages were most welcome in the hands of Mr. Meihuizen himself, along with his consul and his secretary. (Mr. Meihuizen has a self-confessed sweet tooth.)

So my accommodation is most comfortable although I am restricted to the Residence. It is surrounded by park-like grounds where I can sit and read. Probably not such a bad thing so I can get some rest. I slept only till 4:00 am on the first night in spite of a sleeping pill and retiring that Wednesday evening at 11:00 pm. Fortunately, I brought appropriate clothing. Yesterday it was much colder than today; a sweater was even needed. But as soon as the sun shines it gets quite warm.

On Thursday morning, at 8:30, I was picked up to go to the Embassy so that I might personally telephone the [Iraqi] Ministry of Foreign Affairs and ask for a particular person (the Director-General of the Consular Department of the Ministry of Foreign Affairs). First, I got to speak to his secretary, who asked if I was the "genuine" mother, something which they later asked me again at the office. I was told to be there at 10:30.

The man spoke poor English, his secretary much better, but still hard to understand. They were quite courteous, offered me tea and cigarettes, of which I accepted the latter. Then it became clear from our conversation that they would allow me to visit Lex's grave! "But that's not what I came here for," I answered. I did my best to convince them that my original visa had been issued with permission to visit him in prison. But now, since that was no longer possible, it would follow from my application and from the permission received via Rabbi Pereira that we were now dealing with the retrieval of Lex's mortal remains.

They then raised several objections, in particular an Iraqi law (which they also held to apply to the world at large) which forbids such retrieval within the first year after death. I spoke against that, suggesting that it might be so in their country, but certainly not in the rest of the world, and that I had a friend here who was prepared to concern himself with the resolution of the whole matter. However, they were not to be budged. Then I asked about the exact date (of death) which appeared to have been 6 December. And then the manner (of death) at which point I lost my composure.

(Eds. The date of Alex's death was not 6 December. As Mrs. van Straten-Cohen knew, Alex wrote a note from prison six days later.)

Silence all around, and then: "We have sympathy for a mother; I shall take your concern to the Minister of Health." Then I asked, "Please make an exception and let me speak to the Minister myself." But he said that wasn't necessary because his word was good, and I could count on that. Then once more he asked, "Don't you want to visit the grave?" I answered, "Not now, but I'll think it over." Then he: "You are welcome here, and you can come whenever you want." To this I replied: "Do you think I can amuse myself in a country that killed my son?" I quickly concluded in my own mind that it would not be advisable to visit Lex's grave; it would set a precedent which they might use to their own advantage.

Later, during a visit from the Pakistani Ambassador, I was sent with the secretary for a while into another room. Then the secretary started to give me reasons why Lex had been brought to trial. There had been (in their eyes) objectionable materials. He asked if I had previously been in the Middle East, in Lebanon. "No, but in Israel (here a forbidden word) with your enemy; we are cousins!" Then followed a discourse about politics during which I kept quiet.

Back to the Minister who asked where I was staying in Baghdad. "At the (Dutch Ambassador's) Residence", I replied, only to get a disapproving glance. "What do you expect? I am a Dutch woman." In leaving, I asked again that they put in a good word for me. We arranged that I would call for a reply. I also told them how hard it had been for me to adapt to their terms and that I couldn't really leave my husband alone (to say nothing about the cost of the journey).

The whole time the car had been waiting (about two hours). There was a consultation with the Chargé d'Affaires at the Embassy, who agreed with my actions. Then back home and a hot meal. Mr. Meihuizen drove me around a bit. Never in my life had I expected to see the Tigris. At 2:00 pm on Thursday afternoon the day off began; it lasted until Saturday morning.

Later, in the garden, I made some drawings of part of the house. Mr. Meihuizen had a nap; that evening he would be receiving a delegation from Italy at the "Club." I resolved to go to bed in good time, but didn't manage to do so until 10:30 pm. Before he went out, I prepared some tea for Mr. Meihuizen which we took together while talking everything over once again. He gave me an article by Renate Rubinstein [referred to in Postscript]. He also mentioned that Mr. de Graaff had been asked to report on what had happened. I asked if I could also speak with Mr. de Graaff myself. I told him everything, and he said I had done well. We agreed, then, that he would now make contact with the International Red Cross, both in Holland and in Geneva. He asked with whom I had talked at the Iraqi Embassy in The Hague. (Ms. Rosemarie had told him that I did not get to see [Iraqi Chargé d'Affaires] Said al-Khadi.) Thereupon he promised to make contact with Rabbi Pereira concerning his conversation with the aforementioned....

For me the question remains whether we are doomed to failure because our initiative has come from Dutch Officialdom. Indeed, that is the question, agreed Mr. Meihuizen. Would it help or hinder? Personally, I was considering writing a letter to the President of France requesting mediation. So much for now. It is now Friday afternoon, 1:30 pm. The office here is closed on Sundays.

After lunch in the afternoon, Mr. Meihuizen always has a nap, which is in keeping with the local custom here. I did not do this because I feel worse after getting up than before I lie down. Later on, we went to a wooded area of palms that lies in the middle of Baghdad where you can find some peace. Baghdad itself is a witches' cauldron.

Mr. Meihuizen wanted to sell his horse which is stabled at the park, and we met the Danish Chargé d'Affaires who appeared to be the aspiring buyer. He had two young children with him in riding gear. A little conversation ensued. After that, we drove around a bit and saw some beautiful houses and in between them clay huts which were also inhabited.

Today the weather was summery, but generally speaking it is still very changeable, and it is always advisable to carry a sweater. That night [Friday] I could not sleep, and I took more than the usual quantity of sleep medication. Mr. Meihuizen had gone out after we had tea together.

Friday is just like Sunday in Holland. Along the Tigris, you would see many men sitting in the cafés. The next day there was no sign of the sun. I forgot to mention that Friday evening during tea, Mr. Meihuizen spoke by telephone with Mr. de Graaff who had in the meantime had contact with Said al-Khadi who claimed to have heard officially that I could go to Baghdad "to supervise the transport of the body of my son." Al-Khadi would have needed absolute assurance from the authorities to make this possible.

The next day telephone contact was made through Mr. Meihuizen with Mr. Khazraji... about this matter. He later called back on his own (which was most remarkable!) to summon me at 11 am to see Mr. Sibahi, Director General of the Consular Department.

Mr. Sibahi started with a bit of small-talk about what I had been doing in Baghdad. Had I been to Babylon? Had I been to the Baghdad museum? What had been interesting for me? Then I showed him the letter and asked if he would endorse it with his signature, so that I would not have to go home with empty hands because from the letter it appeared that the bodily remains would be released. However, when he saw the letter he became angry and said, "You can spoil everything with this. We don't know any Leendert Aronson; who is Leendert Aronson?" So saying, he handed back my certificate. With this my hopes of leaving matters in the trustworthy hands of Mr. Meihuizen and returning home on Sunday were completely dashed.

I now knew what I had suspected from the first: that I — and I alone — would have to see this matter through to the very end. This became completely clear in the ensuing conversation. I asked what I would have to do, and he replied, "You see, I kept my word. You can get your son if you do what I tell you, and don't involve Mr. Meihuizen." Then we discussed K.L.M. schedules. I would have to make contact personally with Dr. Felix of Public Health who in turn would contact the municipal authorities in Baghdad. Then it might be possible to transport [the remains] on Thursday.

I: " That would be extremely difficult for me because of my observance of *Pesach* [Hebrew, Passover]." He didn't know what that was, but he had a pocket calendar in which he checked the date to see if my assertion was correct. "O.K. You are right; but never mind, you can go to your people here and be together with them [for the Passover]."

In the meantime, I had given Ms. Verkuyten [the Chancellor at the Dutch Embassy] my *Libelle* [a Dutch magazine] to read. She was overjoyed with it, just as she had been with the latest newspapers which I had brought from the plane. For that matter, they are happy here with everything in the way of food, etc.

After nightfall, I drove with Mr. Meihuizen to a *shul* [Yiddish, synagogue] which had been shut down and was no longer in use. Some Iraqi Jews directed us to another *shul* where a service was being held. We arrived there just after the service; however, three men and a boy were still standing around talking. *Matzos* [Hebrew, unleavened bread for the Passover] were lying piled on the benches; they were very different from ours. I asked about their having a *minyan* [Hebrew, a quorum of 10 men, required for public prayer]. "Yes, there would be around 15 people." Would it be possible for me to attend the service on Wednesday evening? And would they be holding a *seder* [Hebrew, a Passover meal]? Yes, I could join a certain family for the *seder*. It was agreed that I would be there. According to Mr. Meihuizen, this is the oldest Jewish community in the world, having begun roughly 700 years B.C.E.

On Saturday afternoon, Mr. Meihuizen sent a telex to Holland to indicate that I would personally finish off the business here and to let my husband know on Sunday that he should hold a kosher seder away from home and that I would be responsible for my own according to *shaliach mitzvah*.

(Eds. Mrs. van Straten-Cohen uses this Hebrew phase to explain to her husband her own failure to observe all the ritual requirements of the Passover. In extraordinary circumstances, the fulfillment of one religious duty {recovering the body of one's son} would take precedence over the ordinary observance of a Festival.)

Sunday, 11 April 1976

Last night I went to bed very late due to much talk with Mr. Meihuizen. I am getting the impression that he is pleased with my presence here. I could be his mother, he is the same age as Lex. We had a bit of drink and watched T.V. Nothing to suit me, just some trashy American movie. All the while I was making some of my rough notes. I didn't sleep much. At 9 o'clock this morning, I tried to phone Dr. Felix of the Ministry of Health. Telephoning is a disaster, but I managed to get through.

I was told that Dr. Felix was out of town, but would return tomorrow. Meanwhile Mr. Meihuizen had come downstairs. He called the same number once again to ask if there was a replacement (for Felix) available. Mr. Meihuizen then discussed with him what was left for me to do and that was quite a lot; too complicated to describe here. Boko, the chauffeur, was drummed up even though it was his day off, and off we went in search of a certain address, where we were redirected somewhere else. Finally, after a long drive, we were given a guide. We arrived at the cemetery where there were hassles again over documents, but then Mr. Meihuizen produced the official permission from the Ministry of

Health. It was all too much for me, and Mr. Meihuizen directed me back to the car.

After endless conversation, we were sent to the undertaker. It was better for me not go inside, although I had a photo and items of identification ready. Mr. Meihuizen came to ask first for one thing, then another. On the basis of these things, the undertaker would identify Lex. Apparently it was true that in this country exhumations were indeed not allowed during the first year after burial, so they had made an exception after all. Again we sat there for a long time; it was very hot in the car.

From the cemetery, we went to the K.L.M. office to deal with the details [of air transport]. It was all quite difficult because of Passover and because a corpse can't sit at Schiphol [Airport]. So a hearse would have to be waiting at the airport to carry off its burden immediately [after landing]. I asked myself who would be able to do that on *yomtov* [a Jewish holiday, when those involved in Jewish burials would not be working]. And where would the corpse be taken? To me the best place seemed the CIZ [central morgue?] although I did not know which undertaker would be able to do that. I wondered whether it would not be better to ask Mr. Sibahi for permission to leave earlier in order to facilitate the arrangements in Holland ahead of time. He had no objection to this, but would have to arrange another meeting with Dr. Felix to ensure that no further signatures would be required of me and that all the formalities were indeed completed. That will be done tomorrow.

Sunday evening, after an elaborate afternoon tea with Mr. Meihuizen, we went to the English library where he returned some books and took out some new ones. When we returned we were both hungry, and I looked after the evening snack. Mr. Meihuizen was delighted with K.L.M. buns and raisin bread. Although I had resolved to retire early after such an emotional day, I offered Mr. Meihuizen a glass of coffee. He was already settled in the T.V. room and, yes, he would love some coffee. The same went for me, so we had some coffee with baked goods from K.L.M. which are highly prized here. I stuck around to watch William Wyler's 1952 movie entitled "Carrie." Not bad for its time! Finally, at quarter to twelve, I was in bed and slept unexpectedly well. In the meantime, I had resolved to go home on Tuesday if we were assured that Lex would be sent along the following Thursday. At the same time, I was racking my brain to figure out how I would manage to observe Pesach in the time available.

Monday, 12 April 1976

As arranged, I phoned Dr. Felix and got through after much difficulty. You could not possibly imagine what I was told: some objections had arisen. Two problems with the city of Baghdad had developed. [Dr. Felix] was not able to explain them to me, but they would prevent the transport from taking place. At least it would not be possible this Thursday.

After this news, Mr. Meihuizen called some other authority to ask what the problems were. He was able to ascertain one thing, namely that the matter would now take three or four months. I discussed this with Mr. Meihuizen, and we determined that it would be best to go back to Mr. Sibahi.

Tuesday, 13 April 1976

I was so discouraged yesterday that I had no appetite to write on. [Today] I went right away in the morning with Mr. Meihuizen to the Embassy and spent the whole morning on this report, with several interruptions for telephone conversations. So I continue.

(Eds. Here Mrs. van Straten-Cohen turns her attention back to the events of the previous day.)

I called Mr. Sibahi who had offered me his help in case there were difficulties. I told him what I had heard from Dr. Felix — that there were two problems having to do with "local law." He was not able to tell me precisely what those problems might be. However, he appeared to know about them already, and he promised me to do his best to solve them, but, from the manner in which he spoke to me, I felt very little hope. Now what? Again I phoned Dr. Felix and, after some floundering talk, Mr. Meihuizen took the phone and maintained firmly that he had seen with his own eyes the permission from the Ministry of Health. But now we had to deal with the "local advisor" who insisted that the law could not be overruled in spite of the exception that the Minister had made. From this it is clear that there are always higher authorities who insist on butting in.

Mr. Meihuizen thus aired his views — he was really quite angry — but he got no further. When I called Mr. Sibahi once again, he had nothing new to report, but said he would keep on working on my behalf. Furthermore I told him (at the prompting of Mr. Meihuizen who did not wish to speak to him personally) that I would not leave the country without Lex, and that I hoped he would be able to convince the Ministry of Health that the transport would have to take place on Thursday. The question is, however, whether this would be enough time, because, according to Mr. Meihuizen, the only authority who could now give the release order was the president of Iraq himself.

The government of this country is a very complicated network of authority. There is a Revolutionary Command Council and also a Baath Command... I can't make head or tail of it. There is also a vice-president of the Command Council (being Saddam Hussein) who appears to have all the power in his own hands.

To return to the conversation with Mr. Sibahi... Well, he had nothing further to say other than that I should call him the following day (today, Tuesday) at 12 o'clock. So for all intents and purposes another day had gone by because all the offices close at 2 o'clock. Finally I told Mr. Sibahi that I had come to the end of my strength. According to Mr. Meihuizen they don't care one bit about that.

Mr. Sibahi then repeated his earlier comment that "I have feelings for a mother." I do believe that he is making an extra effort for me. Yet, I had the feeling that I was "fighting against the brew" [Dutch metaphor = "paddling up-stream"]. Apparently that is the norm here. Even Mr. Meihuizen remains pessimistic as long as Lex is not yet in the airplane. In the meantime, it was time to close shop, and we went home to eat. I was very tired, and, after sitting in the garden for half an hour (no sun all day but not cold), I did lie on my bed for a while. Generally speaking, I find that there is little opportunity for fresh air here. Not my style....

At about 5 pm, Mr. Meihuizen and I happened to get up simultaneously so I made some tea. (The cook and his son arrive here at 4:00 am in order to get space on the bus. Everyday, an enormous flood of people comes into the city from their village. When they arrive at the Residence, they sleep for a couple of hours after which they begin their work, cooking and cleaning up, father and son. Then in the afternoon at around 3:30 pm they return home.)

At the Embassy, there is an attendant who looks after all the little errands including the supply of coffee and tea. Yesterday I drank some Turkish coffee there for the first time; I actually prefer it to the instant coffee which they use here at the Residence.

Well, where was I? Oh yes, we had tea. As Mr. Meihuizen had several things to do, he asked me if I minded staying alone. I had plenty to do and of course I let him go his way. I told him that I would finally be able to go to bed early and that I might even be in bed when he returned. However, that was not to be the case because I had just started the dishes when I heard Mr. Meihuizen coming home. (I always leave the kitchen immaculate even though, according to Mr. Meihuizen, I might just as well leave the dishes alone, but I don't like that....) He appeared to be ready for a glass of coffee, like I had made for him previously, and to keep him company I also took half a glass.

Mr. Meihuizen had been in touch with Mr. van den Oord of K.L.M. who had been able to tell him that the casket maker had been given the red light by the authorities. It was not good news. Nothing to do but wait; later I will phone again, now it is almost 12 o'clock. I am glad to report that Mr. Meihuizen told me last night that in his opinion I was conducting myself very well, especially in my conversations with Mr. Sibahi which, for example, I would begin with: "You are speaking with Mrs. van Straten from Holland. Can I have a few minutes of your time to speak with you about the following question?...".

I often have to think of father in this regard, who always said: "Knowledge is power; the more you know, the better you are equipped for life." And indeed, my 40 years of experience in the office are standing me in good stead.

(Eds. At the most difficult times, Mrs. van Straten-Cohen thinks of her father who perished in Bergen-Belsen. Alex did precisely the same thing, for one of his last notes from prison mentions his maternal grandfather.)

Tuesday, 13 April 1976, later in the day, 4:00 pm

This morning I did manage to get Mr. Sibahi on the line, friendly as ever, just like myself, but I was devastated by what I heard from him: "You spoke on your own with Dr. Muttar." (Apparently Dr. Muttar is a civil servant with the municipal secretariat; I had mistakenly spoken to him, thinking I was speaking with Dr. Felix.) "Now everything is spoiled," continued Mr.

Sibahi, "I told you explicitly that only you as mother could act in this affair, and you have not done that."

I replied: "Mr. Sibahi, I could not understand the speaker; that is the only reason I gave the telephone to somebody else. Listen, Mr. Sibahi, let me come to your office right now. I shall explain everything to you." Then I hurried to his office where they let me in right away. I was very nervous, took his hand and held it tightly, begging him to understand that I could not be held personally responsible for what had been said by someone else. What case was being made? I guess I knew that already. I didn't agree [that I had done wrong], but I couldn't set it right anymore now.

(Eds. From the following remarks, it is clear that the Iraqi authorities took a dim view of the interventions of Mr. Meihuizen. In particular, they seem to have resented his getting angry on the telephone with Dr. Felix the previous day.)

Yesterday, Mr. Meihuizen said in his agitated state that surely there was a ministerial decree and that permission had been granted. He had further implied that these complications never would have arisen in our country. In short, he had been critical of their procedure. And they were not about to take that, especially from the mouth of Mr. Meihuizen, he being the Dutch Chargé d'Affaires. Moreover, it was now plain to them that he was involved in the whole business.

At this point, I have to emphasize that I would not have been able to carry on without Mr. Meihuizen "behind the scenes." I would have been totally lost in this strange land all on my own; however, evidently his support was not to be tolerated.

In the rest of our conversation, I avoided using Mr. Meihuizen's name. Then Mr. Sibahi said: "But you could have called me." To this I replied: "But Mr. Sibahi, you are a busy man, why should I disturb you only because of not understanding somebody? I have a good relationship with you and, believe me, it is not my fault. What can I do now?" He: "You understand that we cannot allow ourselves to be insulted."

I agreed, but he went on to say that this business was now beyond his area of competence. The final decision rested with the president and of course that could not be given very quickly. "In your country, is it not also impossible to speak with your queen within one or two days?" "Indeed, you are right," I answered, "and therefore you doubt that our business can be completed by Thursday?" There was no direct reply. "What about Thursday of next week?" I asked. He: "Does K.L.M. fly only on Thursdays?" "Yes, Sir," I replied.

The strange thing in all of this is that I am not thinking at all about Lex when such conversations are taking place. It is just as if I am talking about some business deal, and it is exactly that which gives me strength even though in reality I am dead tired, especially after being terribly disappointed.

Finally, I added that I couldn't stay away from home any longer; my husband couldn't be left alone any longer; on Thursday I would have to leave. He: "You can get the coffin. We will take care of the transport; you will get a message from our Embassy in The Hague." Then I asked: " Can I write you directly from Amsterdam?" No, he said, that would not be possible. I would have to go through Mr. al-Khadi, who would send my letter on.

Back to the car, where Ms. Verkuyten, who often accompanied me, and the chauffeur were waiting. Once we were seated, she asked, "Did you remember to renew your visa?" (I should have done that in the office because it is only valid until today.) I went right back into the office. I made excuses about being nervous and forgetting to renew my visa. They asked me to leave my passport with them. It would be looked after, and I could call tomorrow. I agreed. As the official was leafing through the entire passport, he asked me what my name actually was. Mrs. Cohen? No, Mrs. van Straten, first name Sara. "In Holland a married woman takes the name of her husband," said the person who would take care of the renewal. I: "You see, I am an old woman." He: "Nonsense, (with gestures) you are beautiful!"

Back to the car, where I relate some of my misery. Ms. Verkuyten: "I must say, we three [Mr. Meihuizen, Annemarie Venekamp and Ms. Verkuyten] are completely amazed by how well you are handling everything. I mean that from the bottom of my heart; you are a most remarkable woman."

At the Embassy, I brought Mr. Meihuizen up to date and impressed upon him, with my index finger waving in his face, "Remember, not one single step from Dutch Officialdom as long as Lex remains outside of Holland!!" He had already been planning to send a note of protest. After Lex is home, I don't care what they do. Tomorrow a telegram will go to Foreign Affairs [in Holland] relaying these sentiments.

Wednesday, 14 April 1976

Yesterday we returned home between 2:00 and 2:30 pm. Mr. Meihuizen had a nap after lunch. I could not sit outside because of nasty weather. At any rate, there was little time; I was busy making the rough notes that I always then type up the next day. I also tried to read a bit, but, before I knew it, tea-time had arrived. I usually get changed for tea.

So it is Wednesday, a regular office day, and I wanted to pick up my visa, bid farewell to Mr. Sibahi and ask him what he would want me to say if the press were to accost me. "What do you want?" was his answer. "Just say how you have liked it here. You have been our guest. Can you say anything bad about us? Are you satisfied?"

I: "No, that I cannot say. You received me politely, and you personally did everything to steer matters towards a good ending. However, if I could take the body with me [when I leave], then I would be satisfied. As it is now, I am disappointed. But since you promised me that you would be willing to push and push so that my son will follow me soon, I shall be hopeful."

The question is, of course, whether Mr. Sibahi will be allowed any influence. It won't be up to him. Mr. Meihuizen came up with the good idea of leaving with Mr. Sibahi a personal letter from myself to the president (with a copy in my possession). I asked Mr. Sibahi to make use of it. Whether he actually does remains to be seen. I suspect that the verdict will be yes or no without many preliminaries and then such a letter would be of little use. However, Mr. Sibahi did ask to read the letter. Of course, I had left the envelope open, and I had to help him with some of the English words that he did not understand.

Then I returned to the question of publicity. "You can say what you will," he repeated. Then again the tiresome tale about their hospitality etc. I thought to myself I will end this quickly and put in writing what I want to say. Immediately I was referred to a Mr. Ali, who had responsibilities for such matters. This one understood no English whatsoever, and the whole conversation was translated into Arabic by Mr. Sibahi, for which he apologized. Once again we drank their strong tea in cocktail glasses with a layer of sugar on the bottom. I said to him, "I like your tea", and offered him a mint. Then I wrote down what I would say to the press and read it aloud:

"I have been received here politely. You did everything to arrange the matter to a good ending, that means that I could take the body of my son together with me [on the same flight home]. But there are problems — raised by local and health authorities. They will try to make an exception [in this case] and have promised me that the body will follow me within a short time. I am disappointed, but satisfied with this promise."

I do not know if I can believe their promise. There was still some discussion about the practical questions that I had raised, especially with regard to the appointment of an undertaker and a casket-maker. I told him that I had understood that someone had already begun to work on a casket. This was a shock to Mr. Sibahi. "Who would that be?" I mentioned the name of Mr. William Hanna and explained that I had already been to see him. I asked whether I should continue on with that man or whether I should cancel the arrangement. "Do you know the address of this man?" "No, I replied, "but I can give you his address and telephone number when I call you afterwards." That was all right with him.

Then Mr. Sibahi began to ask me all kinds of questions concerning Lex himself. No doubt he saw on my face that I wasn't keen to pursue this matter, and so he re-assured me that it was only for his own personal interest. Did I have other children? "No, he was my only son." I told him that before the war I had been divorced from Lex's father and had re-married in 1948. I told him that I had been with Lex in a concentration camp. He knew nothing of these. Where had that been? "In Bergen-Belsen." He had never heard of it.

I told him that Lex had saved my life there; that we had been liberated by the Russians; that we were returned to Holland by the Red Cross more dead than alive. How old was he at that time? "He was 11." And did he stay with you? "Yes, sure."

Then I told him about Lex's restlessness and his obsession with helping people. Well then, was he a doctor? "No, but he was a nurse, and he knew a lot about medicine. He helped everywhere, all over the world." I named Greece, Bangladesh, India, Pakistan whose ambassador had been to this office this week. Mr. Sabihi had never heard of Albert Schweitzer!

"But here people said..." and he did not know how to describe it and instead pointed at his head. "You mean, you think he was mad? No, he was not mad, although he was a strange boy; no ordinary human being." Was he unbalanced then? "Perhaps the war-experience had affected him. He did not listen to me when I told him not to go on his travels. I warned him. He was a restless man. He could not stay long in any one place; neither with me, nor with his wife."

He had been married? "Yes, but not with a Jewish woman. I have a little grandchild." And still the burial will be in a Jewish cemetery? "Indeed, he remains a Jew." In Amsterdam? "Of course, and I will not be satisfied until I can visit him there and I hope it will be soon".

We shook hands, and I got my passport back.

Back at the Embassy there was a pleasant surprise for me in the form of two telexes from my family. I gave a detailed report of the morning's activities. Then there was more to do. We had to look after another formality whereby Mr. Meihuizen would act as the official representative of our state and by which I was presented with the official death certificate. In this the date of death was given as 27 January 1976, which did not agree with the previously given date, but Mr. Meihuizen had read himself the date of 27 January in a declaration of the Iraqi Minister of Health, and we felt it would be best to accept the date as such.

I said goodbye to Annemarie, the secretary, who kissed me on both cheeks and would be happy to visit me in Amsterdam. Back at the Residence, after lunch, I went to pack because at 5:30 pm I had to be at *shul* [for the beginning of the festival of Passover]. I was welcomed by the community, but they didn't know who I was and they were very surprised that a Dutch Jewess would have come to Baghdad. So I explained it all to them. Some of them spoke English and/or French. At the service, there were 25 men and 6 women. There was some free time after the service and before beginning the seder which was now being held at the shul in my honor, for they were afraid to receive me in their homes. Those who stayed were 6 or 7 men and 4 women. I don't think they were orthodox although they did keep the festivals.

There used to be many synagogues in Baghdad which had 150,000 Jewish inhabitants before 1948. Now only one *shul* was being used; it served 300 people, many of whom were elderly. I had no trouble following the seder in a mini-*haggadah* [Hebrew, a booklet containing the ritual for the Passover], even though it was very different from ours. I was very moved when they offered a *yiskor* [Hebrew, prayer for the dead] for Lex. I was asked to light one of the *yomtov* [Hebrew, festival] candles. And they allowed me to decide for myself how long I wanted to stay.

I told them about our customs both before and after the *seder* meal, and indeed that's how they also did it. So keeping in mind the time, I asked if they would agree that I [leave right after] the meal. It was agreed that I would be taken to the Embassy, and from there the Embassy chauffeur would take me back to the Residence. Mr. Meihuizen had already started to worry a bit because it was getting late. I suggested to Mr. Meihuizen that he should phone his wife, which he found most delightful. They will come together to visit me [in Amsterdam] at an opportune time.

Because of the bustle at the airport the next morning, it was not possible to bid a proper farewell to Ms. Verkuyten and the Chargé d'Affaires who had nevertheless both come to escort me. The service in the K.L.M. airplane was exceptionally good, just like on the journey to Baghdad. I will certainly write them a note of thanks.

I felt more than relieved and overjoyed when at Schiphol I set foot again on Dutch ground. According to Mr. Meihuizen, my mission had not been in vain, for my efforts put things into motion.

Postscript:

My own impression now is that Lex could not have been rescued from Iraq through normal channels because of their lack of understanding and reason, their deficiencies in internal communication, their totally different mentality, and their apparently unwitting hatred for everything Jewish. I would say that I agree with Renate Rubinstein (see article in *Vrij Nederland* of 3 and 10 April) that our silence was disastrous and that something might well have been accomplished by shaking up the powers-that-be around the world. After all, there were people everywhere who knew about this business.

[translated by Hans van Nie]

(Eds. Alex's funeral took place on 21 May 1976 at the Jewish Cemetery in Muiderberg, on the outskirts of Amsterdam. We have obtained copies of two eulogies which were delivered on that occasion. The first was given by Alex's mother; the second, by Rev. Ype Schaaf. Elisabeth, Alex's widow, had agreed that Alex could be buried in a Jewish cemetery — providing that a Christian could also speak there. The second eulogy, then, was part of that arrangement.)

EULOGY by Sara van Straten-Cohen

My beloved son,

In Baghdad, I stood at the entrance of the cemetery and had the opportunity to visit your grave. At the time, I could not bring myself to do that. It was not just for emotional reasons. I did not want people to be able to say that [a visit to your grave] was the only reason for my journey to Iraq and therefore allow the rest of the business to lapse.

However, the Iraqi authorities have kept their word and now that we stand by your final resting place in the land where you were born, I will bid you my proper farewell. It goes without saying that I am doing this with a wounded heart. For a long time, we were closely bonded in our shared life together... until you started to find your own way which took you into the service of humanity.

Given the risks that you took for your belief in justice — and especially when you told me you wanted to go and help in Kurdistan which borders a country whose name alone gives me the shivers — you gave me great cause for anxiety. And I suppose that you didn't fully realize that this trip might lead to the end of your well-spent life.

You have left us with the certainty that you lived your life exactly how you wanted to live it, and I realize that few of us can make that claim. We will not forget this as time goes on.

We did not see you all that often, but you did come regularly, and you were always a welcome guest at our table, especially on Friday evenings when you showed us you had not forgotten the *benchen* [Yiddish, grace after meals]. May God give your soul the rest that you have earned.

I want to thank Bets, my daughter-in-law, for the support and the help that she was able to give you as your wife while allowing you the opportunity to serve humankind in those places where help was needed.

Rabbi Pereira, permit me to thank you again, and this time in public, for your many initiatives, your mediation, the huge amount of work and your active support that ultimately led to this result. I sincerely hope that Bets, Lex's father, and I may now finally be at peace with the whole matter.

I am aware that on behalf of our Government, Mr. de Graaff is here representing [Foreign Minister] Mr. van der Stoel. Mr. de Graaff, for months we were in close contact, and I want to offer you my sincere thanks for coming today and for all the trouble you took to help. Please convey my deep gratitude to the Minister. It goes without saying that I also include in this Mr. Meihuizen and his staff in Baghdad who helped me in every possible way "behind the scenes."

Last but not least, I cannot leave unmentioned the co- operation of K.L.M. which was offered to me in so many ways, and for which I express my heartfelt thanks with special mention of Mr. van den Oord and his superiors.

Dearest Lex, I close by telling you that I will miss your ringing laugh and the unexpected appearance of your robust figure framed in the kitchen window till the day of my own death.

[translated by Hans van Nie]

GOODBYE FROM ALEX by Rev. Ype Schaaf

Talking about Alex Aronson in ordinary terms is impossible; for he was anything but ordinary. He was a special kind of individual, and that made his life risky.

For nine months he helped us out by training volunteer telephone operators for the nightly S.O.S. telephone service in Friesland. Then, suddenly, he called me with a question: Could I find him a place as a volunteer at a disaster somewhere in the Third World?

Was restlessness part of his natural disposition? Was it the result of damage he sustained in his childhood? I do not know. One thing is clear... It was not a simple desire for adventure. He was too intelligent for that.

Anyway, I asked my contacts in Dutch volunteer agencies about the need for emergency help. At the time, there was none.

Two days later, Alex told me that he was going to Kurdistan. My reaction was immediate: "Alex, you cannot do this. You will not survive, for you are a son of the Old Nation."

He replied that just because he was a Jew, he wanted to show that it could be done. It was as if he were ready to give his life to prove that humanity exists. For in an emergency nobody is an enemy or a stranger.

And with his big smile, he added: "You know me. I am a Jew and therefore a survivor. I'll manage."

When Alex first wanted to help us out at the S.O.S. telephone service, I made inquiries. Every organization for which he had done work praised his qualities, while warning me to be careful with him. They were right. Alex was very suspicious of organizations and bureaucracy. "They see people as objects, as files, as cases," he used to say.

Alex could analyze the weaknesses of the Dutch welfare system with the insight of a scribe. But he also opposed these organizations with their rules and procedures by acting as a clever loner in unorthodox ways. He could fight them in the interest of one single human being. And that brought him into conflict with the welfare establishment. His only answer was a grin.

I first met Alex in prison in the Cameroons in West Africa. He had been on his way to meet Albert Schweitzer in neighboring Gabon when he was arrested for travelling without an entry permit. Schweitzer appealed to him because thinking and doing were as one for him. Alex also did what he thought. Right or wrong.

That is Jewish, for in the Torah the Hebrew word dabar means both word and deed. Alex did what he said in this Biblical way. Therefore it is right to bury his body in a Jewish cemetery. But he will not rest here as an orthodox man. He was an outsider, who understood more of the prophets than of the priests. And if he should have heard me say this, he would have laughed his big laugh and said: "Ype, you will always remain a preacher."

And yet, when he left the S.O.S. office to go to Kurdistan, we wanted to give him a history of Friesland. He refused it and asked for a concordance of the Old Testament.

In these last months of uncertainty, his wife once said to me: "I often don't know where he is. But it's nice that we have been able to do some things together, even though we have been unable to discuss them." She was referring to the adoption of an Indian girl whom he had sent from Calcutta to Holland with a passport carrying the name of Wilhelmina Aronson.

And this morning Mrs. Aronson said to me, "I have supported this man, this complicated man. I stood by his side. Because of this, the emptiness will be very great."

At this point, Alex would say: "Stop this. It's enough." All right, but I would like to say one more thing. Alex Aronson lived his human potential. He burst the balloon of our inhuman drive for organization. He wanted to cross unjust human borders. For this he died.

(Eds. An unveiling of Alex's tombstone was arranged to take place on 31 October 1976. Four days before the ceremony, Alex's wife, Elisabeth, wrote to Alex's parents explaining why she would not be able to attend. In many ways, this is a very personal and moving letter; the editors are particularly grateful to Mrs. Aronson for her permission the publish it.)

I don't know if I can explain my absence; that I am not able to be present. It is not that I am removed or that I don't want to be present for certain reasons. I have been absorbed with this 31st October Unveiling for a long time, musing on it, trying to sort out my feelings. I am having great difficulty with it and cannot find an answer.

Or I could not until I realized the deep connection I had with Alex which runs through my life like a thread. This has at last offered me a solution. Alex wanted to be known as a Jew, but at the same time he asked for the right to be recognized as different. Rev. Ype Schaaf said it so well. "Here lies buried not an orthodox Jew but an outsider."

Alex could not be thought of as an insider. He could not be placed inside a circle. There had to be an open place, a piece, a part. That open part I call Muktidas in Alex. I never forget about it or stop feeling it. This was and is Alex to me, and I do not want to let him down. I cannot.

If Alex had died a normal death abroad, then I would have respected his wish to be buried in the country where he died. Then there would have been no funeral at Muiderberg. If he had been buried in Siegerswoude, which could have happened, there would not have been a gravestone.

First I accepted your choice of Muiderberg; then your wish that the grave be marked. I went that far, but can go no further. So I cannot attend the unveiling. This is not out of perversity, but because of my feelings which probably no one will understand. But they have grown out of my love for Alex which in part came from the love you bore. Can there be room then for a rift between us?

(Eds. In March, 1978, the following notice appeared in a Dutch newspaper.)

Park for Murdered Lex Aronson in Israel

No Dutch representatives have been invited for the inauguration on 9 March 1978 of the Lex Aronson Park in Modi'im near Ben Shemen, Israel [32°N, 35°E]. The Israeli government will be represented at the opening of a plot containing 4,000 trees, planted in memory of the Dutchman murdered in Iraq in 1975. The Dutch have not been invited because of their lack of action at the time. Directors of the Dead Sea Works who were supporters have been invited.

Appendix: Chronology of Alex Aronson

20 December 1934 Born in Amsterdam.

1937 Parents divorced; both father and mother re-married subsequently.

1940 German Occupation of Holland.

1943 Deported via Westerbork Police Transit Camp to Bergen-Belsen Concentration Camp with his mother and maternal grandparents.

Early Summer 1944 Death of Alex's grandfather, Herman (Tsvi) Cohen, in Bergen-Belsen.

1945 Returned to Amsterdam with his mother.

1945-47 Recuperation from tuberculosis in Switzerland.

1948-51 Hogere Burger (Jewish Secondary) School, Amsterdam.

1951 Father and step-mother emigrated to Israel.

1952 Certificate in chiropody.

1952-55 Nursing student in Jewish Home and Hospital, London.

1955 Left London to join father and step-mother in Israel; worked at Rambam Hospital near Haifa for a few months.

1956-60 *Wanderjahre;* extensive travel including India where he worked with followers of Gandhi; published booklet of poems, *Surrendering My Love.*

26 April 1961 Arrived in Lambaréné; studied and worked with Dr. Albert Schweitzer for 4 months.

Spring 1962 Met Sharon, an American studying at Hebrew University, while she was on vacation in Athens; visited Sharon in Jerusalem where he met Alan Mendelson, a fellow-student.

Early July 1962 Sharon and Alan visit Alex in his cabin in Fannari (Thessaly, Greece); Alex returned to Amsterdam in late July.

Late August 1962 Sharon and Alan arrive in Amsterdam where they stay with Alex in his mother's house.

October 1962 Correspondence with Alan commences.

October - November 1963 Alex returned to Fannari, Greece.

End November 1963 Met Elisabeth van Dieijen in French district of Dordogne in an Albert Schweitzer Village; they married 2 months later. Alex and Elisabeth moved to her father's farm in Poortugaal, in south Holland.

August 1964 Joan Michelson visited Alex in Poortugaal.

14 December 1964 Son Alwin born in Piraeus, Greece; the family returned to Holland, living in Poortugaal and then Friesland.

From December 1968 Spent 8 months in Gabon, Biafra, and Nigeria; aid work for International Committee of the Red Cross and Terre des Hommes.

8 February 1970 Arrived in Chicago for 3-month stay in U.S.A.; fund-raising for International Emergency Brigade.

November 1970 - January 1971 In India.

1971-74 Diploma course in social work with maltreated children.

Autumn 1973 - June 1974 Trainer of S.O.S. (lifeline) volunteers in Leeuwarden.

Spring 1974 Alan visited Alex in Friesland.

25 July 1974 Last letter to Alan.

Late August 1974 Began his drive to Kurdistan.

Mid-September 1974 - mid-December 1974 Worked for three months in Iraqi Kurdistan; with the arrival of winter he travelled to India and Pakistan for medical supplies.

Mid-February 1975 On his way back to Kurdistan, Alex was imprisoned in Pakistan.

Early March 1975 Returned to Kurdistan.

13 March 1975 Last letter to family before capture.

20 March 1975 Had breakfast with Dr. David Nabarro, the last westerner to see Alex alive.

24 March 1975 Arrest by Iraqis and imprisonment in Baghdad.

August 1975 Efforts to find Alex intensify.

11 October 1975 Revolutionary Tribunal held.

12 October 1975 Transfer to another prison, 20 miles south of Baghdad.

3 November 1975 News leaked that Alex had been hanged in Baghdad; report soon denied by Iraqi Embassy.

12 November 1975 Dutch Chargé d'Affaires was refused access to Alex in prison.

November 1975 International efforts to gain release; International Red Cross Committee's request to visit Alex was refused.

12 December 1975 Wrote last note from prison; note smuggled out. Alex was executed sometime between the writing of this note and mid-January 1976.

15 March 1976 Iraqi Embassy admitted that Alex had been executed.

April 1976 Alex's mother travelled to Baghdad to obtain the release of her son's remains.

26 May 1976 Burial in Jewish Cemetery, Muiderberg.

31 October 1976 Unveiling of Alex's tombstone.

9 March 1978 Inauguration of Aronson Park in Modi'im (near Ben Shemen), Israel.